ARAB WOMEN
VOICE NEW REALITIES

An anthology co-edited by
ROSEANNE SAAD KHALAF
and DIMA NASSER

With an introduction by
ROSEANNE SAAD KHALAF

turning**point**
BOOKS

Published by Turning Point Books
14th Floor, Concorde Building, Dunan Street
Verdun, Beirut, Lebanon
PO Box 11-4932
Tel: 00961 1 752 100

www.tpbooksonline.com

First edition: November, 2017

Layout and graphic design copyright © Turning Point, 2017
Front cover image copyright © Myriam Boulos

Co-edited by Roseanne Saad Khalaf and Dima Nasser
Introduction by Roseanne Saad Khalaf
Design and layout by Sinan Hallak
Printing: 53Dots

ISBN 978-9953-972-06-0

To inspiring Arab women writers and the bold spaces they create.

INTRODUCTION

Eleven years have passed since I edited *Hikayat: Short Stories by Lebanese Women*. Sadly, the Arab world today is a vastly different place. As wars continue to rage with horrific consequences, the region is fast becoming darker, more volatile, and dangerous. Violence and devastation have assumed a haunting presence, harshly intruding upon and shattering the daily lives of millions. Yet in the midst of such oppressive times, and in stark contrast to the prevailing mood of pessimism, comes a watershed moment for writers, particularly Arab women, the beginning of a deep, long term and thoughtful attempt to re-imagine, reshape and restructure a culture that has long sidelined and silenced their crucial voices. A vibrant creativity that is fluid, constantly evolving, liberating, and never confined, has burst upon the landscape.

Another striking difference between 2006 and today, is the availability of shorter forms of fiction and nonfiction. The novel is no longer the culture's favored literary form. Previously, Arab women writers chose the novel over the short story, embracing the expansiveness and verbosity of the former genre as opposed to the economy and brevity of the latter. Consequently, in selecting stories for *Hikayat*, I had to include a number of novel excerpts. Thankfully, this is no longer the case. Now there exists a wealth of original and diverse short works to select from.

This collection which gathers stories and prose pieces by gifted women from across the region, reflects how uncertain, troubled times empower writers to frame their own values, to construct texts that explore complex human experiences, paradoxes, and contradictions. They can be obedient wives, daughters, mothers, and sisters at home, yet disruptive, bold game-changers elsewhere, given the need to function differently in opposing spheres. Ironically, consumerism is rampant and highly accessible to all, yet many women remain excluded from other hugely important segments of society, suffering mindless constraints and exclusion when it comes to education, jobs, and politics. For them, although multiple identities may not offer long-term solutions, they are, understandably, not considered contradictory. It's hardly surprising that currently authors occupy spaces of skepticism and hope. In this fluid landscape of shifting possibilities, they become boundary pushers, writing compelling stories that have the power to change how we see, and equally important, how women see themselves.

In a region known for its restricted freedom of expression and repression of women, there is an urgent need for risk-takers who explore unchartered territory and move others to uncomfortable places. These boundary pushers force readers out of their comfort zone by crafting stories that are often shocking, raw and fearlessly infused with moral purpose. Arab women writers have become daring disrupters who are way ahead of our courage. The pure act of telling is destabilizing. Each brave voice raised and heard ultimately has the power to change the game.

Precisely because the contributors to the anthology dwell in uncomfortable places, resisting strictures in countries that often deny their presence, they possess the power to dislodge us from a life of complacency, to connect us to other, often unimaginable, "new realities." Even if these "new realities" are merely old realities rendered darker and more complex, they define a history of gendered and generational struggles over identity, voice, place, belonging, conflict, and war by individuals historically confined to the margins. And by doing so, their work, generally not widely available, is vitally important, cutting edge, honest, poignant. They focus the lens on a fast-changing, volatile region, crafting stories that hold transformative powers, that offer an entirely different, more nuanced understanding of how Arab societies function.

The anthology brings together works of fiction and nonfiction by a talented mix of women writers from across the Arab world: new voices, relative newcomers, and established authors. All have crafted original, previously unpublished pieces. For some, this is a debut, a space to tell stories that aren't usually heard, voices coming fully into their own. For others, like my three aspiring creative writing students at the American University of Beirut, overwhelmed by possibilities, but not yet lodged in the necessary comfort of having discovered the shape of a story, or having located their own voice in it, this is a way to nurture young creativity. Their nonfiction pieces are taken from memoirs crafted and workshopped in my Creative Nonfiction courses. No matter how accomplished or fresh-faced, these writers have one thing in common: they are inspirational forces whose ever-widening, vibrant work is fast reshaping and redefining old realities. By pushing against yet remaining in conversation with the societies they inhabit, these game changers have rapidly created "new realities" throughout the Arab literary and cultural landscape, with stories that provide unique possibilities and ways of seeing.

Although compiling any collection is a huge challenge, it's clearly best for an editor to step aside, to let the stories speak for themselves. But I cannot resist offering a few remarks particularly because each piece is infused with a certain immediacy that captures what it means to be a woman living in the Arab world today. Given the rich diversity of texts, it would be misleading to reduce them to a single perspective. Instead, I have grouped them according to eight unifying, salient themes none of which are mutually exclusive. Here are the twenty-seven stories, six of which were originally written in Arabic, selected together with my co-editor Dima Nasser. Far from being a chorus of voices, they reveal distinct individual experiences, show deep, witty insight and explore profound "new realities" as experienced by women throughout the Arab world. I hope you will find them as enticing and inspiring as we have.

Bold Journeys

Adania Shibli's story, "This Sea is Mohammad Al-Khatib's," explores a number of options available to twenty-year-old Mohammad Al-Khatib who, together with his friends, wants to reach the sea either in Gaza or Yafa from his hometown of Al-Khalil. All available roads are perilous and end in disaster, a grim reminder of the relentless intimidation and humiliation young Palestinians are tragically subjected to. "Ameera's Journey to Andalusia" by Amany Al-Sayyed is a strange, wondrous, and rambling tale of Abe, a rich forty-something "halal" tour guide and Ameera, a complex, intriguing woman of many talents who cannot focus on any one memory nor can she find a suitor to satisfy both herself and her tiresome family. Determined to escape from "Toxic Beirut" and "from one loss to another: best friend gone, husband left, work crashed," Zena El-Khalil journeys to an ashram in India. Now that her life is in shambles, nothing short of a miracle is needed to rescue her. There is great honesty, pleasure, and inspiration in this evocative and delicately unraveling narrative. A truly bittersweet ending brings much-needed closure to a remarkable and tender relationship with her soulmate, Maya. Inaam Kachachi's "Nude in Waziriyya of Baghdad" is a moving account of a French woman who travels to Baghdad on a sad mission. Once there, she explores pathways as mysterious and unknowable as a dream. What transpires at the end is the story's boldest, most dazzling, delirious achievement.

Shattered Lives

Aisha Isam's "Mayhem" is a harrowing piece of narrative tension, a powerful shock to our senses, an urgent, desperate, catastrophic account of the ravages of war, of airstrikes, artillery fire, and landmines that turn cities and lives into rubble. This is the story of a woman, searching for her children, being slaughtered silently, recording the atrocities of brutal regimes and terrorist groups. As the nameless woman comes into focus, politics and region recede. The dead, shot or buried alive, crushed by debris, dismembered by suicide bomb blasts—eerily overwhelm the living. "A Paper Nest" by Irada Al-Jubouri is the tragic tale of an Iraqi woman who lives with her abusive husband in "a state of suspension" and excruciating silence after an explosion kills the most precious person in her life. "The Illusion of Us" by Shahd Al-Shammari and "On the Seventh Floor" by Raya Hajj, focus on the lives of two highly successful professional women in entirely different circumstances. Both have had the privilege of shaping careers that should normally provide identity and give purpose. Unlike the vast majority of women in the Arab world who don't have the time, money, or ability to follow any of their dreams, these two professionals appear to have it all until circumstances and the public gaze turn relentlessly critical, with serious consequences. In "Close Enough" Youmna Bou Hadir's exhausted protagonist is entrapped in a stressful job, pressured by her family to find a husband and utterly unable to form lasting, real-life relationships. Not surprisingly, she escapes to the world of social media, to dream-like states of virtual reality, to chat rooms seen as hugely inappropriate for a well brought-up Arab woman. Hanan Al-Shaykh's "The Angel" is a perfect masterpiece of short, narrative tension, tightly wrought, skillfully executed with an intriguing plot, an understanding of how to engineer suspense. Al-Shaykh knows how to make the reader wait and speculate and precisely when to deliver the final blow.

Magic Moments

"Saying Goodbye to Yuki" by Fatima Bdeir and Fatima Mahmoud's "Omran and I" are two works thematically related. Both are coming-of-age stories that transport the reader to dizzying, imaginative worlds. In the former, a young woman who feels out of place finds comfort in books and reading, retreating to a captivating realm of adventure and fantasy. Never feeling like herself around real people, she bonds more easily with fictional characters. Besides, fictional characters don't instigate trouble, and "when she came to know the world for what it really is," she wisely decides to "ignore a lot of it." Mahmoud, revisiting the enticing landscape of her childhood, relates a touching tale about her dazzling and intriguing cousin Omran, who steals the moon and hides it under his bed. She soon finds herself taunted by spiritual questions, caught in a fierce competition for knowledge that rages on and off the playground. The story is all the more compelling in what is left out, cruel and startling in its abrupt reversal, a dream gone bad, tragically veering out of the magical realm of childhood.

Courageous Voices

Gabi Toufiq's "Silent Letters" unfolds as a graphically confessional and shocking series of letters addressed to her Iraqi missionary parents. Courageously, she moves beyond making her rapist pay, or focusing on survivor's shame and self-doubt. Instead, she centers herself, the victim, in her own narrative to instigate a more complex and deeper conversation. For decades, stories have explored the rape of women by directing their attention to some man's story. Instead, Toufiq makes us see exactly what it looks and feels like when the lens doesn't turn away. "Dry Sludge" by Huda Al-Attas is unremittingly and chillingly dark. Evil pervades this work: the evil of misogyny, ignorance, repression alongside blind adherence to primitive and harsh rituals, customs and traditions. Cruel and haunting in the telling, it unleashes a destructive and horrifying narrative energy. Zeinab Al-Tahan's "The Lady in the Black Veil" dips in and out of the past to recount a tragic life with devastating clarity and an equally grim ending.

Marriage and its Discontents

"Amira's Mirror" by Mishka Mojabber Mourani and "Mantra" by Nisreen Sanjab provide a bracingly bleak view of marriage. Outwardly, the couple in "Amira's Mirror" seems a model of traditional respectability. But a marriage, as seen from the outside, is only one thing. From within, it can be quite another. Because divorce is unacceptable in a conservative society, the pair drone on paralyzed by the twin gods of failing matrimony and inertia. The reader is privy to what it really looks like when the layers are stripped back; the murky, ugly undercurrents of relationships when infidelity and betrayal erode the mutual bond of trust forever. The only glimmer of hope occurs when Amira's life is briefly interrupted by a young Syrian refugee. In "Mantra," a woman bright and bored, and drowning in the daunting responsibilities of marriage and children, reveals her innermost self while meditating during yoga. She laments how much of her time is spent lost in thoughts of the past or future—

or sideways, in all those things she could or should be doing. In "Grooming Rana" and "The Way Back Home," both Reem Rashash-Shaaban and Yasmina Hatem, hone their lens on the never-ending pressure young women face when it comes to marriage. Shaaban's lighter, more humorous prose playfully mocks the heavy handed, manipulative schemes of mothers determined to find eligible suitors for their daughters. But beneath the lightheartedness lurks the profoundly shocking realization that young women's lives can be treated with such nonchalance, with complete indifference and total disregard of their desires and feelings. Returning to her family home in Beirut, the narrator in "The Way Back Home" is haunted by her past alongside the pressures of being single, of feeling locked in a futile struggle against the conservative values of Lebanese society. Despite becoming unhinged as the narrative unfolds, her feelings of alienation and exclusion glow with warmth and humanity, ultimately ushering in a totally unexpected reversal as the story comes to a close.

A Place Called Home

"Hyphenation" by Nadia Tabbara highlights the immigrant experience replete with physical displacement and challenging linguistic differences. For Sabah, it's not simply a matter of adjusting to the new realities of *Amairka*, but of forging a different reality in which at least a tenuous balance can be made to happen. In the end, she achieves some semblance of belonging by making a rather surprising choice. Cyrene Bader's "Skin Map" unfolds in a series of chronological memories. Pleasant and deeply painful moments are coiled into view culminating in a touching realization of what home truly means. "Come Back Home" by Sima Qunsol is a tale of two cities: Amman and Beirut. As Qunsol shuttles back and forth between the two, she digs deep into her experiences and thoughts, questioning what it really means, and whether it's at all possible, to fully belong to any one place.

Body Language

In a powerful prose poem, "The Half-life $T_{1/2}$ of the Body", Hind Shoufani applies a mathematical and scientific analysis of exponential or gradual decay to the parts of a woman's body. The pared-down, direct, quantitative language releases an overwhelmingly unexpected array of powerful emotions. Zeina Abi Assy in her moving narrative, "Body as Home," revisits the years before she moved from Lebanon to Brooklyn, a time when she was body shamed, her confidence far from ironclad. The focus on her figure rapidly became a source of debilitating insecurity as she felt increasingly persecuted under the magnifying glass of social, public, and family scrutiny. Abi Assy's rare and vulnerable telling of how she began to accept dysmorphia, taking notice of her body in a powerful way, is disarmingly arresting.

Disturbing Reflections

During a trip to South Africa, Rima Rantisi in "Here and There in a Time of Terror" is suddenly traumatized by raw visions of savagery and new brands of terror. Pregnant and gripped with fear at the responsibility of bringing new life into the world, she movingly agonizes over how to protect her yet unborn child from an unpredictably violent world. Nisreen's life in "An Article" by Zaina Erhaim is harsh to say the least. She endures an impoverished existence with her five children, her husband, and his extended family, in a country ravaged by war. Burdened by endless domestic chores and forced to stay mostly indoors unless granted permission to leave by her tyrannical husband, she dreams of a better life. Something happens, of course. A sudden opportunity arises, offering her the freedom she never had. In "To Myself," Hafsa Bouheddou links the past to the present, descending into a delirious state of creative chaos, an unbroken chain of happenings each flowing from the other. The remarkable fluidity of her voice and its disturbing insight is rendered more immediate by the stream of consciousness technique used to depict the multitudinous thoughts and feelings which pass through her mind. Themes of disenchantment, despair, estrangement, and rage race through the narrative with alarming speed.

Roseanne Saad Khalaf

CO-EDITOR'S NOTE

The discourse of Arab women speaking out, refusing to be silent, and voicing their experiences, is alive and ever-growing. These narratives are moving, raw, and acutely attuned to reality, but they are not exempt from being co-opted by larger forces. Therefore, as researchers and curators in a position of power, it is our responsibility to continue to add to this significant body of literature – to do so critically and with attention to cultivating fertile grounds for new voices... Far from claiming to be comprehensive and representative of the vast cultural diversity in the Arab world, this collection is nonetheless an attempt at capturing the pulse of as wide a regional scope as is possible at this moment. Readers are asked to take in these stories with a grain of salt and an awareness that their intention is not to reduce the multitude of experience among women within any particular Arab country. These stories are instantiations, records, and they will never be told in the same way again.

Seldom do we get the chance to see a literary project through in a relatively short period of time, especially one which involves many writers, translators, artists, designers and publishing members. It is difficult to imagine this collection coming to fruition without the facilitating support of the publishing team at Turning Point Books, based in Beirut, the critical lens and expertise of my co-editor Roseanne Saad Khalaf, and the many colleagues, friends, and family members whose conversations contributed to the story between the lines. A debt of gratitude is also owed to the literary translators, Michelle Hartman, Rula Baalbaki, Amahl Khouri, and Yasmine Haj, who kindly lent their time and literary skill in an effort to translate the Arabic stories, encoded with their own complex cultural and linguistic subjectivities, while taking care to preserve the authors' voices. And last but not least, our deepest admiration extends to the writers themselves who have entrusted us with a most precious gift: their stories.

Dima Nasser

NOTE ON THE TRANSLATION
AND TRANSLITERATION

Readers will find specific Arabic words and expressions that appear in certain stories transliterated with an explanation or translation in the footnotes, or explained in the context of the story.

Some Arabic words, expressions, and combinations that are common among several stories are translated and explained here.

Amairka/Amreeka; variations on the Arabic pronunciations of "America"

Argeeleh; a hookah, a single or multi-stemmed instrument for smoking flavored tobacco

Baba; father

Dabkeh; Arab folk dance performed at weddings and other celebrations

Habibi (masc.) *Habibti/Habibteh* (fem.); my dear, my love

Haram; that which is sacrilegious or forbidden in Islamic law; an expression of pity

Mama; mother

Teta; grandmother

Ya; a form of address in formal and informal communication usually followed by a noun

Ya binti; my daughter, my dear

Yalla; hurry up, move it

Za'tar; thyme or the preparation of thyme, sesame seeds, and sumac

THE STORIES

GRACE

ZENA EL-KHALIL

For those who stick it through, for those artists, storytellers, and lovers who are willing to shed everything, the universe has been known to present them with miracles. The miracle of truth. And, it was nothing short of a miracle that she was looking for.

4:30 a.m. Dubai Airport. 2017. In Transit to India

Never India. That's what she promised herself after Jo's brutal murder there, 15 years back. She was always attracted to the food, culture, and colors that came with that nation, but had decided that in this lifetime, it was a no-go for her. How was it that she now found herself about to take this journey on her own? Just like Jo did. She had heard that India is where the desperate run to when there is nowhere left to go. And since she had made multiple unsuccessful attempts on her life, there was nothing left to fear, nowhere left to go. She was as desperate and broken as they came. Heart ripped out, shredded, humiliated to the point of no words. A vacuum of pain. An effigy to catastrophe. The last outhouse on the edge of the universe, where alien shit stains piled high on squat toilets. That's where she left her heart. In a squat toilet, 500 million miles south of Jupiter. She had heard that sometimes people "wake up" there and then disappear... choosing a life of solitude, meditation and reflection, abandoning the material world. Sometimes, it was not even their decision. The all-pervading underlying energetic blanket created by generations upon generations of *rishis* (seers) were known to wrap up these wretched truth-seeking souls, providing them with the warmth and comfort they had come to find. To outside eyes, they looked mad as they shuffled around in ruffled loincloths and matted hair. But upon contact with their eyes, one could see an extraordinary light showing through. Call it the Divine, in manifestation. The formless within form. That which cannot be described. That which was never born and never died. That which is beyond attribute and description. She wondered if this would happen to her. She made Hiba and Hind promise to come get her if she wasn't back by the end of the month. She promised herself not to get attached in any way. Not to stay for too long. Not to make any friends. And certainly not to fall in love.

The last ten years she had spent in toxic transit. In Beirut. From one disaster to the next. From one loss to another. She swore that after the bombs in 2006, she would never get stuck in one place for too long. Always moving. But, things caught up. And when they did, it was bad. Nothing worked; nothing stuck. Not her work. Not her marriages. Nor her home. During the 2006 July War, she chose to remain in her city, under the bombs, to find a way to help. The slow reporting by Western media made her decide to fight back with words. The "blog" had recently been invented and a friend helped set her up with one. Her writing soon gained an international following making her one of the first largely followed bloggers in the Middle East. She was married, had a home, a dog, dreams, plans, life goals… and a best friend, Maya. But all that was gone now. All that was taken away within weeks of the war's end. What the international media always fails to report is the emotional massacre that happens during a war. The breakdown of relationships. The illnesses that multiply. The speed at which death comes. The depressions that follow. The endless supply of drugs taken in order to soothe and help one forget. Forgetting is a Lebanese national pastime. Wine. Coke. *Argeeleh*.

Electro-*tarab*.[1] At the time, it seemed like the entire world was interested in her life, even wanting to help. But the day the media stopped reporting, moving on to a different crisis somewhere else in the world... people like her were left behind. There is no interest, no money, that can be made telling the story of each personal life-dissolve that follows a post-war, post-bomb, post-situation, comma-situation-period. And she got left behind in a big way. Best friend gone. Husband left. Work crashed. Left with a big apartment, and no children. Dog, however, thankfully, still around. She had her dog and her grief. People like to think that crisis spurs art. From chaos comes creation. But there is a fine line between crisis and depression. In depression, no work can come. Only the dream of death. And auto immune body-mind-soul failure.

The airport was quiet. She liked this airport. Liked the diversity of people. The melting pot of the world. Compared to Beirut, it was refreshing to see so many people of different nations, also in transit. Everyone here had their story. Their unbelievably heavy coffins of memories and loss that had stained them, like thick dark mud. Everyone hoping that the next plane would finally take them to the purpose they had been seeking. A place that provided a warm bed and a shoulder to rest upon. "That's all I need," she thought. "A body to cave into. A softness to fall into, forever." A warm breath on her neck and her ears. A hand, perhaps, that ran through her hair from time to time. She didn't need much. Except maybe some arms to hold her up. And some lips to remind her that she could still feel. She had forgotten what it felt like to be held. To be touched. Her body had become flaccid and it happened without her even realizing, as Beirut continued to loom above her. "No place for grief here. Everyone is grieving all the time. Nothing special about yours," Beirut constantly

---

1 A hybrid and relatively recent genre of music that combines electro sounds with *tarab*, a genre/concept in Arabic music said to have a trance-like or ecstatic effect on the listener.

hissed at her. "Seventeen-thousand people still declared missing. Families torn apart and no one talks about it. Where massacres once happened, people now built nightclubs. Nightclubs that hosted premium oblivion; lines of coke on silicon seas of breasts and lips and asses… and you are crying over one best friend?" As shame and depression took over her life, she found it easier to just dissolve into the background. Just like Beirut concrete. Humiliated concrete. Raggedy. Putrid. In Beirut, everyone and everything looked the same. Aged, rotten, depressed. Paint peeling. Nicotine stained teeth. Decades of mold upon mold, growing through cracks, bursting, bourgeoning mold. Her furniture. Her bed. And even her body. Everything was mold. Even the men she was attracting into her life. Dark, and equally broken and insecure. Mold. Even her grief was mold. She could not grieve properly there. Years and years of crying, and still, it sat in her gut like a rock. Maya.

She bought herself a hot cup of tea, found a spot near her gate and slumped down. She was thankful that her journey was East. With fascism on the rise in Europe and the USA, she was grateful to know she would not be greeted with fingerprinting and interrogations. Even 2006 didn't manage to strip away her dignity like that. The news about Muslim families being torn apart at US airports made her furious. It had now become illegal for citizens from Sudan, Yemen, Somalia, Iran, Syria and Libya to fly into *Amreeka*. But maybe this was a good thing. Maybe the Arabs would finally find a way to stand together and boycott the countries that made bombs that killed them in the first place. "*Amreeka*, land of the free, you make bombs to drop on me. *Amreeka*, land of fear, **** you, I no longer come near," she mumbled to herself. Only six hours to go until she could melt into the backdrop of the Himalayas. Over there, no one knew her, and no one would care how much she cried. She could grieve without being judged. Salvation was possibly at hand. She ripped open her tea bag and dumped the green tea leaves into her cup. Since giving up coffee, she found herself drinking daily heaps of green tea. Toufic, a veteran tea drinker, had warned her that bleached tea bags could lead to ulcers and cancer, and that doing away with the bag was the only way to drink tea in this day and age. Tears were already welling up in her eyes. *Just hold on*, she whispered to herself. She watched the tea leaves sink to the bottom of her cup. *Only a few hours to go and then you can cry as much as you want. Breaking down now would mean hours on the floor covered in a pool of tears and snot, a possible panic attack and a shit load of embarrassment. Hang in there.*

5:30 a.m. The Morning Call to Prayer Begins

No one could understand their friendship. This love. This loss. No one. Not even God. Her hands rattled as she lifted the cup to her mouth. For years, she thought about how horrible this day would feel. For months, she dreaded the big ten-year anniversary. She thought perhaps she should do something great and meaningful with all their friends and family. She thought to write something powerful, possibly even reactivate her blog. That would be a great way to honor Maya since she had written about her so much then. She thought she would commemorate it through some sort of act. Hold a vigil at home and have an international Skype-based wake. Her dog would be curled up beside her and they could all weep for an eternity. She had been crying for ten years. So it seemed appropriate to continue for another ten. But no. Something had been slowly changing. She could no longer be around people. She could not stand any sort of attention or acknowledgement. The death of a soul mate and the betrayal of not one, but two husbands can, indeed, leave one face-down in a pile of their own viscera, entrails, and shit. It was the burden of humiliation she carried around with her. Shame. Failure. As she gave so generously of herself to the public, betrayal climbed into her bed back home. How could she have been so blind and… yes, stupid. The embarrassment became a disease. She stopped going out. Stopped seeing people. Tenderly closed herself off until the phone eventually stopped ringing. The few friends who remained did not even live in Lebanon. Over the past ten years they had all emigrated for better jobs and saner lives. She was alone. In a city where everyone knows everyone and social incest is high; friends sleeping with friends, who have slept with friends, who are sleeping with friends… she managed to disappear. Slipping through the cracks. "It's better like this. It's better to be a nobody," she thought to herself. The call to prayer came to an end and she closed her eyes for a brief moment. Maya.

"Miss? Miss… wake up! Are you going to board or not?" Jolting up, she stared at the attendant in a daze. "Last call. Are you getting on?"

She jumped up, grabbed her backpack and ran towards the plane. How could she have fallen asleep? As she ran, a wave of nausea hit. The wine from the night before sloshed in her stomach. Not that it made a difference, but as usual, she cursed herself, vowed never to drink again and picked up her pace. She boarded right foot first, and following her flying ritual, tapped the side of the plane three times as she stepped in. Settling into her seat made her feel like she was already in India. The smell of Sandalwood body soap and rose oil from the elderly woman next to her was like a warm hug. The acid in her throat and stomach began to settle. She gave the lady a smile.

Maya hated drama.

She dreamed of becoming a writer one day. While at university, she used to leave her funny little notes in her mailbox. Sometimes they were lines from their favorite movie, *Airplane!* "Stop calling me Shirley!" No one ever used those archaic metal boxes except for them. In 1994, the Civil War had just ended and the postal system was far from up and running. No one expected letters in those boxes. But she got them. Hundreds of them. Letters, notes, and even paintings. Maya saw it as her daily creative offering to Beirut. At some point, she got into drawing with crayons. For weeks she would copy Degas paintings of women bathing and women dancing, all with crayon. She called it Post-Modern-Crayola-Deconstructivism-Ism. It was something she was very serious about. After living through 21 years of Civil War, she believed that art could help heal, that reverting to a childlike mind, using childlike materials, was a big statement against the post-war capitalist art machine that was on the rise. War is over! Burger King has arrived! Let's buy art! They make wars, she believed, so that they can make money. They make plastic out of oil and they fight for oil. Crayolas were the closest thing to drawing with plastic. Maya believed that her medium had to represent her message. If only she were still around, she would have had a field day with contemporary conceptual art. At the time, she thought Maya's drawings a bit naïve and didn't find them very interesting. But when Maya copied a Nirvana album cover for her, she saw them in a new light. Now, they were punk. And that, was anti-establishment. And that, was cool. And that, was exactly what they were; post-war Arab women punk poet rockers. Sid and Nancy meets Rumi and Shams. On Acid.

Midnight. Rishikesh, India

Arriving at the ashram late at night, she was received by a grumpy night guard. "You are late. Check in ended five hours ago."

"Yes sir; I am very sorry, but the bus broke down." The 14-hour trip from Delhi had left her cold and hungry and she was determined to get a room.

"Sorry mam, no more rooms tonight. Come back at 7:00 a.m."

"Yes sir, I understand, but really I have nowhere else to go."

"I'm sorry, I don't have any keys. I can't help you."

Fuck! She had flown all this way, planned every step of the process, except for this. She began to feel the tears welling up again and fear was slowly creeping in.

"Please sir," she pleaded. Then whispering to herself, "I just want a corner to die in. Nothing too fancy. Just a corner where I can finally die."

"No keys! No rooms! No corner!!"

She felt her heart fall to her knees, and she followed it to the ground. Panic was beginning to rattle her wicked tail. She felt a flash of heat sweep through her body. Maybe this is how Jo was killed. Left out in the dark. Her breathing quickened and she fought back the nausea. Most people faint during panic attacks, she on the other hand, vomited.

"You want to die like Sadhu, you sleep on Ma Ganga like Sadhu. Come, I take you to temple. Get up. You sleep there and come back at 7:00." He pointed at the small temple by the river. "Come. I open temple for you."

"Yes... yes, okay. Thank you..." She picked up her backpack and followed him down to the river. "You are sure it is okay? Really, thank you so much." She took a few deeps breaths and tried to calm down.

"You don't touch anything, okay? You just sleep on floor. I lock you inside and open at 5:00 a.m. Okay?"

While opening the temple door, the guard whispered a prayer

and knelt to the floor. She followed his gestures, quickly doing the same. He walked in, lit a small candle, and placed a flower on a smooth round stone in front of a sculpture of a blue deity with many arms and a crescent moon on his head. He was beautiful. A strong, chiseled body with eyes closed, serenely meditating. Wearing nothing but a loincloth, with a serpent around his neck.

"Okay, you sleep here," he said pointing to a straw mat on the floor. "You want to be Sadhu, you pray to Shiva like Sadhu and then you die. Okay?"

"Yes, yes, thank you. Thank you."

He lit a small candle for her next to the mat and lit a stick of incense. "Aum Namah Shivaya!" Say with me, he instructed. "Ommm Shiiiivaya," she answered.

"Good enough," he assured her. "Don't touch anything. I lock now," he said walking out.

As she lay down her backpack, she wondered how many women the night guard had saved in this same way. Beirut seemed so far away now. It was a relief. She could breathe again. Beirut, the whore monster. Devouring and being devoured. Her legs open to any who would have her. At the crossroads between East and West, since the beginning of time, from debauchery to massacres, to million-dollar weddings. Maybe that's how the city survived. Favors, here and there. Secret despot dictator bank accounts. It's so easy for Beirut, the slut that she is. She is generous. Sick sweet honey sludge, generous. People succumb to her bitter bounty. They try to leave, but her seduction overpowers, and in the end, all that is left is pleasure pastimes to numb the pain. To forget. To partake in her fury and fervor. One more drink. Once more nip and tuck here and there. One more bastard child left on the street to beg and rot.

For the first time in months, she began to feel a sense of space. And rather than tears, a smile crept across her face. Maybe here, she could finally lay back and surrender once and for all. Here, with no attachments, her soul could freely leave her body prison. Self, combustion. She imagined the guard opening up to find her body cold and lifeless. He would probably instruct the villagers to build a funeral pyre and have her body burnt on the Ganga River, like all the others. She would be just another burnt body, a heap of ash returning to the Earth that made her. Her soul would look for the next shirt to slip into for another 80 years or so. That would be a great way to leave. But then images of her parents, dog, and friends flashed in her head. Maybe not tonight. She could not be that selfish. Here, death was acceptable and dealt with gracefully. How she wished it could have been easier to grieve in Lebanon, rather than worry about showing face, acting strong, accepting God's wishes. Bullshit.

They used to fight as passionately as they used to laugh. When Maya died, she was at first very angry with her. What was she supposed to do now? Who was she supposed to grow old with? Who was she going to walk through the park with pushing their babies along in Rosemary's Baby strollers? Who was going to answer her 2:00 a.m. calls when she needed to share ideas, dreams, and crushes? Who was going to dance to Cindy Lauper with her? Who was going to hold her hand during her next heartbreak? Who was going to say the words without her having to speak them? With Maya, she believed everything and anything was possible. With Maya, she felt strong. Invincible. The room would light up when Maya walked in and she would be transformed into Xena, the Warrior Princess. Unafraid of anything or anyone. Maya was her rock and her muse. Her Pythia, Oracle of Delphi, her Amelia Earhart, her Ishtar, Isis, and Zenobia. Her Maya.

Singularity.
Then came silence.

Followed by,
Retraction.
Expansion.
Explosion.

And then... the quiet bitter vacuum.

A supernova is an astronomical event that occurs during the last evolutionary stages of a massive star's life, whose dramatic and catastrophic destruction is marked by a final titanic explosion. Best friends occupy that dense sacred space that is closer than family. Maya's departure was followed by such an event... an explosion so cataclysmic that the void that followed was a living death. And she did die in so many ways. And it was so easy to die in Beirut. Beirut thrives off her vampires, ghouls, and doomed souls. In Beirut, space is darkness deranged and stars die a million deaths leaving no trace of light. Violence is present in her genetic coding, and her people blindly accept the PTSD passed down through their genes. If stars destroy themselves only to be reborn, perhaps it is only natural for humans to do the same. Constantly churning and spitting out starstuff. From the ashes, we rebuild. From fire, we create life. All Starstuff. All holy. The cosmic dance. The cosmic wrath. The underlying power that sits underneath the sublime universe. That which you can't put your finger on. That which escapes you. That which is completely elusive. All one.

As a fallen entity, she wandered and hovered in grim corners of abandoned houses. Lost, fallen, in search of the Styx. And now, she had arrived. She had come to India to cross over. She would die in order to wake up. And it was only in India that she could do this. Beirut was too selfish to allow for such an act of kindness. She peaked through the window. Across the river, barely visible, she traced faded orange embers, leftovers from earlier burning bodies on Ma Ganga.

1:00 a.m. Shiva Temple. Ganga River Bank

"I am still here, Maya." She looked up at the Shiva sculpture. The stillness on his face kindled a sense of peace within her. "And, maybe you are here too. Only different now. Maybe." A cockroach scuttled across the temple floor. Her first instinct was to reach for her worn-out sandal, but she imagined killing the creature here would provoke the wrath of the entire Indian pantheon of Gods. Big time. She was well past malfunctioning and simply could not deal with that thought. In her tiny two-by-two-meter temple, she conceded to share her sacred space with her new friend. Pulling her backpack towards her, she mumbled at the cockroach, "If I don't die tonight, I want to find a new way to live. Not just survive like you, Mighty Cockroach, but to truly and fully live."

One does not quite recover from a supernova... that type of pain seems to stretch on for eternity. So one learns to live with it until it becomes a natural extension of oneself. It was cold. She pulled her scarf out from her bag and wrapped her head, remembering that 40% of body heat is lost through the head. She brought the candle closer. Shadows danced across the temple walls, and in the distance she could hear monkeys chatter. She wondered why they were awake at this hour. She stood up and walked around the sculpture that stood at the temple center. She was an artist. But the art world is not kind to artists who disappear for too long. They are forgotten as quickly as they are discovered. Trampled over and brushed under the carpet to make way for new money-makers. She was learning to respect the pain she carried, thinking that perhaps if given time, it would eventually evolve into something else. And in the meantime, she waited. Sacrificed lovers. Gave up exhibitions. Anything that could distract her. She clung to the pain because that was the only way she knew how to be close to Maya. And with time, the pain began to transmute into love, becoming two sides of the same coin. In her solitude, she became softer and more loving. She worked on herself, stripping away inherited violence imposed by society, expectations, and her growing self-hate. She grew quiet, but that taught her to listen better. And because of that, perhaps she was becoming a kinder person. However, the will, the need, to die, still pressed on. She stretched her arm out and gently caressed the sculpture. A shiver ran down her spine, almost like electricity. She missed being touched. Being held. She put her hand on the sculpture's hand. The stone was cool and hard, yet something warmed up in her heart. A release. The tears finally came and she let them fall. She let herself cry. No neighbors or family to judge her pain. She put her arms around the sculpture, held it tight and sobbed. And sobbed. Slowly she fell to the stone feet, heaving. She placed her cheek against its feet. Total submission. It felt good. She cried and cried and when she was done, she allowed herself to pass out.

3:00 a.m.

She jolted up, confused, trying hard to understand her whereabouts. A strange humming filled the temple and a light flickered outside. She crawled towards the door and peaked out the keyhole. She could make out a small fire and in front of it sat a man. He looked old, with a long white beard, but his face was smooth and young. He was bare except for a white cloth around his waist and a thin rope hanging diagonally from his shoulder, across his chest. He was chanting in a language she could not understand, pausing occasionally to throw things into the fire that made the flames flicker and dance. His voice was tender and enchanting. It was the most beautiful thing she had ever seen. Or heard. He was quiet, but strong. Emotional, but firm. There was so much tenderness in his voice. And she knew it. She knew that sound. But where from? Or When? She gazed at him for some time, in awe of the aura of peace that surrounded him. As he sang to the flames, he was as focused as the sculpture in her temple. Longing. It was the sound of longing. Of yearning. In the past few years, she had come to know this sound very well. It had become second nature to her. Wanting to go past the limitations of her body and senses. Wanting to go past, go through. Wanting to break free of the space-time matrix. Yearning for something more. Something bigger than her and her speck of a life. Yearning for a devotion that she had yet to discover. The water to quench the pain of separation. The water that was unity. But unity with what? With Maya?

In Sanskrit, Maya means illusion. It is that which conceals the true character of spiritual reality. It is all our temporary worldly attachments that convince us we have everything we need. This subsequently masks the pain of separation from the universe that encourages duality. Artists, truth seekers, lovers and poets know when they've hit the wall of Maya. That is the point when yearning sets in. And the need for something more, something bigger… is born in order to transcend. She sat up with her back to the door and let the sound fill her. Fill her heart. She had read once that if one allows their ego to dissolve completely, falling into a state of perfect self-surrender, then one may become tuned to Divine Grace. One finds a joy that never fades, a life that never decays. One reaches the shore of fearlessness, which is beyond darkness, despair, doubt, grief, sorrow, pain, and delusion. That was what she wanted. The death she was seeking. It wasn't to die in this corner, but to wake up. To burst with love again. To meet the Universe face-to-face and wrangle out what little life was still left in her. To love. To be loved. To receive grace. The chanting softened and she could hear him fumbling around with the fire. She trembled at the beauty of his song. As her eyes looked up at the sculpture, she felt her heart open even more. So, was this truth? Was this the invisible tug that pulled at her all her life? This sound. She tuned herself to this timber. The sum of fundamental tones and overtones, she allowed to reverberate through her. Melding with the moment, the movement of the Earth and all those who were tuned in to that frequency. To the Sadhus around the world and on different planes of existence. To the bells ringing in temples in Nepal and Rome. To each and every other person chanting this sound in the past, present, and future. To the moment she let go of everything. Melding into the morphogenetic field of sacred sound.

This deep raw sound entered her body, which she allowed willingly. She looked down at her hands and felt as if she were holding the entire cosmos in them now. She could touch it. Pull it apart and reassemble it in an instant. Maya. She could feel her again, but this time there was no pain. It was love, a sense of oneness. That they were the same creation, the same entity. She allowed her mouth to hang open and slowly began to sing along. Maya was a good person. A great woman. Kind. Gentle. Caring. Affectionate. She thought of others. She always put her friends and family ahead of her needs. She never forgot birthdays or anything like that. And she loved unconditionally.

4:00 a.m. Brahma Muhurta. One-and-a-Half Hours Before Sunrise

A man sits by the fire. Lost in song, in the music of his soul. He sings to the stars from which he came. Kissed by light, he sings to the Universe that created him. A young woman gently traces a door handle and finds that the door swings open very easily. The door that was never locked to begin with. She walks over and shares his fire. He passes herbs and oils for her to throw in. She wills her pain to leave, no longer wanting to identify with it. It had become her whole life. The *only* thing in her life. But now she was singing again. She didn't know the words, but she sang anyway. The Sadhu's eyes never left the flames. They were a blue grey, and she thought it strange for an Indian man. His face was so soft, not a single crease or wrinkle. But his hair, white as ash. He didn't speak to her, didn't ask her name. Was not even surprised when she sat down. It was complete acceptance. The most normal thing in the world.

He kept passing the herbs and as I threw them into the flames, I saw Maya's face. I saw gratitude. I saw love. I saw Maya's beautiful smile. The one where her slightly crooked front side tooth showed. The smile she flashed a million times as if to say, "Seriously, dude? Hanging out with Sadhus in the middle of the night... very cool." That smile where she used to place her folded finger on the corner of her mouth, trying not to burst into laughter at my usual overemotional outbursts. "Woe is me; time and space have collapsed on top of my head. Again!" The one she used to make when she was angry with me too, but loved me too much to be really angry. The one I loved her for, more than words, because. Because, that is what it was. Unconditional love. A love without condition. A rare and beloved union of souls. Though now separated by the illusion of death. I am determined to find you, Maya. We will pay for river crossings with song and sift through dimensions with hearts open like the beautiful warriors that we are, filtering through Nirvana and Gomorrah. We will trudge through the dense fog of separation. I will never let go of your hand as we walk through sleeping forests of nightmares and dreams. And war. One step at a time. Our reunion is the end point of the journey that they say does not exist. We will prove them wrong.

And we will sit by a fire like this. And we will laugh and laugh when we realize that our individual journeys have never been separate. They have always been together.

Beirut. October 26, 2006

I wore pink today so you'd see me as you left. So you'd know that I knew you were leaving. And that you'd know everything would eventually be okay.

Nude in Waziriyya of Baghdad

INAAM KACHACHI

The day I printed my electronic ticket to Baghdad, Adam told me it was a crazy idea that would only end in disaster. Adam is my son. I know what I raised. He is a rational French engineer given to addressing the minutest details. He takes after his father in one thing only: he has a thin black moustache – the same moustache that caused me to fall for an eccentric Iraqi sculptor forty years ago.

When I first saw him at the Centre Georges Pompidou, he was contemplating, like a person possessed, a certain painting. He looked at me. I looked at him. Our communication was accomplished by signs and several nods of the head. I addressed him in my sophisticated French which years of studying literature at the Sorbonne had perfected; he answered with simple words stammered before giving way to long looks that completed his ideas. His black irises and sharp gazes possessed a super-human ability to formulate meaning. How was I not to be drawn to him when he was the living embodiment of everything that contradicted the bourgeois traditions and stupid etiquette I was raised on?

He completed his art degree; then we got married and he carried me off to Baghdad, a strange and energetic city. I loved the sun and palm trees but failed to get familiar with Baghdad's dust. We lived there for a scintillating few years, during which Adam was born and my husband realized his dream of teaching at the Academy of Fine Arts. Unnecessary wars however forced us to return to France, and we took residence in a small house in the South, which I had inherited from my parents. Adam grew up; we grew older, and then my husband – ever a pillar of steel – succumbed to a strange illness that reduced him to a husk. Could it have been nostalgia for his country?

An hour before his demise, we were summoned by the nurses to say good-bye. He had become an emaciated and motionless wraith. Adam and I stood at his bedside. We tried to figure out the words which the tubes protruding from his nostrils and mouth were camouflaging. He muttered that we should have his body cremated and the ashes strewn in the pathways among the graves of the English cemetery in the Waziriyya quarter, not far from the Academy. Adam's eyes grew round with alarm, whereas I felt a sense of relief since cremation is less costly than burial. But neither of us understood what made our dying beloved want to torment us with this silly will of his. Waziriyya indeed; what nonsense!

My husband, having reduced both his cigarettes and nerves to a smoldering mass, died at Hôpital Européen Georges-Pompidou in Paris. Pompidou seemed to have united us then set us asunder. As his deep-set eyes were turning to ashes in the oven, the Iraqi press was already busy writing about the passing of the great sculptor, Salem Al-Shazri. His friends were publishing articles calling for organizing a "national funeral procession for the artist who passed away in exile after presenting an honorable image of Iraq's contemporary sculpture at international quarters." His students were sending appeals for transporting his body to Baghdad. That was what was being written. But no one contacted me, neither from the embassy nor the ministry of culture; they must have been occupied with more pressing matters. And so, one sad late morning, I poured out my husband's ashes into a large copper urn made at Souq Al-Safafir in Baghdad, which Adam had brought back from his one visit to Iraq. My son had not traveled there to know the country of his ancestors; he was merely accompanying a French builders' firm that was seeking contractual opportunities. His father's name was used as bait for such transactions.

I carried the urn on the plane. I had secured its lid and covered it with wax paper then wrapped it with a pillow case. The cloth case passed through security check at the Charles de Gaulle airport without a hitch, but difficulties started at the airport in Amman.

"What's this?"
"An urn."
"What does it contain?"
"My husband's ashes. He wished for it to be strewn in his country."

The official at the Transit section looked agitated and hurried to fetch her supervisor who luckily only wanted to let sleeping dogs lie. He allowed me to pass through with my suspicious luggage. I took a taxi to Baghdad.

The artists gave me a warm welcome, but as soon as I took the urn out of the case and placed it on the minister of culture's elegant desk, he gave a jerk and yelled, "I seek Allah's protection! We are Muslims, not Hindus, and cremation is taboo. *Haram*! Take this thing away from here, madame, I implore you!"

I placed the urn back in its case like material of a dubious nature, Anthrax, or drugs. The minister resorted to invocations and stating submission to the might and power of Allah, and seeking refuge in His protection. That repeated several times, he took a kerchief and wiped his desk clean, still looking disgusted while advising me to go back to my country. He implored me not to mention the case to anybody: the country was not safe, and chaos was everywhere, and someone might kidnap me because I was a foreigner, even assassinate me. I did not know what to do and so remained at the Grand Hotel for three days, until I became sick with boredom. On the fourth day, I took a taxi to Waziriyya.

"The English cemetery, please."

The driver was unable to reach our destination since a file of American soldiers passing through had stopped traffic on that street. I was eventually dropped off at the Academy of Fine Arts, at the corner of the street. That was where Salem used to teach his students the art of sculpture for many long years. I thought I would enter the academy and look around the old building so that I might try to find traces of my husband's existence there. A guard however accosted me and asked to search me.

"Where are you going?"
"To see the dean."
"Do you have an appointment?"
"Yes."
"What's this?"
"An urn containing some earth that is good for planting mint. I am asthmatic and need the plants for treatment."

The guard gave me a skeptical look but waved me in. A student who had been standing behind me and heard the conversation, followed me. She asked me where I was from, and I answered with my orientalized Arabic that I was from France. She froze, opened her eyes wide and whispered:

"You are the wife of the late Mr. Salem Al-Shazri!"

At that very instant, my Baghdad visit was transformed: it sprouted wings and a beak like no one could ever imagine. Waziriyya was a refreshing quarter that looked nothing like the area where my hotel was located. There I had passed burnt cadavers; homeless drunks who puked on my shoe; drug addicts who seized the strap of my shoulder bag; blind people chugging away in a train-like chain; a demonstration of people with amputated ears clamoring for compensation; and children with filthy feet busy scratching their heads as they ran after me yelling, "One dollar, please... *Hajjia*,[2] one dollar!"

I succeeded in reaching the cemetery but was only partially able to execute my husband's will. I scattered one handful of ashes over General Maude's mausoleum, maybe because the grave looked imperious. It was a beautiful and quiet place despite the distant echo of gunfire volleys; normalized music in a non-normal country. There were fat cats and stray dogs and epithets smeared with marks of aged excrement, as well as luxuriant trees daring all odds. Upon returning to my hotel I started studying the plan that had suddenly hatched in Nasima's mind after our conversation. Nasima was the little student of sculpture, who became my guide here.

I got my things together and checked out to find an old Toyota waiting for me outside the hotel. Two young men were waiting in the car; Nasima waved at me from the back seat. We exchanged abrupt greetings like well-trained commandos and took off to Waziriyya. My husband was not born here; he was born in a poor town divided by a small river. He had told me how his little boy's fingers first kneaded mud on the banks of that small river. He would make figurines of people with flattened heads and hollow eyes. His

---

2 Used here as a title of respect for an older woman.

mother would give him a beating, saying that statues were only for infidels. He thus received frequent beatings but never stopped. At age nineteen he joined the Academy of Fine Arts to study sculpture, but was discontinued in his third year because the statue he sculpted of the president had uneven eyes. An envious student had accused him of intentionally making the leader one-eyed, and thus he spent three months imprisoned in secret vaults before making his escape through the northern roads. What happened after that I fully knew, since I was witness to every event henceforth.

I lived in a rented room in a house in a back street of Waziriyya. Those houses were spacious and at one time luxurious before the dust of years distorted their crumbling exteriors. They once were encircled with gardens and low fences, and little swampy puddles left by the winter rains. I thought of spring making its first pounce on the city accompanied by the first white florets of lemon and bitter orange trees. They call that scent "*kaddah*" and it all but overpowers the perfumes made by Dior and Chanel. Evenings witness the slumbering perfume of the *kaddah* and the awakening of the intoxicating fragrance of afternoon lady, a bouquet emanating from tiny blue or violet flowers that grow on an oblong stem, only unfurling their petals after sunset to intoxicate the heart and mind with their heady scent.

In those long-gone days, lovers would come out of their student residences, holding hands and promenading along the side streets. A certain brave student might have dared to break some street lamps with a bird noose, engulfing the streets with darkness and allowing for stolen kisses behind the luxuriant eucalyptus trees. Nowadays darkness is all in place: power failures abound due to the bombing of power plants. Lovers no longer need to shoot lamps with bird nooses.

I filled my nostrils with the fragrance of afternoon lady and walked through the place which I used to frequent with Salem, at the top of the road that goes down from the metal bridge. I looked for Restaurant Gardenia, with the low green ceiling, where, according to my husband, they served "the most delicious green fava bean pilaf in the whole world." Instead of the restaurant I found a modern building with a hideous façade that looked as gaudily rode up as a gypsy bride. The sound of drunken singing reached me from under the bridge; they had to be surreptitious drinkers who managed to buy raki cloaks and daggers after liquor bars had been banned by the government. Is this your Waziriyya, Salem?

For a whole week, Nasima would come daily to accomplish the stages of our plan. She would carry to the house quantities of moist clay and pile them up in the back garden.

One evening her two young men friends arrived with a big sac like that used for flour. The white powder was plaster, which I watched them mix with water and some clay. Every now and then the door would open to admit more students, who would tread carefully lest they attract the neighbors' attention. As soon as their work was done, they asked me to pour into the mix what remained of Salem Al-Shazri's ashes. It wasn't only Nasima who dipped her hands into the plaster mixed with clay and ashes; Salem's students took turns immersing their hands in the basin, to the accompaniment of the girl students humming folk songs and letting their long braids hang down over the basin. Their locks were plastered to their sweaty foreheads and arms, and I couldn't help feeling a shudder at the strange ritual.

Later, after Waziriyya fell asleep to the soothing lullabies of distant shooting, the hands of girls and boys – all shy of twenty years of age – extended to smear with dark plaster the body of Nasima, who stood naked in the bathroom, and who looked like a Sumerian goddess iridescent in candlelight.

On a clear dawn at the beginning of summer, people in Waziriyya woke up to the statue of a naked woman looking down on them from the rooftop of the Academy of Fine Arts. It was a life-sized statue that defied every rule that decreed covering women, banning sculpture as a sin, and banishing song and music as curses. The scandal sprouted legs which ran through the streets and banged on doors. The scandal asked people to come out and look up at the academy's rooftop.

Children woke up and followed the source of the racket. The soles of shoddy plastic slippers stomped over the afternoon lady plants in gardens. Traffic cops dashed along with their hands securing their caps on their heads. University students arrived one group after the other to the old building and cheered out loud when they saw the sculpture. Scarves covering the heads of female students came loose as they clapped their hands gleefully. Mothers took off their black 'abas and twirled them in the air. Waziriyya, for long saddened and suffocated, wanted to breathe. Waziriyya wished to reclaim its festivals, books, colors, as well as the lovers of its alleys and back streets.

And then arrived an armed squadron. The policemen started to climb to the rooftop, except that the students of the sculpture department had blocked the stairway with podiums and class desks. That left the attackers downstairs with one means of assault: they attempted to catch the nude statue with ropes, just like wild horses are reined. They attempted to pull it down by the neck so it would collapse and fall face first. The collective rush jerked one of the late drunks awake. He raised his head and rubbed his eyes.

"Is that another statue of Saddam?"
"No, this is the spirit of Salem Al-Shazri returning to Waziriyya."

Translated by Rula Baalbaki

This Sea is Mohammad Al-Khatib's

ADANIA SHIBLI

Who is Mohammad Al-Khatib? We know he is a young man, twenty years old, and that he is from Al-Khalil. And he wanted to go to the sea with his friends. We can then assume that he deliberated at length over the question: how to get there? We can imagine, under the present circumstances, two possibilities of a sea that Mohammad Al-Khatib might visit.

The first possibility is the sea of Gaza. As its name quite literally indicates, the sea of Gaza can only be accessed, at the moment, by whomever finds themselves already there. So how can Mohammad Al-Khatib get there? He would first need to reach Allenby Bridge in order to cross the closely controlled border to Jordan, and so would his friends, one of whom will be denied entry to Jordan, then head to Amman airport, and from there, to Cairo airport. But before that, Mohammad Al-Khatib needs to obtain a visa to enter Egypt, which is very difficult to get, but he could try nonetheless, and he will, and so will his friends, except for one who is on the Egyptian intelligence list. From Cairo, he must head to Al-Arish, but without his friend, who is denied entry to Egypt despite having a visa because he was unfriendly to security services. Then he will arrive in Rafah, where he will find the crossing closed and be ordered to return to where he came from.

But he might find someone to bring him to Gaza through the tunnels, and from there to the sea. This is getting more and more difficult to do these days, ever since Egyptian authorities waged their war against tunnels leading to Gaza. And so, after three days of travel, Mohammad Al-Khatib will arrive, without any of his friends, at the sea of Gaza, on September 1, 2016 at around 5:00 p.m. and will have one hour before night encroaches and with it, the naval artillery. But that hour with the sea is what counts. It counts for sixty minutes, or three-thousand-and six-hundred seconds; an infinite time. Who could ever count up to three-thousand-and-six-hundred, except for the waves of the sea?

The second possibility is the sea of Yafa. And to get there, we can imagine, under the present circumstances, two possibilities.

The first is that Mohammad Al-Khatib's father, or his uncle or cousin, or one of their close friends, or a close friend of an acquaintance, has a connection to someone who occupies a high position at one of the Public Administration offices. That connection would get Mohammad Al-Khatib a permit to enter area D between 7:00 a.m. and 7:00 p.m. which will allow him to visit the sea. But what about his friends? Well, they are his friends, and they too could get a permit, except for one who is on the Palestinian intelligence list. On September 1, 2016, they could all start early and be the first to stand at the Bethlehem checkpoint. They will get delayed a bit, and one will be turned back for no reason, but at around 5:00 p.m. after having been stopped and searched, with one arrested here and another arrested there, Mohammad Al-Khatib will arrive at the sea of Yafa; a name which is not quite accurate, since Yafa is many kilometers away. He'd have one full hour, excluding one for the road back before his permit expires. But that hour with the sea is what counts. It counts for sixty minutes, or three-thousand-and-six-hundred seconds; an infinite time. Who could ever count up to three-thousand-and-six-hundred, except for the waves of the sea?

The second possibility is that Mohammad Al-Khatib's father dies, and his uncle, cousin, their close friend, or the acquaintance of a close friend with a connection to someone who has a high position at one of the PA offices, who also died a while ago, is survived by the son of his neighbors, who needs none of these connections to get "inside." He works there without a permit, and he knows how to get there without one. Mohammad Al-Khatib will spend all night with the neighbors' son in order to learn the "illegal" route that will allow him to get to the sea.

And we can imagine, under the present circumstances, two possibilities for this "illegal" route.

The first is to drive with a yellow plate number on his car. Mohammad Al-Khatib has a friend with such a car and a desire to go to the sea. He'd leave early in the morning, with his friends, except for one because there isn't enough room in the car, from Al-Khalil to Wadi Annar, or the fire valley way, until they reach Beit Jala. One passenger will get car sick due to the many twists and turns for which Wadi Annar is known. They'd take out their sunglasses and head to the tunnel checkpoint just as rush hour hits, the settlers of the south on their way to work in Jerusalem. And since the soldiers wouldn't want to disturb any of the settlers, or delay them, the car will pass through. Alas, halfway to the sea, the car will overheat, and after a couple hours of failing to cool it, the driver friend and another person will stay behind while Mohammad Al-Khatib rides the bus to the sea. He'll arrive at around 5:00 p.m. on September 1, 2016, and would have one full hour before he'd have to ride back to Al-Khalil during rush hour when his chances of going unnoticed are greater. But that hour with the sea is what counts. It counts for sixty minutes, or three-thousand-and-six-hundred seconds; an infinite time. Who could ever count up to three-thousand-and-six-hundred, except for the waves of the sea?

The second possibility is being unable to find a friend with a yellow-plated car number in the area of Al-Khalil, so Mohammad Al-Khatib and his friends will have to use the on-foot "illegal" route to get to the sea. He'll prepare himself, along with his friends, to leave before dawn. They will head south, rather than north, to the area of Al-Ramadin. There, among the hills, they'll pass the wall route, still incomplete and in the form of wired fences. They will jump out of the rented stolen car and run to the fence. They'll run and run, all reaching it except for one friend, who loses a shoe and goes back for it. Then, as they jump off the fence, another friend might rip his jeans all the way up to his thighs. Blood gushes out, and he will be left behind. Mohammad Al-Khatib cannot be delayed, otherwise they'll be caught, so he'll keep running until he reaches the small white bus with a driver from Rahat, who will be waiting with the doors open. Once Mohammad Al-Khatib enters, they'll quit the scene at full speed. But the price is high, and Mohammad Al-Khatib will have enough money only for a third of the way. With no money left, he'll have to hitchhike to the sea and arrive at around 5:00 p.m. on September 1, 2016. He'd have one full hour before needing to hitchhike back to Al-Khalil. But that hour with the sea is what counts. It counts for sixty minutes, or three-thousand-and-six-hundred seconds; an infinite time. Who could ever count up to three-thousand-and-six-hundred, except for the waves of the sea?

Finally, he'll be standing before the sea, where he will finally shout out loud: "This sea is mine." And we can imagine, under the present circumstances, two possible responses from the sea.

The first is that the sea might panic upon hearing Mohammad Al-Khatib's shouts (in Arabic obviously), and glimpsing in his raised hands as he runs towards it, what resembles a knife. The sea will think Mohammad Al-Khatib wants to stab it. Young men from Al-Khalil suspected of planning knife attacks are often covered in the news. That's why the sea cannot be cool about it. The sea will call the police to inform them about this shouting and running. But prior to their arrival, the sea will attempt to neutralize Mohammad Al-Khatib, pulling him to the ground, and dragging him in to contain the danger. But misfortune happens and Mohammad Al-Khatib dies in the process.

The second possibility is that the sea, upon hearing Mohammad Al-Khatib's shouts (in Arabic obviously), will open its heart, since this is the sea of Yafa and it has not heard Arabic in a long time. It might glimpse in the raised hands of Mohammad as he runs towards it, the hug he intends to give it. Like a lover's ear and eye, the sea won't confuse what its beloved is about to say... But like in love, once one claims another is theirs, the other is bound to claim the same.

As the sea hears Mohammad Al-Khatib shouting, "This sea is mine," it will call back, "You are mine." And the sea will not let go of Mohammad Al-Khatib ever again.

AMEERA'S JOURNEY TO ANDALUSIA

AMANY AL-SAYYED

"And this is my *fitna*:[3] women!" he jokingly says to her and the entire Lebanese tour group on the Alpujarras mountains in Granada. Women are Abe's addiction and joy. Love is not a weakness that needs staving off, and this is the city of women, of dolls, of pious virgins and cute bitches in one body. They come by the dozen each year to the south of Spain where Abe's job is to show them around as a *halal*[4] tour guide (she's never heard the Muslim story of Granada). Send these goddesses his way, O God, the Maria's and Lina's and Fatima's and Ayesha's-formerly-Britney's. The hybrids of past and present male fantasies combined, Abe has unlimited yearly access. Behind the infinite layers of moral cool, of Abe the great revivalist of a forgotten golden age of Islam, was this fact: he can be seduced. Walls and walls of Catholic-Muslim palaces surround Alhambra where this companion of kings threads every day in the fierce summer heat, where his desire falls. But this isn't a cheap kind of whore-saint sexual fantasy, or a secret desire for white flesh, brown and white, yellow and brown, or a combination of all. It isn't even a colonial inferiority complex riding as sexual weakness on his dark conscience. It is, rather, a desire without parameters unlike the reign of Isabella or the Moor's last sigh.

Abe's annual income is in the six-figure bracket. He works ten months a year, rests one, reads another. "Porsches and Lamborghinis do nothing for me," he says during lunch. Abe is single and forty-five but he isn't without love; quickly his unsolicited chivalry rises in his

---

3 Problem.
4 That which is permissible, as opposed to forbidden (*haram*), in Islamic law.

words to Ameera. "I did call to check up on you. I do care about you," he says after leaving her behind during one of the tours. She isn't furious, but she does communicate a clear won't-shop-if-you-won't-buy attitude from the first time they met, twenty-four hours ago. Not open to the ecstasy of a holiday in an imagined country on top of a real one, Andalusia on Spain, or was it the other way around? Was he fantasizing or was she? *Furious Desire is coming after me again*, he thinks when he sets eyes on her the second morning of the tour, in the breakfast lounge: orange hijab, pink organic lip-gloss, perfect combination, like the hues of Alhambra, he thinks; newly kindled flames are hard to deny. He withholds his fire, stands safe behind a fortress of moral cool. Everything about her conspired against him. She was five-foot one, had olive skin, dark eyebrows, and naturally pouting lips. She spoke five languages, finished his sentences when he struggled in translation between Spanish and Levantine Arabic. A dedicated fashionista, a fabulously inventive cook, an avid reader, singer, traveler, culturist, writer of short stories and a superb people watcher; a living Khadijah. *Ameerat Al-Andalus!*[5] Ameera loves her power over men, but Abe can take it all away if she falls in love. Difficult choices must be made here in imagined Alhambra located in real Spain, or the other way around.

O Dream-Andalusia!

Where does fury go to hide before the fall of true love? What sound makes the Moor of Spain on the hill of ruin? She had joined this tour (Granada, Orghiva, Cordoba) from Lebanon where she lives as a guest, (previously a migrant guest in Canada, before that Malta a guest, pre-birth in Ghana where her parents were guests, before that Lebanon, where her ancestors were guests. Lebanon was

5 Princess of Andalusia.

the first host after the Exodus from Home – Acre in Palestine. Here, it was we who received guests though some folks insist it's the other way around). But her mother is Lebanese, her father Palestinian, which is why she cannot claim Lebanese citizenship by law. Hers is a history of migration, refugees, global movement, a fluid life. Fast forward, twenty or twenty-five years later, and she has returned a grown woman to the Middle East to dig up her Arab heritage. She moves to Lebanon and embarks on a mission, observing olive trees and Palestinian people who have been there for a very long time. She was just in time to watch the 2012 Arab Spring unfold. She watched aunts, refugee camps, Tripoli, grape vine leaves, hummus, pollution, smog, village life, power cuts, water mafias, riots, protests, revolutions, police brutality, journalist bravado, photo albums, cappuccinos, lost recordings, Arabic *fusha*. This goes on for nine years. Does Ameera find an answer to "Who am I"? Maybe after death I'll have a story to tell you...

But the Palestinian story is the Andalusian story is the Arab story is the Universal fairy-tale. Ameera grew up on the Island of Malta in the early 1980s where she devoured the television set, Italian cartoons, in escape from her own picture-perfect life. She found places and historical sites on the Falcon Island too grandiose and golden-age, so she transformed La Meravigliosa Isola with concoctions of allegories and metaphors, contaminations of invention, alternative worlds, Beauty and the Beast. O how her heart sobbed for Belle. She did real things there too, like learn languages, make friends, and go on fieldtrips to the catacombs where she peered into the walled-up graves thinking a zombie will jump up and eat her alive. Miss Camilleri said those whom the gods want to destroy, they first make scared. She was scared. But she loved the vastness of cathedrals in Valletta where she looked high up, straining her neck just to see the tip of the renaissance ceiling. On Sundays, there was one tiny *masjid*[6] in Luqa where she went for Arabic lessons. She remembers two things: the ruler and the Libyan teacher. "Open your hands," he used to say, *whack*! because "homework means homework, *ya binti*."

Her Maltese was better than the locals', she memorized almost all of the pages from *Il-Denfil*, the book of poetry, just by sitting in class and listening silently like a thief. Her father warned her, "You're going to lose your Arabic with all this Maltese," or was it the other way around? Rescued; they say this isolated language is an uncontaminated form of Tripolian Arabic from long ago. The guest-stop in Malta lasted just over fifteen years, during this time her father was a soldier. Of tales. Once upon a time there lived a beautiful princess in a building in Lebanon, born to a traditional family. She grew, then grew older, then she wanted sex. Her father was distracted with loving her mother, the princess brought shame to the family, married the concierge. The end. Father's stories were always about shame, or women who can't tell the difference between love and sexual abuse; Ameera never really understood them but she pretended to. Dad and Ameera against the world; he was a poet, journalist, radio broadcaster, novelist, businessman, but no one heard of him; he was one of a kind. He lived in cities mostly, but his soul resided in stories.

O Father...

Growing up in Lebanon in the late 1950s, everyone knew he was simply too attractive. It would take the wits of Ibn Rushd[7] to decipher his mysterious allure. Have you ever seen someone – *a man* – actually stop traffic? Like arrest the motion of motor vehicles

---

6 Mosque or Islamic place of worship.

7 Averroes; a medieval Andalusian polymath who also wrote about Aristotelian and Islamic philosophy and theology.

and other mechanisms just by being present? He had that power. He would walk into the room and everyone jolted up in cadet salute, including elderly women and newborns. When he read poems in public, especially in the refugee camps, all the shops would close, even cafés and schools, just to hear him. Once, he walked home whistling his favorite revolutionary Darwish poem about bread. When he glanced back, hordes of people were following him, mesmerized by his tune! I once heard he could seduce an entire *harem*[8] without lifting a finger. They say he takes after his own father, the Mighty Peasant – a Palestinian from the West Bank. Her father is the eldest of six, but unlike all his siblings, he quickly developed unrequited love for formal education which was hard to pursue given his struggling financial situation. Still he chased his dream, under the dim light of the lamp-post in the middle of the night, he'd later tell his daughter, he would read books every day without fail. In 1948, when Palestinians were dispersed throughout the world, he moved to Lebanon's refugee camps. In time, he started attending university in Beirut and got a job teaching Arabic literature in Tripoli.

Mother...

The Princess. Not to say that wealthy princesses did not exist in the early 1960s in Tripoli's merchant town of tobacco mafias, weapons, and delightful Hallab sweets. But her chase for perfect beauty in almost every aspect of life, like satin white dresses and the Diana-of-Wales-highlights, wasn't easy to admire. Maybe because on her seventeenth birthday, somewhere between preparing breakfast and making fresh goat cheese, her mother decides to say, "Oh, and your real father is dead; this man who raised you is your uncle, his brother." The uncle married her mother (Ameera's grandmother) a

---

8 The women, wives, or concubines of a polygamous man.

few months after her father's death. Some say he'd always been in love with Vida, or Hayat in Arabic, who changed (translated, moved over) her name when she arrived in Lebanon before the Civil War as a fourteen-year-old bride. It was useless, she believed, to thrive on Venezuelan descent in an Orthodox Muslim family. Hayat-formerly-Vida's daughter (Ameera's mother) got her good looks from her father-uncle. Delicious roasted brown hair paired with chestnut eyes and porcelain skin, it was all him-them. But at the ripe age of two months, the girl was sent to live in Jordan with her father-now-uncle's parents (until this day, Ameera's mother hates this truth; how cruel of them to send off an infant into the unknown). She grew up and settled down into a good life on the reef of Jordan's desert and developed an admirable devotion for her grandparents; it all kept her from searching for anything beyond the next satin dress to show off to her jealous and unattractive friends. Meanwhile, Hayat-formerly-Vida and father-now-uncle visited sometimes. She came back to live for a while in Lebanon as a teenager because school was important to the family. Soon after, Hayat-formerly-Vida set off on a *niqah*[9]-crusade to find her daughter the prince she deserved, so she boasted about her to the entire elite community as a prize to be won only by the best man in town.

The Palestinian continued to thrive. He exceled at everything on the curriculum and he liked journalism. After school, he would interview prominent political figures in Beirut and publish their stories in local newspapers. He was Palestinian and she Lebanese. Hayat-formerly-Vida was in pieces when he proposed to her daughter (how they met, well it was at a school for traditional *dabkeh* dancing somewhere in Beirut; his knees locked in lust with hers somewhere between the first and third hop – one, two, three – hop,

9 Literally means conjunction or union. In Islamic law, it implies a marriage contract in the presence of two male witnesses.

hop, hop – step routine). She was supposed to marry the best man in Tripoli, definitely not a Palestinian. "Look," she told her daughter, "there are three wealthy Lebanese suitors asking for your hand. You must choose one." The answer came way too quickly, "I don't want any of them. I want the Palestinian."

O Father tell me...

The little princess from Tripoli married the Palestinian man, and from day one, father and mother became perfect strangers. Does it matter that she is pregnant with their fifth child on this forgotten island over there that belongs nowhere really, neither to Europe nor Africa? Still attractive as ever, she sports her gorgeous highlights with the flair of a princess and tightens her jeans like a soldier. Every single morning after fifteen years of marriage, she pens the darkest eyeliner around her warm chestnut eyes with feather-like precision so that her porcelain skin shines bright under the hot sun. One day in Catholic Malta, out of nowhere it seems, her five children watch her cover her hair with a scarf. Her skin, white as snow, shows no more. Her daughter says, "Mommy, it's too hot. Don't wear that." But in time, the girl comes to obey mother's discipline when it's time to memorize parts of the Qur'an, or go to the only *masjid* around, or play with the kids of the only Sheikh on the Island. Father is hardly there. Mother-now-veiled cleans, cooks, and keeps pretty for him, but his heart and mind and spirit grow elsewhere. Not with her. He joins the Palestinian political party and on the weekend, he sits at a quiet café to read the news or discuss pressing political issues or explore his words of poetry – sometimes while she sits there, quietly. He reads to her all the poetry his heart can bring, and all the news about Palestine he can find. For some reason, in Malta no one follows him spellbound, walking into lampposts, not even the cats. Keep going, Father, the daughter would think in her little mind, keep going, she'll like it one day, she'll get it one day. He tells her all about the seagulls of Acre, the salt in the sea, the sand at his feet, just in case it's true that two souls do become one. Even on his death-bed after thirty years of life with a Lebanese wife, it never came true that two could become one. Simple is the song of a peasant's daughter. Companionship, love, community, the world, these interwoven realities split in two cold fronts inside Ameera: saint-sinner, Palestine-Lebanon.

But Abe of Andalusia knows none of this. He doesn't ask; he's not into this sort of history, this autobiographical connect-with-your-dead-father's-story shit. As far as he's concerned, Ameera is his own fairy-tale come true. The weather changes, last day for the tour; it's time to go home. Alhambra suffers the heat of a fierce summer which has given way to a disturbed, pattern-less climate. There are many clouds and too much sun, and hot mornings that abruptly turn cold after brunch, sending shivers down the spine of the Muslim girls on the bus in their summer hijabs and dresses, snapping picture after picture, flowers, rivers, murals, insects, benches, dogs, cats, ice-cream cones, tables, streets, pizza slices, leaves, bridges, cars, men, women. *What a waste of time*, Abe thinks, with their Hermès handbags and iPhone 7's, dishonorable materialism, "Who do you think you are? What is the use of my lecturing on the wrath of Ysabella and Fernando who robbed us of our golden age, of the Nasiris, Abdallah Abu Sud, the Last Moor's Sigh, the companions of the beautiful Prophet, Mount Tarek and the Murabitun[10] of Morocco, the Slave Kings and La Reconquista, pigs and alcohol, and the celebration of May 3rd to spite Moriscos?"[11]

Tears stream down Abe's face unabashed. True love cannot be

---

10 An imperial Berber dynasty centered in Morocco, established in the 11th century and stretched over the western Maghreb and Al-Andalus.

11 Former Muslims who converted (by force) into Christianity after Spain outlawed the open practice of Islam in the early 16th century.

denied; these heroes must be loved. Another photo click, the girls chuckle while Abe lectures on about the lattice windows in Qasr Al-Saʻada in Alhambra. In that moment, he imagines a part of his own dream for the future, the future in which he too would break through the barriers that hold him back from becoming without horizons, without cold fronts and halves, without changing names of streets in Granada, or catacombs turned from *masjids*, without lines that cut through him. A future with no parameters where only desire falls. He imagines he saw a part of his Limitlessness going up in that awful flash of the iPhone 7; click, gone.

"The Andalusian is destined to last," Abe says to himself, his eyes locked on *Ameerat Al-Andalus* standing with the girls at the end of this journey.

Mayhem

Aisha Isam

My chest is drowning in worry. No room for fear is left within me, just sorrow filling my heart to the brim; overflowing like bitter coffee dregs dribbling down the edges of a small floral cup, the same cup once used to serve dear and esteemed guests. The cup and the company have long disappeared. The dull hum no longer resembles death but salvation to us all.

They whistle as they drop; one, two... seven. The pounding through my veins travels to my toes, climbs up my legs, curdles my blood, and shakes my spine. The picture frames rattle against the walls. They can only hold on for so long. I grab my prayer clothes to cover my hair and bosom just in case. Always just in case. The ticking clock on the wall infuriates me. How can it be so dedicated? Restlessly and continuously counting down to something – so mechanically genuine and with absolute disregard for everything else.

I gather what I know. There is no time to waste. I run like I taught you to. Run like I used to see you do, dashing across the dirty alleys, trying to catch someone or something. Run towards darkness, where death might be deceived into not catching you. You do not have to put sandals on. No, you cannot look for your doll. The faster we leave, the faster we'll be able to come back and turn the TV on. Go! I am sorry I keep lying to you.

The staircase has always been endless. One-hundred-and-twelve steps. I count them every time to distract my aching arms from the heavy onions and eggplants. I count them in anticipation as soon as the clock hits 1:30 in the afternoon and the kids burst out of the school gates and run across the city. But it is different this time. Everything is different this time '– the steps have multiplied by a hundred. The metal railing, turquoise for the most part, but silver where memories were forced on it, goes on forever. Are we running up or down an endless circle? Everything mixes together. I no longer know whose name to call.

When will we reach the last step? How long until my feet can touch the loose and shaky tiles of the ground floor? I want to assure the universe that we are still here, that my feet have yet to take multiple trips back and forth through the entrance of our building. Is it going to rain? The July sky has been sullied by all of this mushroom-shaped smoke encroaching upon the skyline. Grim and opaque, it summons memories of winter – not the best, but they will do for now. I force my memory back, for the sake of distraction, to when the first raindrops trickled shyly down my windows as I placed small pots where the ceiling was most likely to leak. This time, however, the sky is shameless about what it is hailing. Audaciously pouring a different kind of rain that no one prayed for. Pieces of something or another, possibly scraps of furniture and flesh, flying around so recklessly that they could be mistaken for flocks of pigeons.

A unified roar and a wave of sweltering heat bring us all to our knees. A buzz fills my ears. I fight it as I try to listen closely, but my ears are filled with yellow noise and pebbles. Sacks of rubble render the outer world mute. Maroon colors my vision as I inspect my surroundings with what's left of it. Nothing. How am I so alone all of a sudden? I taste something sour on my tongue. I spit it out, again and again. Nothing can choke back the bile that is fear. I swallow some of it down. My forehead rains and I allow it to, for jasmines may grow here next spring. Why are you so alone?

It still smells like home where I am, where it was moments ago. The distinct scent of cumin intertwines with that of woe. *Za'tar* mixes with dirt so agreeably. The aroma of coffee vanishes from my surroundings as if the walls were never soaked with its scent. My nostrils clog and I am certain this is the end, or near to.

I feel the wreckage around my bruised body which I caress with my remaining nerves. It is coarse and difficult just like my daughter's hair. These walls, with all their secrets, weigh heavily against my shoulders, heavier than the guilt I have borne for so long. A woman, unmarried for a long time. A woman, with three girls. A woman whose husband fled. What a shameful fate. Secrets and afternoon gossip have made these walls weigh heavier than they are meant to withstand, and I wish they would speak to me, I to them, to alleviate this weight. From wall to woman – and woman to wall.

There they are, stepping on top of me, asking if I can hear them. My throat bursts. There is nothing like a call for rescue. I wonder how many times I have wished I were dead, but not this time. Is it not curious how a woman's voice is shameful and she is forced to keep it down at all times – except at times like this? No man can touch a woman either, until war breaks out and all laws crumble, making you untouchable no longer. Yes, this time, you are touched, no, yanked, out of the folds of death and carried with love and prayer. All intimacy is permissible in times of war.

I forget it is daytime until the sun pierces my olive eyes, my pupils shrinking to the size of a sesame seed. Where to now? I absurdly dust my prayer skirt and think of how to cry when I cannot yet find my voice. There are so many faces and different sounds of wailing around me that I do not care for. I have only one concern but, much like my own heart, I cannot yet place it. So I wave fiercely, one hand slapping against my chest, the other drawing a figure in the empty air. They ask me how many. They want to know how many of you there are, and I forget how to count. Four, I finally exclaim. Four children, ten years in total. No, their father was not home, I remind the rescuers and myself. He had to attend to another, smaller, fresher family a year or two ago, I do not care to recall. I still cannot count properly. After living under fire, you lose everything; from lovers to the ability to articulate, from your gold earrings to yourself. They all go somewhere out of sight. And in the rush of it all, I never stop to wonder how it is possible for all this to fall upon me, me of all women. I, who was deemed fragile and weak, here I am, rising from beneath the boiling ashes of my recent past, my arm is a sword, my ribcage a shield. How am I so unbreakable?

I still do not know which names to call. *Ya Allah. Ya Lateef.*[12] My eyes catch those of strange men, and naturally shy away. Do they feel what I feel? The scene around me paints itself into an ugly picture, the kind that ends up on the front page of a newspaper, and gradually turns into a makeshift tablecloth for a group of construction workers somewhere other than here, who could not care less about my aching bones for they have their own to worry about.

My chest is a drum, deafening me from hearing anything but the moans of the earth beneath my feet. I watch my steps – someone might still be there. Soon, blocks are going to be lifted, and old furniture will rise from the rubble as if to announce that life once existed here. It will amuse someone with a camera and a twisted taste for art. How sadistic. Soon after that, fingers will slowly appear,

---

12 An expression meaning, "Oh God; oh merciful one."

braids and souls. I call your names, one by one – oldest to youngest. The earth continues to moan, motionlessly.

I see you. Why are we so far apart? I asked you to stay near me. I count your limbs. Three and a half. God is great. I assure you that the doctors at the local hospital will look after you, but I have to stay and wait for the fate of your siblings. I walk through the rubble hoping to identify something or someone myself, but how is that possible when the last thing these faces had seen was a suffocating, hideous darkness screaming at them as it snatched the life out of their damp eyes? Another one is grabbed. Not mine.

My voice knows no bounds, but it is now confined by the walls of fear and memory. The world slowly turns orange and my shadow is now enormous. Look at you! With three hundred walls collapsed against your back, your spine is still as stiff as a palm tree. Your neck is resilient atop your golden shoulder blades. Invincible.

But just as the clock on the only remaining wall continues ticking, a blatant truth emerges. I lose hope and with it, my balance. A wooden stick formulates in my hand without warning. I kneel and my mother's perfume comes to mind. I start poking holes into the dirt, "Breathe, my dear." It feels as if I've been silently weeping for ninety-two weeks.

I drag myself further until I am completely squatting like a beetle. I cannot see the sun; all I see are a hundred clouds gathering, sneaking up to observe me in my naked agony. I sense that what is left of the city's trees has been set on fire, although no smoke or flames can be seen, just a wild smell lingering among white shrouds hanging from a clothes line.

"Have you ever heard of phantom pain?" I ask the earth just as I pierce a hole into it.

"No," the earth speaks softly. Its tenderness repulses me.

"It is pain one feels from a body part that is no longer there."

"How do you know this?"

I cackle. You should not ask such questions.

"Where are you keeping them?"

"Within."

"Can I speak to them? I need to make sure they are warm."

"You do not want to speak to them."

Restless, I try to remind the earth that I am mighty, that although I am made of clay, my bones are still intact. The earth does not yield to my stabs. It is clear to me now that neither earth nor man have any mercy left. No heart except mine, as bloody and weary as it is, will survive, as it has always done.

"Is he under a tree? My son?"

"I do not know. There are too many of them."

As I wade through the layers of earth, my wooden stick encounters clots that have grown too rough. I spit to soften them, and they break. I did not know the earth was so weak, but I remain silent to not set it off. Unlike the clock, the earth is far too unpredictable.

A fire ant appears from the eastern side. It crawls towards me, drawing its insignificant body nearer and stings me. I shriek as it bites further into my thigh. I scream, cutting my lip. The ant is now walking away to its kingdom, carrying a chunk of my flesh in its mouth. It's at this point that I realize I am never going to be whole again.

"Do you cry?" I revive the conversation.

"No; the skies do," the earth responds nonchalantly.

"But I swear I heard you cry the other day, underneath our apartment building."

"It is not I; it is they."

"Why do they cry?"

"It is a collective cry of joyous laughter; do not be fooled."

"Does my son laugh?"

"I do not know. They are too many."

With every hole I make, the earth swallows its damp dirt deeper into its underbelly, silently and without a trace, in the same manner it swallowed my children's broken bones. I cry to the earth to bear responsibility, but it feigns innocence. I slowly learn that the earth has a habit of letting things slide, hiding stolen treasures within. Like gold, all they were and all they were meant to be is hidden.

"Tell me, will they remember the smell of our kitchen? Of olive oil and bread?" I ask impatiently. The earth does not respond so I shove my face into it. Dirt fills my still bleeding mouth and I have no spare second to spit it out. The holes I poked should make it easier for my eyes to sneak a look. No use. I immerse my face fully and attempt to speak. But the earth's thick layers ricochet my injured voice, and it only comes back stronger and deeper to splice through my upper lip. I cough out all of the worms and dead roots.

I stand up straight to widen the holes but the earth swallows my wooden stick. Resentment courses through me. The earth chooses to remain silent, persisting, just like my yearning for an answer. I stab the dirt with my bare hands. The earth slashes any flesh that comes its way. And yet, with my naked hands, I tug at all that I can salvage. I dig deeper and lose three fingernails. "Does it not scare you how livid

I am?" I ask as I grasp the earth and smother it within my palms. I scream into it. Milk gushes out, a fountain without a source. Pain is no longer a phantom; it is present in the very color of grapes. I gather what I can of the damp earth with my bleeding hands, and hurl it at the clouds to scatter and diffuse it.

This is what I will remember of you. You are a rogue; a vile thief. This is what I'll remember about the earth the day it betrayed me. Despite it all, the sun comes out, this time with a bang, screaming obscenities at every living thing save for me and the dead beneath me.

Perhaps I, too, am dead.

A Paper Nest

IRADA AL-JUBOURI

Waseem left early that day without having breakfast. She called after him. He came back, hugged her, and kissed her forehead.

"*Mama*, I'm in a hurry."
"Let grandpa take you to school."
"No, Mom, let grandpa sleep."

Seventeen minutes later came the sound of an explosion that shook the whole house and shattered the kitchen window. She had already left the kitchen to get her purse and go to work. She froze at the blast. She had no recollection how she left the house or how she ran in the street while her father followed in his car. She jumped in without even realizing it was him driving. They neared the school and found the street blocked by the police. They wouldn't let her get any closer. Dust and clouds of smoke made it impossible to see anything, and the throngs of families and people pushing to get through created uncontrollable panic. Policemen fired shots into the air in a desperate attempt to hold back the crowds and disperse the human tide, for fear of another explosion...

Yusra got out of the car and made her way forward, paying no attention to these warnings or to her father's plea to stay where she was. She told the officer, "You can't stop me from finding my son – you'll have to kill me first!"

He tried to make her understand that the fires were still burning, and that going in could impede the rescue operations. He took her by the hand, led her over to the fire truck, and asked her to wait for him there. She had no choice but to believe him and simply wait for the moment when she would see him bringing her son out to her.

He told her that her son was fine and she just had to stay calm. She stood there, unable to figure out what the different movements of the firemen and emergency workers meant. Slowly, these images faded, mixed in with the noises, and moved further away. She couldn't understand what they were saying... she heard whispers nearby... she could make out her father's voice and another one she recognized, but she couldn't remember where she'd heard it.

She tried to lift her head to see whose voice it was. But it felt heavy and nausea overtook her, making her rethink trying to get up and finding her bearings. She felt a hand touch her forehead. "Don't tire yourself out, *habibti*," her dad said in a muffled voice, kissing her forehead. When his lips grazed her brow she felt a pain piercing her side. She had fled from the blood-stained sports shoe that an EMT was carrying on a stretcher, next to a burned body.

With the nurse's help, Yusra pulled herself up with difficulty and sat up straight. She opened her eyes. Her husband Nabil was standing there confused, not knowing what to do. He tried to say something. She closed her eyes: "The best thing you could do is to get out of my life." Her voice sounded strange. It was as if she was hearing it for the first time. The husky voice that he loved had left her forever, and a harsh new one replaced it. It was so coarse that it hurt her throat when she uttered those words. She couldn't see his reaction. She didn't know if he stayed for some time or left at that moment. She said those words and sank back into her own world that was flickering with memories and the remnants of nightmares.

She spent days in the hospital, cared for by her father's doctor friends, surrendering to the sedatives they pumped into her. When it came time to return home, she went with no objections, questions, or comments. She simply left one bed at the hospital for another at home. Her oldest friend, Basma, and her cousin, Zeina, took turns sitting with her, and always stayed until her father came back from his clinic in the evening.

In the short periods of time between the girls' shifts, she'd call out to Waseem to feed the cat – the cat he once fed that started waiting for him every day at the kitchen door. The cat's meowing was like hot water being poured into blocks frozen in her memory in forms ready for oblivion. She'd call out to him before getting out of bed, "Waseem, the sun's up, you're going to be late." She'd call him and go next door to his room, where her hands would freeze on the handle of the locked door.

Basma and Zeina packed clothes, books, and everything else belonging to Waseem into suitcases they left inside his room and locked the door. But they couldn't box up his absence to make her forget his laughter, his comments, his sense of fun, his voice filled with needless apology every time he went to sleep over at his father's house, and his excessive happiness whenever he came back to his room and his world, saying nothing about what he did during his time away. They'd always shared a true mutual understanding without having to make the effort to speak. But he would blush whenever he saw Hiba, Zeina's daughter, and this would make Yusra smile. Sometimes when she'd sing meaningful songs about love, he'd lose his temper and shout, "Mom, don't act like this." Then she'd quarrel with him and ask with feigned innocence, "What... is singing forbidden?" He would accept defeat, fearing the conversation might lead to areas he didn't want to delve into. Those were some of her special moments with him; they filled her with joy and happiness...

Everyone was worried about the way Yusra was acting. She didn't cry. She didn't do anything that would have been appropriate considering what she'd gone through. She didn't even ask to be taken to her son's grave. She never asked what had happened to him, the school, or the other students.

She used to avoid any hint of the incident or her son. When she forgot, went to Waseem's room and found it locked, she neither asked for the key nor objected to it being locked. She would sit and watch television advertisements endlessly. She ate, drank tea, and watched ads that were repeated dozens of times a day.

One Friday, Baba Mahmoud woke up and found her in her usual place staring at the screen without batting an eyelid. He observed her for a few minutes without her noticing. That was when he became sure she was stuck somewhere else, that she couldn't even see what was right in front of her.

With no explanation, her father told her to get dressed. She didn't resist or ask why. She simply did what he asked. She got into the car next to him. She sat down and looked out at the road calmly; he searched for a good station on his car radio. Then he switched it off and stared straight ahead.

As soon as they left the center of town, he avoided the anxious looks she was giving him. Condensed corridors of eucalyptus trees loomed ahead as did the woman selling rosewater and sweets. She closed her eyes and shouted, "*Baba*, go back!"

He paid no attention to her pleas. He kept driving and bit his lip so that he wouldn't start crying himself. He stopped the car. She had hidden her head between her knees. He got out of the car and opened her door, imploring, "Come on, *habibti*, let's say hello to Waseem."

"No, *Baba*."

He burst into tears and started pleading with her, "It's okay to cry; come on."

He walked away and sat down near his grandson's grave, crying bitterly while also talking to his daughter, "Come, *ya binti*, pay your respects, come and cry over Waseem's grave. Don't leave me here all alone. Come over and let's try to get through this together."

Her father's trembling voice moved her. She went over and tried to comfort him. Concerned about him collapsing, she ignored the ceramic headstone, which bore the name of her only child, along with the date of his birth and death.

When the sun had begun to set, they were still at Waseem's grave. Her father finally stopped crying while she was arranging stones around the grave, as though she were fluffing up sofa cushions. Her face was drenched in sweat as she moved the stones around, rearranging them, her lips tightly pursed so she wouldn't let a moan or wail escape. Her father stood up and in a sharp voice ordered her, "Yusra, enough. I beg you in the name of our beloved Waseem..."

She ignored him and continued her futile act of moving stones from one side to the other. He approached her and grabbed her face, "This is Waseem, your son Waseem. Read his name written here."

"No!" She screamed loudly, violating the cemetery's silence.

He embraced her and whispered gently, "*Habibti*, what you are doing to yourself and to me is wrong..."

She fell apart in broken sobs and threw herself onto the grave. The sun was almost completely gone, and it had started to get cold.

He whispered, "Let's go... It's hard for me to drive at night." "But how can we leave Waseem here all alone in the dark?"

Gently, he pulled her towards the car and they drove back home in silence. At moments she sobbed in anguish, at others she sat quietly. That night she got out their family photo albums, searching for Waseem's features. When she couldn't recall them she stopped. She passed her fingers over his face tenderly and affectionately; she stroked his hair and hugged his photos. She was careful to avoid the pictures that showed Waseem's father. She avoided mentioning his name and all connection to him. She tried to erase every trace of him as much as she tried holding on to any trace of her son.

Waseem's absence meant a much greater presence of his father/ her ex-husband, as she insisted on calling him. Referring to him was unavoidable when she had to describe his connection to her and her son. Her feelings of anger towards Waseem's father recently had transformed into pure hatred, and she stopped desiring him, even when he exhibited his usual prowess during sex. As if searching for additional reasons to hate him, she'd started blaming him for Waseem's tragic death. She'd felt hostile to life itself since losing him.

The strange and confused years of her marriage didn't allow her to break with life completely. But she kept herself at a clear distance from "having a life." In the end, she rebelled against that lonely state of hovering between having one and having none. She thought of it as a state of suspension. If she wasn't able to actively live, she would keep herself on standby. She engaged with life like she engaged with the rules of Arabic. At the end of the day, there were the rules of grammar and there was breaking them.

Ever since she was married, she had felt forgotten. No one knew what she was living through – not her father, not her female relatives, not her girlfriends, not her colleagues at work. She never shared what happened to her and would remain silent when one of them talked about a problem with her husband or boyfriend. Her pride prevented her from disclosing anything.

Only as the water from the shower spilled over her body did she allow herself to reveal her pain. She wept bitterly, sometimes repeating, "What have I done to myself?" She spent time in the bathroom without fearing that it would arouse her husband's suspicions. He always watched how her features changed – when she was silent, when she was sad, when she laughed. In their last years together, she was no longer able to laugh or be sad at all. Calm silence was chiseled onto her face. He used to repeat his sole wish in her earshot, "How I wish I knew what you were thinking!"

In amicable moments, he never failed to mention that it would take more than her rare smiles to distract him from her damaged mouth, which was no longer good for kissing or telling secrets. He liked to point out what was lacking in her so he could feel better about himself.

Her silence gave her girlfriends and cousins the illusion that her marriage was perfect. She was never brave enough to tell anyone that her life was on hold indefinitely, but she knew it deep down. Nestled inside her, waiting, was that moment from which the secrets of her marriage would burst forth, never to return.

He once told her that he would kill her if she thought of leaving him. The truth was that he was both obsessed with that moment and ignored it at the very same time. "You will never live in peace if you leave me. Don't think that you will get together with another man. No one would consider marrying a divorced woman."

She calmly answered him, "A woman doesn't necessarily separate from her husband in order to marry another man."

Her calm indifference provoked him. The way she talked while changing the television channels, as if she were lazily commenting on a talk show she was following.

"I won't kill you; I'll kill him," he added with growing anger.

"You'll kill who?"

"You know who."

"No, I don't know who you're talking about." (She'd found the channel that carried her favorite program, "Oprah").

"Look at me when I am talking to you!" his voice rose threateningly.

He made for the television set, and stood between her and the screen looking at her anxiously. She left the remote and went into her bedroom while he sat smoking greedily, following the news and reports of wars and violence in the world.

He sent her a message that he wouldn't divorce her. She didn't reply. The loss of Waseem made her lose all desire to respond. "I won't go back to his house," she said. And the matter was closed.

When her father's health worsened and he was advised to go abroad to recuperate, she needed her husband to come to the passport office so she could get a new passport. That's when she lost her sense of balance, calm, and any shred of patience she had left. She shouted right in the face of the employee at the passport office that he was no different than the ones who killed her son – corrupt murderers, they all were, who enjoyed abusing their authority over innocent people, and especially women. She screamed at him and left before he could figure out how to respond in front of all the people lined up at the window waiting their turn. In an attempt to deal with his confusion and embarrassment, he said, "Poor woman!"

She left the passport office with no destination in mind. She walked on roads where the fumes of melting asphalt were rising as the temperature exceeded fifty degrees Celsius. She just wanted to walk and walk until she fell unconscious under the wheel of a car, got hit by a roadside bomb, or by stray bullets hailing on the streets like rice thrown at a bride and groom in a summer wedding.

She felt no sense of victory when her father's assistant brought her new passport to her. Her father knew what she was thinking and said, "We had no choice except to pay off an employee..."

*

Yusra returns ten years later, some of these years were spent as a refugee; others as a citizen. She'd been working as a translator in refugee camps, which were proliferating to absorb the Iraqi, Syrian, Libyan, Yemeni, and Sudanese Diasporas. Basma doesn't dare pose the question that any person – known or unknown – would be eager to ask: "Why did you come back?"

She had known Yusra since they were teenagers. She knew Yusra would come back some day and was surprised when she didn't return after her father Mahmoud died only a few weeks after they'd left. She expected her to bring his body back and bury him next to Waseem. But she didn't. She got in touch only on specific occasions that meant something to the two of them: after the first time they'd quarreled in middle school, they were never apart again; their birthdays; their children's birthdays. It hurt Basma to call Yusra on Waseem's birthday but she found not calling her even more painful. They didn't really talk during such calls. They only reached out so that one of them could say to the other—I am with you wherever you are...

The sun spills onto the kitchen table where they are sitting enjoying their afternoon tea. Yusra had always loved winter afternoons. When she was living outside Iraq, she'd shed secret tears for these very moments. She missed the blazing heat and the cool breezes of harsh August noontimes. She sits with Basma, watching the way the bulbul bird is hopping around restlessly in a cage hanging in a corner of the kitchen. When the sun starts to sink lower in the sky, she gets the urge to tell her friend the story of Nisreen who at twenty fled an arranged marriage she'd actively resisted. She paid the price of being married; her body bore the scars of beatings and torture. She escaped her marital house and Iraq with smugglers who advised her to reinvent herself as a Yezidi, and create a story about fleeing from a family who enslaved her. But she told her true, unembellished story to Yusra and the interviewing committee.

She briefly wonders if it's right to talk about what Nisreen revealed to her, the ways she suffered as the lone female on a refugee journey from home until the moment they met? Instead she reminisces about their lives and secrets together.

"Remember when we used to drink tea during the embargo?"
"Ha, ha... We'd have to wait for Abu Yasser to bring tea and soap from Jordan and then we'd distribute them like Eid gifts, using only a

tiny bit at a time so they'd last longer."

"Poor Abu Yasser! Did you know that his son Yasser was in love with my little sister? Then he disappeared on the road to Jordan, at least that's what we know of the story..."

Absorbed by Basma's story, she becomes aware that she'd heard it before and it was going to make her cry. She was very conscious of how conversations unfold between Iraqis who have not seen each other for a while. She thinks of changing the topic to Europe, to the bathroom in Robin Hood Square, or maybe to the homeless man who loved her jet-black hair. This would surely make her friend laugh and then she'd want to encourage her to talk about her adventures in different cities and countries... the memories that fill her like salt fills a sea breeze. She'd certainly ask, like she does every time she calls, "Aren't you tired of it yet? How much longer are you going to be homeless and husbandless?"

Yusra swallows her answer and looks out through the window at the sky. She tries to catch the rattle about to escape her throat by asking a question, but fails to make it sound like a joke, "Can I change the question?"

On the other side of this conversation, Basma is aware that there's no use continuing her line of questioning when it sounds more like reproach than advice. So she stops asking. She notices how pale her friend's face has gotten and what this means to both of them. So she changes the conversation so they wouldn't be forced to deal with the past, steering it instead towards grandchildren and their worlds.

"Can you imagine Riyam, not even five years old, telling her father, 'Daddy, don't interfere in my life!' He didn't know whether to collapse in a fit of laughter or act like a serious father."

As she watches the bulbul in its cage, Yusra asks her friend unexpectedly, "Does Nabil still like birds?"

"Not like he used to... we've had this female for two years now and he hasn't thought of finding a male for her." The bird is busy tearing the newspaper lining the bottom of the cage into strips.

"Does he call you guys?"

"Sometimes he gets in touch. He tries to seem spontaneous and asks for a friend's number that he knows I'll have. He'll keep circling around different subjects and people, which will lead to you. Sometimes I'm in the mood to play along; other times I cut him and the conversation off. I know he still loves you, though. Don't you have any regrets?"

The question comes as a surprise to her.

"No," she replies – sharp and sure. Basma waits for her friend to continue talking, but she'd effectively silenced this line of conversation.

"Even now I don't really know what happened..." She keeps hoping to drag her back into the conversation but receives only silence in return and glances that seem directed at the birdcage but go beyond that...

Yusra wants so much to be able to share what had happened. There were no words to express the sting of what she'd lived through with him, how she'd lost a bit of her soul each day. Like the olive tree she watched for months through her bedroom window, its fruits falling off before they'd ripened. It started withering and slowly lost its leaves until termites destroyed it, and all that was left was a hollow tree trunk which couldn't resist that one autumn wind... The olive tree collapsed in the middle of the garden that day, smashing into the rose bushes that lay bewildered beneath it. On that same day she decided to leave and never return. She realized she would lose whatever self-respect she had left if she kept ignoring her self-loathing whenever he touched her body after a quarrel over her "inappropriate" behavior, which usually ended with apologies, kisses, and promises of eternal, unconditional love. She allows her mind to drift to a distant memory of Waseem...

He stood in the doorway as if he knew what she was thinking, "Mom, I know."

She turned to him and realized that her son had grown up in the blink of an eye. While she was getting ready to leave the house that day, Waseem waited for her at the door, holding his school bag and staring at the fallen olive tree, which had dragged the electricity lines tangled in its branches down with it. The different colors of the wires helped the neighbors distinguish between them in case of a breakdown in the generators that supplied power to the houses in their area.

"Why are their last days always filled with signs we don't notice until after they're gone?" She surprises herself by saying this aloud.

"*Habibti*, Yusra... I don't know what to say. Waseem is one of thousands of innocents who've left us... I only wish he were the last!"

Any words spoken now would be tinged with sorrow. Basma doesn't know what to say or how to manage these moments. She pours a little tea into her cup and notices that Yusra hasn't touched hers yet.

Yusra wants only quiet. Once words are spoken, you can't take them back. That's why she sought out silence and the frenzied search for fun and jokes she shared with an enthusiasm unmatched by her girlfriends and acquaintances. She wants only to talk about Nisreen: about the light that shone on her face when she sang songs in broken Arabic by Salima Murad, to whom she'd listen only to humor others at first, but then it transformed into a real love and passion for

Murad's music. She wants to talk about the strength Nisreen gave her. She wants to tell Basma about how she had put her life on hold for as many years as Nisreen was old.

The light of day is now gone. Basma closes the kitchen curtain. The female bulbul sits in the corner of the cage picking at newspaper bits balled up to the side. She almost tells Basma about Nisreen and her decision to return. But she changes her mind at the last minute and gets up to leave. She kisses her friend and says to her in a voice filled with the warmth of the sun, "Tell Nabil to bring the female a male or else set her free."

Translated by Michelle Hartman

The Angel

HANAN AL-SHAYKH

The woman asked her guests to leave at once, instead of inviting them to eat the food laid out in the dining room. She managed only to say, "My son, my son," before hurrying back to the bathroom, where her 28-year-old son lay, still high. He was crumpled like a dead leaf in the corner. The needle lay on his thigh like a baby's dummy, his belt squeezed around his arm, and a soft-drink straw for the white powder was discarded on the floor.

The woman bit her lip, regretting the dinner party which she had hoped would transform the atmosphere in the flat. As she served the guests, she had kept an eye on the front door, feeling the keys to the locked bedrooms safe and sound in her pocket.

She had imagined her son finding the rooms locked and retreating to the bathroom to inject himself, not caring that he couldn't lock himself in. Then her heart throbbed as she imagined her boy startled by the unexpected appearance of a guest, barging through the door, the needle going astray in his surprise and harming him.

So she had prayed for her guests' bladders to remain empty as she refilled their glasses.

And there he was, his arm swelling like an elephant's foot, red blood oozing from it. She howled, silently scolded him, pitied him, pitied herself. Her recriminations were like water repelled by a steel eardrum. He had constantly warned her to stop pleading; her weeping infiltrated his veins and urged him on.

She decided to pack a case and leave. But coming out of the bathroom, she found her guests' eyes upon her. They rushed in with sympathy but she pushed them away, like a swimmer upstream. Then, embarrassed, she pretended to seek their help, mumbling, "There is no hope for my son, he is slipping out of my arms. He's finished. Nothing can wean him off his habit except divine intervention."

"Let us say a special prayer for an angel to come and save this poor boy," one of the guests whispered.

A second protested, "Let's not waste time waiting for angels. Let's get him to a clinic now and we'll all help you with the cost."

"I wasn't talking about angels with wings, but angels who will bring God and meaning to this boy's life," the first guest insisted.

A third guest said, "Just give me fifteen minutes and please try to do nothing."

"No doctors or policemen, please," the mother whispered.

The third guest took hold of the woman's hands. "No doctors or policemen, I promise, just wait. Fifteen minutes and I'll be back."

Fifteen minutes or fifteen centuries, the mother couldn't go in the bathroom, worried that her son would wake and shout abusive insults at her. She couldn't stand the whispering, the praying, the questions of her visitors who were crammed in the corridor like sardines in a tin.

When the third guest returned he was shrouded in a white bedsheet, holding two feathered wings.

Adjusting the wings, he said, "I used to flutter them every time I had a date in college, the girls went crazy, now hurry and get me flour." When no one moved, he went into the kitchen himself, opening and closing the kitchen cabinets, until the mother went in, reached into the cupboard and handed him a bag of flour. He poured it over his head, transforming himself into a white angel.

He pushed the bathroom door open and closed it behind him. The mother and the guests were nailed to the floor as though birds were perched on their shoulders. They heard the boy exclaiming, "Oh you've found me, lovely angel!"

Noises came from the bathroom: running water; breaking glass; jumping footsteps; and the boy's only words, "This and this, and this."

Then silence gave birth to stillness. The mother took a few soft steps towards the bathroom, like a cat, and went in.

"Mum you're not going to believe what happened! An angel found me! He held my hand with his two wings, then a strange light drained my arm like an alligator nibbling fingers. I found myself bringing everything out from its hiding place, stamping on the syringes and needles and pouring the heroin down the washbasin."
She resisted the urge to embrace her son.
"You don't believe me, do you?" he said, "you never believe a single word I say. I'm telling you that an angel came in to the bathroom..."
"But where is he?" the mother said, looking around.
"What do angels do?" said her son. "They come and live among us. Angels fly..."

The mother looked out the open window and into the night beyond.

On the Seventh Floor

RAYA HAJJ

She was humming to herself in the shower that day, a surprise even to her. She always woke up pissed off and never wanted to leave her queen-sized bed. "But today is different," she told herself while drying and straightening her hair. She carefully put on her makeup, still wrapped in her warm towel. She always made sure her eyeliner wasn't too thick and her lipstick wasn't too bright, but she just didn't care today. "Today is different," she smiled to herself.

She didn't spend her usual fifteen minutes staring blankly inside her closet. She had already chosen her outfit: the grey dress with black lace on the neckline that she had decided to save for a special occasion. With her high heels on, she looked a bit more like her mother than she had planned, but she didn't mind. She thought of her mother as the most beautiful woman on earth anyway.

She looked around the bedroom before going out the door. Her bed was made up, the curtains drawn back letting the light in, the pictures on the wall smiling back at her. She was still humming to herself while cooking breakfast, which she enjoyed preparing today, because she never really had the time to tend to herself. "But today is different," she mumbled while whipping the eggs and pouring them over the meat balls in the pan. She sipped her coffee with a smile on her face, satisfied that she wasn't going to have the healthy breakfast she usually had.

She put away the plates, the cup, looked around her tiny kitchen for misplaced items, and was content that everything was in order. Her small home was rarely so spotless; her mother would have been proud, although she hated the idea of her daughter living alone in the city. She personally liked having her apartment a little messy; it gave it some life. "But today's different," she whispered as she stepped out on her barely-a-balcony on the seventh floor, the one that looked out on the busy highway below. "Today's the day I'll find out," she said a little too loudly, to no one in particular, as soon as she stood on the ledge. And as she was dismissing the ringing phone inside and the little voice at the back of her head telling her to reconsider this decision, she just leaped forward.

Seventh floor, sixth floor, fifth. She couldn't control her breathing and her limbs were flailing about as if they had a mind of their own. The wind was hitting her face hard, and tears pricked her eyes as everything started to become blurry. Being the perfectionist that she's always been, she had planned this day to the smallest detail. The dress, the hair, even the timing. She pictured herself diving through the air like an Olympian would have, her chest open, hair flying freely, with a sea of faces watching her angelic look, for at least five or six good seconds, the time it would take her to hit the concrete ground below. But the thing is, she knew her aimless fidgeting was ruining her moment and she was starting to run out of time. "It should have started by now! It should have started by now!" she thought in a panic, starting to question the integrity of the people who wrote about their near-death experiences, a subject that had consistently sparked her curiosity. She was everything but impulsive you see, so her decision to stand on that ledge that morning was long premeditated. She wasn't depressed; she wasn't terminally ill. But having reached the peak of her career at such a young age, she was convinced that whatever she'd be doing next would only lead her one way: down. So she wanted one last moment of greatness, of freedom, as long as she was on top. And to give herself the recognition no one else would, she'd have the exclusive honor to watch her life flash before her eyes.

She had tried talking to her mother about it when she stopped sleeping, about this very bad feeling at the pit of her stomach, about how she had sacrificed her twenties for a career she was thrown into just to have a constant safety net, and how she had to turn down relationships, friendships, and even acquaintanceships just so no one could jeopardize her position at the firm. She was concerned that her managers were hungry for "new blood," those young leeches they're recklessly recruiting, and she couldn't accept it. She had worked so hard and gone through hell to get to where she was. She didn't want anyone snatching it from her. And all her mother was able to tell her was: "Stop having such dark thoughts sweetie; you're beautiful and smart, and they're lucky to have you. Life goes on whatever happens. Now stop whining and take me to the supermarket." She immediately regretted opening up to her. Don't get her wrong, she loved her mom, but they had stopped talking a while ago. Well, her mother talked and she just listened and nodded approvingly to whatever she said.

She knew she couldn't turn to Alex about this. He had broken up with her a few weeks earlier when she proved to him once again that her career was more important than he was. Even though he was the only person in the world that she trusted, she couldn't imagine herself saying yes to his marriage proposal, because that would mean letting her guard down at the office in order to start a family. She knew she couldn't handle both, and she definitely couldn't risk failing at either of the two. Besides, he kept pushing her and demanding excellence, and in doing so, consistently managed to make her feel like a failure, like she would always live in his shadow. She felt he was ashamed of her, of her lack of confidence. When she tried to confide in him and ask for his guidance, for some words to ease her fretfulness, all he said was, "Babe, you know I'm not into this emotional nonsense. Now, fix your makeup and let's go to dinner; we're running late." She felt terribly disappointed that night but managed to fake a smile for his associates throughout that boring dinner, a skill she had mastered in the first months of their relationship. She just kept thinking to herself that he would be just fine with anyone willing to wear short dresses and look all lovely and cute next to him at his endless business gatherings. "He won't even remember me next week," she kept thinking after they broke up, convinced that he would replace her in a heartbeat. And trying to reach Jenny, her childhood friend, was a fiasco. Jenny was too self-absorbed to even consider postponing her weekly brunch with her in-laws to talk to her. She reminded her of the saying by Dostoyevsky: "I say let the world go to hell, but I should always have my tea." Knowing Jenny, her presence wouldn't have made a difference now. She would never listen, too busy on her phone, sending emails and texts as if the world rotated around an axis that was her. She was alone in this and it was tearing her apart. She knew she had potential and her achievements were outstanding, but she had no one to share them with. No one to tell her that she still had a lot to accomplish.

Fifth floor, fourth floor, third. She was falling at a terrifying speed; way faster than she could imagine. "Come on, come on!!" As she spliced through the deafening wind the blood came rushing through her ears, the adrenaline rush making her heart pound in her chest, and the concrete ground was fast approaching. That's when it happened: time froze for a fraction of a second as everything around her started to move slowly, and pictures of her life started to swiftly unravel in her mind randomly. She was fourteen at her first dance party, then in a flash she was six years old blowing out her birthday candles, her schoolmates by her side. Flash. She was a grown woman, receiving her university diploma. Flash. A teenager with braces on smoking her first cigarette. She had always thought that she would watch her life as though it were a movie from start to finish. But she couldn't control what she was seeing. Time stalled for important events, like her first kiss or the birth of her godson. One particular episode clung the longest. She was twelve years old again, standing in the doorway of the living room at her parent's house, watching her mother sobbing on the phone, sputtering words she couldn't understand. It was the day the hospital called to deliver the news she had been dreading for months: her father had lost his battle with cancer. He was gone.

She didn't know what to feel, or how to react to this news. She would show the world that she was sad, devastated even, but what she would never admit to anyone is the sliver of relief she felt. She loved her father on his good days, but his strict nature made him an intolerant man. He would lash out at her if she came home with less than perfect grades, scold her if she broke a plate or stained her dress, and worst of all, mock her if she cried. "Crying is for the weak; it will get you nowhere," he once told her. "You should be strong, independent, and courageous and find a way to get what you want without being *that* emotional."

Subconsciously she had turned it into her motto for life. But at the time, she was only five years old, waiting alone in a big empty schoolyard until he finally showed after having forgotten to pick her up. It was a terrifying place for her, even in the daylight with children running around everywhere. He never apologized, and he never comforted her. But what he did inadvertently made her tougher and colder even at his deathbed when he made her promise to be strong and be the very best at what she does no matter what.

Her heart sank as her memories shuffled once again. Flash. She saw herself holding back tears when the workers came to take the piano her mother had to sell to get by. Flash. She was applying to business school, convinced that the degree will put bread on the table. Her heart broke a little because she couldn't pursue her dream of becoming a writer. Flash. She was breaking up with Alex after a relationship that survived five years, arguing that she wouldn't make a good mother given her long hours at work. She wasn't ready to compromise her career yet. Flash. She was talking to her priest about her fear of not knowing what the future holds, her terror of failure and her dread of dying alone. Time lagged again, and his words came back to her once more: "Don't be afraid my child; you don't need to worry. Doesn't the good book say, 'Look at the birds of the air; They do not sow or reap or gather into barns – and yet your Heavenly Father feeds them. Are you not much more valuable than they?' You have so many gifts to be grateful for, a mother who sacrificed a lot for you, a job that feeds you, a man who loves you. Focus on that and invest in them. Have faith and everything will be okay."

But she had forgotten how to actually live. Even worse, she couldn't admit to anyone that for the first time in her thirty-four years, she actually needed help. She wanted someone to hold her hand and tell her what to do, or at least share the weight she was carrying on her shoulders. But life had taught her to never depend on anyone.

Third floor, second floor, first. She wanted to scream, still unable to see where she had gone wrong. But no sound came out of her mouth. Her throat hurt, choked with tears and regret. Then for an instant, the fear was gone, replaced by disappointment, disappointment in herself. She was going to die in less than a second and all she could do was make herself feel worse. She wasn't enlightened, she wasn't proud. Flash. She was in the library helping a group of friends study for their finals. Flash. She was in an evening dress at a wedding where she met Alex. Flash. She was hugging her mother at her father's funeral. Flash. Her parents were clapping their hands, looking happy and proud, at her very first piano recital. Flash. She was standing in her father's hospital room. But the bed he had occupied the last three months of his life was empty. Looking around her, she saw him standing next to the window, seeming healthier than ever, smoking a cigarette with a serious look on his face, the one he would give her when he had something important to say. She was confused because this had never happened between them. Catching her reflection in the glass behind him, she saw her present self, wearing her grey dress. "This isn't a memory," she realized, "this is a vision."

His presence filled the room, as it always did when he was alive, and once again she felt intimidated by him. "Oh, sweetheart," he told her. "What have you done?" She felt so ashamed at the tone of his voice; even in his afterlife he was reprimanding her. "I just couldn't take it anymore," she cracked, without looking him in the eye. "I'm tired of being the strong one, the independent one, the heartless one. I ruined my life with Alex for the sake of my career, for executives willing to replace me now with younger candidates. I wanted to make you proud, to show you that I can be the best. But I've failed."

He took a few steps towards her, making the space around them warmer and more intimate. "Honey, you've got it all wrong. I never asked you to sacrifice your happiness. I wanted you to know that life is hard but it's full of opportunities. I needed you to learn how to be self-sufficient, to do the best you can to achieve what your heart desires without being taken advantage of. I knew my time with you was running short. I should have taught you how to deal with defeat; sometimes losing is crucial to growing wiser and stronger."

And for the first time in a very long time, she broke down in tears, realizing that, before standing on the ledge of her balcony on the seventh floor, she was still in control of her life. That all she needed to do was have the courage to change where her life was headed and not be such a coward and end it. Flash. She was hiking in a green meadow, somewhere in the mountains. Flash. Alex was on one knee, proposing to her. Flash. She was on her laptop at work on New Year's Eve, trying to finish some report she couldn't care less about. Flash. Ground floor. Crash.

In that moment of intense darkness, the silence was too loud. Her soul was being crushed with every breaking bone and could no longer fit in the corpse lying on the concrete. Unwillingly, aggressively pulled towards a bright glow, she suddenly felt so light and fully aware of every sound, color, and emotion surrounding her. The crowd was gathering quickly around her motionless body. She stood there unnoticed, among the panicking neighbors and curious passersby, looking at her blood-stricken face and lifeless eyes. With a crooked smile and a shake of her head, she turned her back to this awful scene and made her way up towards her home on the seventh floor.

"Today was indeed different. Oh well..."

CLOSE ENOUGH

YOUMNA BOU HADIR

Dust floats about aimlessly in beams of light filtering through glass windows. The only interruption comes from dark baggy pants and dirty boots slicing swiftly through beam after beam. He marches towards her with purposeful strides. She looks up from her phone, clutching it closer to her chest. Her eyes widen and her jaw drops slightly. She stands up. He stops abruptly then inches closer, uncomfortably close. His stubby fingers gently stroke the crevices of her face, feeling their way down to her lips, to finally mimic a piano concerto at her collarbone. Her chest moves in steady intervals, drawing nervous breaths as her shoulders quiver in their rhythmic rise and fall. He says something she chooses not to hear as he lets both his hands roam on yet another quest to trace a mental portrait of her face. She stands still, less rigid but still, closing her eyes whenever his index fingers venture near her cheekbones. He drops his hand to hold hers; she retracts.

All he does is reach out to collect the specks of dust that have invaded her periphery.

★

Left... Left... Left... Pause. Cute; chubby. His bio reads: "Happy camper looking to make friends" – maybe this one is not as much of a creep. Right! *Match.* "Hi" – here it comes; the unsolicited, should-be-censored, what-on-earth-were-you-thinking snapshot is underway. A brief "hello" is followed by an upside down smiley face. Okay.

"Jana?" She's called into a meeting she'd been waiting for in the lobby. Jana quickly switches off the phone before anyone sees the shameful red flame logo of an app a well brought-up woman should not be on.

She arranges her frizzy hair into a messy bun while thinking about *teta*'s comments: "Your hair is too messy; no man will want to have you for a wife. How can he know if you'll actually keep your household clean? The other day I saw a news anchor with the same hair, puffed up like a broom, but she had it neatly pulled back to hide her untidy curls."

Jana puffs and shakes off her *teta*'s snarls. She looks around the conference room aimlessly while her boss rambles on about the year's marketing strategy. She takes a pause from chewing on her pen and starts to doodle. "You think you can handle it, Jana?" – "What? Yeah, yeah, sure."

She walks out of what felt like a century-long meeting, leaves a note on her door that says: *Off for the rest of the day*, and goes to Jay's coffee shop for some alone time. Najla is the kind of waitress who constantly wears a smile, making you think her one and only passion is waiting on tables. But actually, she's a musician trying to save up for the guitar she can't afford. She serves Jana her double espresso and places a fresh ashtray by her right hand. Holding her phone under the table, Jana resumes her swiping ventures.

*

A head of curly red hair rests on broad shoulders. A well-built woman sits comfortably in an office chair typing away on her phone.

Light, calculated footsteps slowly pick up pace. Familiar palms rest on her shoulders, locking them in a tight embrace. Her jaw clenches, her back straightens and stiffens, as if wet concrete was dripping down her spine, instantly solidifying. He gently caresses the curve of her thick arms and whispers something – this time she tries to hear but can't.

She leans back into her chair, but the all-too-familiar palms had already retracted. The specks of dust he brought back waltz behind her.

It had been a hectic week. Jana worked through the night, through the weekend, through life; yet she still couldn't manage to meet all her deadlines. "You're not getting any younger, *ya mama*, twenty-eight and single, how will you feel at thirty-five if you're still childless?" She hates it when her mother uses this tone, especially since she does so only when *teta* is around. In any other context, *mama* is all for being a career-oriented, strong, independent woman and all that. After *mama's* comment, *teta* always follows with, "So I won't meet your children before I die?" then, checking Jana out, remarks, "You need to lose some weight before you expire, *ya Janjoun*; men look for slender women. You see, no matter how smart you are; nobody wants a truck in the living room. *Yalla habibti*, promise me; a small effort goes a long way. Look at me! Who would guess I am seventy-seven? I look no older than sixty-five."

Jana nods and excuses herself. She gives her mother a kiss, salutes her grandma from afar as if saluting a soldier, and leaves the house.

She resumes scrolling through the chats, skipping over the cuss words she inadvertently receives from some men, giggling at their ridiculous insults. *I'm sure you have AIDS. Who would want to date you anyway, you fatass c*nt.* She still can't understand why they do that, but marvels at how creative they get with their name-calling.

Happy Camper was nowhere to be found. She saw him a couple of times at Jay's where they had a decent conversation and exchanged numbers. She wonders why he never texted, but doesn't give it too much thought.

*

While typing away on her laptop, struggling to finish her final draft before her eyes give up, her phone buzzes. Happy Camper's text starts off with: *I need to be honest with you.* She doesn't bother to read. Day after day, he keeps apologizing for how he had behaved. Weeks later she reads: *You were too fat anyway.* There we go! She thought to herself. It took him some time.

On Sunday morning, Jana sips on her espresso at Jay's. Najla walks up to her and says, "It's my last day today." Jana beams and congratulates her, asking whether she was traveling or leaving to concentrate on her music. Instead, Najla extends her right hand to Jana, showing off her ring. Jana, unable to hide her disappointment, asks how long they've been together. "Well, our parents have been friends for years. My mother thinks it's for the best."

Jana's phone buzzes. *Hey, so I'm going to get off my high horse, we matched a week ago and nobody has said a word. Your bio reads well. You appreciate literature and good music.* Jana smiles; he said nothing about her pictures. And he took the time to read her bio. *Yes I try to maintain a relationship with art, although I work a full-time corporate job.* Marwan is chubby, dark-haired, teaches social studies at an international high school, enjoys the theater, reads – *click.* Her mother calls; she stares at her phone for a minute, then answers.

"Hi, mum, what's up?" [...]
"No, I don't want to meet him." [...]
"I don't care who he is, or what he does." [...]
"My auntie Wadad can keep her son." [...]
"Mum, stop it; it's 2017." [...]
"I'm hanging up now – bye."

Jana orders the check and exhales, blowing a strand of hair away from her eyes. The strand, of course, does not care for orders and comes back to assume the exact same position. Jana retreats into her own arms. It has been, by far, the most exhausting week of her life.

✶

She impatiently waits for him, looking around the empty room. She closes her eyes, trying to activate all her senses to find him, to allow him to get to know her, to allow herself to get to know him. She struggles to put one foot after the other in a straight line, and wonders how he does it so steadily, with such purpose. He stands at her doorstep watching her waltz around awkwardly and smiles. She looks exactly like he imagined her to be.

Three weeks in and Marwan has been fabulous. After several coffee dates and quite a few inside jokes, he finally asks Jana out to dinner. She puts on a dress, heels, and makeup. She lets her hair down. Her mother comes to her room to stare at her daughter in a little black dress.

"And where are you headed tonight?"
"I'm invited to dinner with... a friend."
"And who is he?"

Jana blushes and smiles. "His name is Marwan."

"And where did you meet?"

"Uhhh... the... we met at the supermarket."

"*Keef?*"[13]

"*Shu mama*, the supermarket!"

"I don't know how you kids do it these days... back when I was your age – no wait, I had you when I was your age, my goodness... and you were my third child, can you believe that? – *yalla, ya mama*, it's about time—"

"You were saying, *mama*?"

"Yes, yes, well, your father, may he rest in peace, was auntie Marianne's son. Our mothers were good friends and he saw me that one time and couldn't stop talking about me to his mother, asking to see me at least three times a week. I was a stunner in my early twenties, with my straight brown, well-kept hair. I always wore dresses – I mean, I could pull them off, I had one set of legs, I tell you."

"Yes, mum, I've heard this story quite a few times – I need to get ready, if you don't mind."

"Okay, okay, you don't need to be so touchy. Is he picking you up?"

"No, *mama*; I can drive myself."

"You strong new women are ruining all the fun; you know?"

"Mum, shut the door."

Marwan is really interested, so far, but she's almost sure he's going to back out the second he finds himself a prettier girl.

He lets both his hands roam on yet another quest to trace a mental portrait of her face. She stands still, less rigid but still, closing her eyes

---

13 "How?" Or, "What do you mean?"

whenever his index fingers venture near her cheekbones.

Jana gets in her car and drives to the French bistro where Marwan had made reservations. He beams the second she walks in.

"My goodness, Jana, you look fabulous tonight."

"Thanks." She smiles reservedly and breaks eye contact.

Dinner goes smoothly; they have a good time. Still, Jana thinks she blew it with him. The next morning, Jana receives a text from Marwan: *Hey, I've enjoyed every minute I spent getting to know you. Can you spare some time tomorrow after work for a quick stroll around the city? There's this great waffle place in Hamra I really want to try – with you.*

Jana smiles but quickly thinks he must be a creep, or a sleazebag who is in this for easy sex, or some psychopath – he can't just be normal.

She texts back: *Hey, thanks you're a really cool guy too, but tomorrow is a bit of a stretch, maybe the weekend? Xx* – "Or do I not send kisses? – why not." *Xx.*

The weekend works. I have a few papers to mark, but they can wait.

Jana doesn't text back.

Marwan texts on Friday night: *Are we still on for tomorrow? Let me know *smiley face* xx.*

Jana doesn't text back.

Marwan texts on Saturday morning: *Hey, if you're not in the mood for waffles, we can always hit up Jay's – I heard Najla left though; poor thing got stuck in an arranged marriage. Let me know what you feel like doing. Cheers. Xx.*

Jana doesn't text back.

Marwan texts again a few hours later: *Are you alright? Was it something I said?*

Dust floats about aimlessly in beams of light filtering through glass windows. The only interruption comes from dark baggy pants and dirty boots slicing swiftly through beam after beam. He marches towards her with purposeful strides. She looks up from her phone, clutching it closer to her chest. Her eyes widen and her jaw drops slightly. She stands up. He stops abruptly then inches closer, uncomfortably close. His stubby fingers gently stroke the crevices of her face, feeling their way down to her lips, to finally mimic a piano concerto at her collarbone. Her chest moves in steady intervals, drawing nervous breaths as her shoulders quiver in their rhythmic rise and fall. He says something she chooses not to hear as he lets both his hands roam on yet another quest to trace a mental portrait of her face. She stands still, less rigid but still, closing her eyes whenever his index fingers venture near her cheekbones. He drops his hand to hold hers; she retracts.

All he does is reach out to collect the specks of dust that have invaded her periphery.

THE ILLUSION OF US

SHAHD AL-SHAMMARI

She was as beautiful as an arrangement of red and white roses. A balance between smoldering fire and the subtle peacefulness of white. Just crisp white. She was like fresh, white, crisp sheets, the tumbling of lovers meeting under warm blankets, the tenderness of trembling hands, and the softness of someone's shoulder.

My world was teeming with voices. My day to day life involved saving the lives of others. I was always on call, rushing from one room to another, picking up charts, and running to the Emergency Room. And yet I was lonely. I was unable to come to terms with the relentless ticking of time. Every night as the clock struck twelve, I looked at the calendar. Another day, another night gone by, and I was still unable to grieve her loss. I'd remember the way we first met and wonder what it would take to bring her back to that day, to that moment, before I gave her up. Before I chose my life, my world, and the voices over her.

She had walked into the hospital one day and I was struck by her long black hair and the thick dark eyelashes that curled like umbrellas above her big round eyes. I was smitten – as were all the other doctors. The nurses couldn't stop whispering among themselves. She would visit us once a week. Nobody knew why, and I could never follow where she went. She was the talk of the hospital but I only heard bits and pieces of her story. Rumors, opinions, criticisms: she was in the medical field; here to evaluate our administrative staff; perhaps she was with Quality Assurance; perhaps she was visiting someone special... Sometimes I wonder if she was part of my disease. She walked into that hospital – my safe zone, the place where I was in control – and took hold of me, infecting me with her presence.

Ali Yousef was a handsome and charming man, but that wasn't why his patients trusted him. Perhaps it was his kind nature, his soothing voice, and the skewed smile that never left his face. When he delivered fatal news to family members he would offer his condolences and support. Unlike most of his colleagues, he managed to strike a balance between professionalism and empathy. He knew his patients by name and asked them to call him, "Ali; just Ali." They told him their stories, fears, and how many children they had. He saved their lives and yet insisted that medicine had saved his.

He had been living alone in a large apartment across the street from the hospital which his parents had left him when they passed away. The apartment was in a tall old building, to which clung the stench of death, garlic, coriander, and dearth... It reeked of sweat and hard work that never paid off. But he grew up there and could never bring himself to leave. He wasn't a modern man in the wheeling and dealing sense. He was content with his lot in life and never readily embraced change.

I was always fighting my way through the masses. I had felt dislocated, suspended in mid-air. I never belonged to the region, although Arab blood flowed through my veins. I was Arab, but my heavy French accent confused people. I was managing too many investment companies and found myself traveling all over the world. I had collected so many points that "Frequent Flyer" could have been my nom de guerre. I always had three phones with me: one for business, the second for family, and the third for my international dealings. That was how I had earned respect and gained power both in the region and internationally. My wardrobe had to change: dress for the job, I reminded myself. The world was not ready to understand that clothes did not define authority. I was fully capable of doing the job, but I had to put on a mask of perpetual seriousness, smile a lot less than I'd liked, and develop a firm tone when dealing with men. And then there was that moment, that day I arrived at the hospital. I was grabbing a coffee at the kiosk in the lobby when I locked eyes, for the first time, with someone who did not look like a stranger. He was a stranger, of course, as most people were, but a moment of recognition passed between us. Something about this man's manner was reassuring, non-threatening, quiet. He carried himself slowly in his immaculate white coat, deliberately, almost like a phantom.

The first time I asked if she would have coffee with me, I was afraid. Not of rejection – which I had learned to deal with. I was afraid of who she was. I had heard the rumors: her passion for her job, the power that she held. She would come and go in a Diplomat's car with a bodyguard lurking around her. She was on her phone most of the time, giving commands in a commanding tone, telling people to finalize deals with a distant look in her eyes. Was she ever really here? It was hard to tell. I, myself, was dealing with the diagnosis I had received a week before, trying to figure out what would happen to my medical career. A sick doctor. The irony was almost too much. There was no mistaking ALS (Amyotrophic Lateral Sclerosis); it was a progressive neurological disease that made my hands shake every time I held a scalpel. The headaches became persistent, the blurriness of vision progressed daily. My feet shuffled across the halls as I went from patient to patient, pondering when I would be the one in a hospital bed waiting for a doctor to come see me.

"I'm just a stranger, asking you out for coffee," I said, smiling at her. "I'm no stalker."

He was no stranger, and I had had my share of stalkers. I laughed at the innocence of his proposition and thought about how long it had been since I had come across innocence. Age is a daunting concept. We age; we change; we lose pieces of ourselves, fragments, in order to fit in with other people, society, ideologies – just to fit in. Just to be accepted. I wanted to let him in. But he didn't know. He didn't know the half of it. He could never know.

For all her professionalism, Nora was, after all, a woman in a society governed by unspoken cultural codes. She could never approach a man like she would in France.

The more coffees we had, the more I realized I was completely taken with this woman whose laughter was like a dose of amphetamines. The rush, the sheen of sweat that broke across my forehead every time we came into close contact... I wonder if she noticed. Chemistry is taught to us very early on and we understand its dynamics, its mechanics, and we memorize the formulas. And then comes one person who crashes into all of you, dispersing your every last atom. She takes a part of that composition and you know there is no going back. The Persians defined *al-ʿishq* as mad love, a love that consumes and deconstructs the self and the ego.

"What type of woman do you like?" she once asked. "Do strong women put you off?"

I wanted to answer her with the truth: she was the only woman I wanted. There was no type. There was no fear of strong women, but I understood that most men hated powerful women. Her power and authoritative demeanor were a scarlet letter she wore around her neck. Not only was she too powerful, I couldn't find one flaw in her. I was a man and I was flawed. Disease and disability don't mix well with men. I knew I would lose my job and become bedridden soon. I'd seen it happen to so many of my own patients. I'd seen them confined to wheelchairs, unable to take care of their basic human needs, let alone their wives. Their wives had all the power. They would bathe them, feed them, and, at times, grow exasperated with them. My medical background didn't help. I knew just how quickly I would deteriorate, and I understood that I would need to hire a nurse. And this nurse could not, should not, be my lover. Love and commitment are made ugly in the face of disability. I thought of *Lady Chatterley's Lover* and how even great literature could not find a place for a disabled man. The character – Clifford or Clark, I can't quite remember – is castrated both by his wife, who has an affair, and everyone around him, the second he is paralyzed. He is no war hero; he's just a man, unable to please his wife, shamed and shoved aside while his wife finds satisfaction in the arms of a stranger.

Nora struggled to understand Ali's hesitance. She saw in him a perfect man. People at the hospital began to notice when her visits extended into longer periods. They soon became the nurses' favorite topic during lunch hour. Ali had never been married and everyone waited to see who he'd choose as his wife. The fact that Nora came from somewhere else unnerved all the local women pining after him. As for Ali's male colleagues, they felt pangs of jealousy.

He looked at me as I spoke, but I knew he saw right through my words. He looked past them into my history, my Arab roots, my war with colonization, my war with society. He asked me to show him pictures of my family, my Mama, my Baba, my childhood home. It's strange when someone asks to see where you came from. It's strange when they listen to you as though they were hearing music for the first time. He wanted my story, my version of the song, unabridged, unreleased, waiting, waiting impatiently. His body leaned forward every time I told him stories of my childhood. We barely had any time. He was too busy and I couldn't fit him into my schedule. Maybe I was afraid of losing. The men in my life had always left. My father had left before ever laying eyes on me. It took years to find a home within myself and now I was a woman of power. I had worked so hard for everything I had, and I couldn't let him stop me. My walls were held firmly in place, and I never thought I would have to worry about meeting someone, anyone. And yet, here he was, asking me to marry him, every time he held my hand, mesmerized with the eight rings I wore every day.

The telephone is a device that can bring lovers closer while inflicting such pain as each waits impatiently for a call. Both Ali and Nora knew the protocol: no late-night phone calls. The affair started simply with words. Words that would expire by 9:00 p.m. each day. Good morning text messages later turned into lengthy calls over the span of a few days. Each conversation broached a different subject. Favorite foods, favorite artists, favorite countries. Politics. Life visions. Goals. They were a pair hungrily getting to know each other, exchanging words until finally, one night, a stolen kiss ignited their love. Ali had asked if he could kiss her cheek on the third day after she had given him her favorite book: Nawal Al-Saadawi's *Woman at Point Zero*. She believed every man should read it and he had reluctantly agreed. He wasn't sure he had time for Arab feminists but here was the woman of his dreams asking him to read. He knew there was more to this innocent gesture.

Every morning I would look at myself in the mirror and find a strange set of eyes staring back at me. Disappointment has a way of penetrating your skin. I rubbed my eyes to see clearer, careful not to smudge the mascara which already made me look tired. But I was here and alive. My mother's voice was always with me, reminding me that I had to stay alive. During my college years I just did it – I tried to kill myself. Depression was as silent as my father was. It expanded to fill my lungs and I found myself unable to go through the motions. Adult life, heartbreaks, men who bolted at the first sign of a serious relationship. I was an emotional wreck. My undergraduate years in Philosophy made my head spin. I couldn't find a balance. Until the day came when I was alive and my father was dead. When he died, it was time for me to stop trying to die.

I didn't belong anywhere, no matter how hard I tried to fit into society. Never finding a home. I must have wanted a home, though. Who doesn't want a home? I just kept putting it off. Marriage, commitment. All of it. I knew that it would stop me... Or maybe it would pause everything. All my friends had said the same thing, that they would pause their lives, just for a moment, find the right man, make it work, and then resume their lives. On the contrary, their lives changed forever. There was no pause and reset button. There was only the pressing problem of my mother. She had paused her own life when she met him. He was a man of tradition, poetry, and an old-fashioned upbringing. He couldn't date her without feeling as though he was sinning. And so they were married. She was endlessly infatuated with his bold desire and his grand gestures of commitment. No French man had ever offered her a ring. He committed to her until I was born. And then he fled Paris, went back home. I grew up far away from the Arab world, in her arms, in the land of the foreign, those that had always remained strangers to Arabs. My father was ashamed of her, and, by extension, horrified to call me his daughter. He died when I was twenty-five, leaving me a fortune. I came here to claim everything he had left me. His will included money in a currency I had never before dealt with, buildings and real estate in a country I had never set foot in. I had nothing to lose so I moved here to discover those hidden parts of me, the blood that pulsated through my veins, and wanted to see the world through the brown eyes I had inherited from a man *called Muhammad. Muhammad, like the Muslim Prophet ("Peace Be Upon Him," Mum always repeated). When I landed in this foreign country, my name was attached to his. I was suddenly labeled as "bint Muhammad," heiress to his empire. His reputation, his business, his house, his servants, even his driver, Khalil. I left Paris and yet my accent lingered. I learned to say "As-salamu 'alaykom"[14] every time I entered a place. The world was different here. Slowly even my friends in Paris disappeared. Distance and time kill even the strongest of bonds. But the Doctor with perpetually fatigued eyes was a bond I wanted to press within me. He always looked like he hadn't slept. He hid the bags under his eyes with eye glasses that threatened to topple off his nose. Inquisitive eyebrows, always asking silent questions.*

I wanted to ask her to marry me on the fourth day we spent together. But I couldn't bring myself to say the words. Four days. Even the skies were built in seven days. Four was a half-life. A half-love. A woman like her would never settle for half. And I was losing myself, my body, my mind, my health, my sense of self. I was a half. And she a feminist.

I wanted him to fight for me. Persistence was a quality I had missed. Men were too afraid of women. I loved his fight for humanity, for change, and the way he saved lives every day. I wanted him to make one move. To stop me from leaving.

She was always slipping from my grasp; I couldn't hold on tight enough. She was unattainable – a dream, a fairytale, magic. A Medusa? Who was she? Dinner plans never happened. I had to rush to the hospital that night, after making reservations at an elegant restaurant. Work called, and I prioritized it. I thought she would

---

14 Peace be upon you.

understand. Second chances did exist.

Nora and Ali spent one night together. One night of endless talking and nothing else. She wondered how she would explain to her friends back in France that Ali did not make a move although the chemistry between them was as electric and tangible as the steering wheel in her Mercedes-Benz. She gripped the wheel tightly as they sat through traffic, and thought about how reliable it was. Sturdy, steady, never failing. A German car knew its way around Arab streets whereas this Arab man resisted the chemistry between them that night.

I put my life on hold, waiting for him to lead, to waltz, to tango, to remind me of the beauty of Arab men. I wanted a knight in shining armor; I wanted my own prince. But I didn't want to say it. When you're in a position of power for too long, you become less fluent at the language of vulnerability and love. That night, my head on his shoulder, I closed my eyes and dreamed of a white dress, of kisses and promises. In the business world, a deal is always negotiable, even if you find no reason to negotiate. For him, a deal was a promise of a world unseen, of a future untouched, of fate dealing your hand. Fate had dealt me someone I didn't want to lose. But I negotiated with the universe. I pushed. I wanted him to fit into my world. I was used to taking the lead. I couldn't relinquish control. He once asked me to stop leading, to let him take care of me. I laughed at his request, his desire to offer me a home, and said, "I'll take a backseat, doc." He grinned at me, fascinated with someone beyond his grasp. My heart beat so fast I was afraid he would hear it.

We couldn't find a way. There was no ticket I could book to go to her world. I was slipping away from my own life, and she was a life force on her own, one I could not reconcile with. I later learned that there was a snake tucked between her thighs. A snake that was part of her, hidden, always unseen. The snake was safely tucked within her, every night. When she woke up in the morning, she would scratch its head, remind it to stay in check. The snake was very docile. It listened to her, remained in place, and did not hiss until it really needed to be released. Only at dawn prayer would she get up and let the snake loose in her bedroom. The snake would circle around her as she prayed wondering if there was a way to enter her, merge within her. I never wanted to ask her about the snake. But if she were mine, if only I had her, she would have no connection with that snake. It would be just us – and that would be enough.

I theorized that if I asked her to marry me she would eventually leave. She would abandon me once she found out how ineffectual I really was. I did not want to be left behind by a woman. Especially her. What could possibly make us equal? At the hospital, I was making mistakes. My patients were not getting the best treatment. Holding the scalpel in my hands was a nightmare. It would taunt me, and I would fail to keep a steady hand. Cutting through someone's flesh is a delicate matter. I put the scalpel down and walked out of the Operating Room. Defeated. Everything was short-lived. My body was on a short-term lease and I could not afford more time. We all get our lot in life. *Maktoob*: it was fated, somewhere between God and the stars, that I would fall in love with a woman I could not keep, and that disease would claim me long before anyone else could. I signed my resignation letter with trembling fingers, determined to step down in order not to harm any patient. My hands would be of no use to anyone. Not even to her. Unless she was willing to give it all up for me.

When I heard her heels clicking as she walked away from me, I knew it was time. She would walk away and I would deteriorate. I would never know what it was like to be hers. I understood that she could have anything and anyone she wanted. Why would she ever want me?

Vulnerability is terrifying. Exposed and naked – just like my mother. Decades later we were restaging the scene on a different continent. Like every addiction, you must wean yourself off it before it kills you. The sound of his voice pleading on the phone, asking me to stay another day. I shut my phone, knowing I had to go. He wanted all of me, all of me, and no part would be mine. Even my missing parts would be his. There was no other exit. We were doomed, and it wasn't a reality I could understand, let alone explain to him. The borders and barriers between us were not illusions. After that final phone call, he never reached out to me again. Neither did I. The longing was not enough. Every night, I lay in bed, reminiscing over the sleepy eyes that held me as I asked, "How do you do, doc?" I went back to my life, to my world, but I sometimes wonder: who was to blame?

Omran and I

Fatima Mahmoud

Whether a little or a lot, I was to most grown-ups truly annoying, and my father was one of the people I annoyed most. But, "Isn't it a parent's job to answer their children's questions about absolutely anything?" That's what my mom would whisper to my dad every time he became frustrated with the downpour of questions. My mother and I had a deal; whenever she felt that downpour coming, she'd refer me to him, saying, "Ask your dad; he knows everything."

There was no doubt in my mind that my dad, in fact, knew everything. He was big, tall, and incomparable to any of our family members or any man I'd ever met! It took me some time to figure out that his knowledge had nothing to do with size; my dad used to dedicate two days a week to teach illiterate men, who were older and sometimes bigger than him, to read. That's what convinced me he was the only one who knew *everything*. Besides, that's what my mom told me, and my mom never lied. Sometimes, my dad would scold me for being too curious but that never put me off. Once, when he ignored my nagging, I said to him, "You're not my *baba*!"

I think my outburst surprised him. He looked at me perplexedly and then gave me the silent treatment. I wasn't just an annoying child; I was also a rude one! But my dad didn't know that I was caught in a fierce competition raging on the playground... Omran, my cousin, the wickedly handsome scoundrel, who would constantly provoke my anger and admiration... Ahmad, my composed and quiet friend, who never took my side when I was mean or stubborn... Najiya, who was older than us; and Sayyida, my cousin, who was the youngest and only blonde among us. She was pretty but spoiled, and would use our game of hide-and-seek for her own benefit. Once, Omran caught her breastfeeding from her mother when we thought she was hiding, like the rules said to. We weren't going to invite her to play again if it weren't for my aunt... Who would want to play with a baby, anyway?! Poor thing, though, she had to give up that habit of hers to reclaim her place among us.

I was ahead in the game, especially when I pretended to be a teacher and made them recite the only lines I knew by heart from a long song, or count the numbers from one to ten. I skipped over nine and ten. It crushed my pride when Omran gloatingly teased: "Ha ha, you don't know the rest!" But my enthusiasm rebounded and defiantly summoned the number nine to my lips: "N-i-n-e." Then he struck me with a fatal blow: "You're older than me but can't count to ten!"

Older than him? Me, older than him?! The difference between us was only a few months. The rascal always knew how to outdo us and when to reap victories with barely any of the effort we put toward receiving some praise from the grown-ups. Omran would mock us when we reluctantly obeyed them. And when we hesitated to do foolish things that could get us into trouble, Omran would do them and walk away unscathed every time, laughing merrily, winning over their grown-up hearts, sparking our admiration and resentment. I don't know how he had such freedom. We were too young to be preoccupied with jealousy; it would have deprived us of playtime which was too enticing to let end. Perhaps we thought we'd always remain young and that our childhoods would remain intertwined and dedicated to the simple things that grown-ups never appreciated; like the rain we ran under with joy. We turned it into a bet to test our skill: whoever got soaked the most would win, not caring that our parents would reprimand us as soon as we caught cold and our temperatures spiked.

We shared tough times too. One night, we fought over the stars, each of us claiming they were winking at them alone. Omran aimed his slingshot at the moon, leaving the stars to us, and dragged me into yet another battle over the sparkly spoils. Our mothers soon intervened, telling us to go to sleep. We woke up early the next morning, looked to the sky and found no moon. Omran laughed, saying that unlike us, he didn't sleep all night and waited until everyone had dosed off, climbed to the rooftop, and managed to knock down the moon with his slingshot. He said he was hiding it under his bed and wouldn't release it until after dinner! We offered him candy, sweets, and all kinds of bribes to show us what was underneath his bed. But he absolutely wouldn't do it. As soon as night fell, Omran's moon reappeared, full and bright as if it were never stuffed under his bed. After that, no one fought with him over owning the moon; he had earned it fair and square.

Omran was an only child, but the entire clan loved him like their own even though they had many sons and daughters. And as much as he intrigued the adults, he stirred our imaginations, us kids, with his unrivalled energy. He had a generous spirit that would rise like a miniature sun in the palm of one's hand, leading us into mischief and giving us the courage we lacked. I loved his friendship, even when he exhausted me with questions I had no answers to.

Omran startled me awake from a nap one time. His slingshot was loaded with a small stone and he was playfully aiming it at me. "If you're smart, you'll tell me how big God is!" His question came at me the same moment he fired the slingshot at a small bird leaving its nest in the huge mulberry tree we used to swing from. I stared at the nest, ignoring his (monumental) question. How come it had never occurred to me before? Ahmad jumped in, my guardian angel.

"I know. I know." Then he pointed with his hand at the hill bordering the flat and wide farmland we used to live on. "God is biiig... like this land!"

Omran's dark face flushed with victory and he pointed his finger at the sky. "Wrong! God is biiiiiig..." he proclaimed, "like the sky."

It was now my turn, but how would I outdo this little swindler? I knew nothing that was bigger than the sky. My other guardian angel, Najiya, intervened: "It's *haram* to talk about God... Whoever talks about God will be thrown into the fire!"

Terrified, Sayyida ran to her mother, recounting Najiya's threat. Omran laughed at her. "Sayyida is going to get her daily dose of milk!" Then he changed the subject nonchalantly, as usual, and continued his pursuit of the birds, completely oblivious to my shock at his unanswerable question. I barely slept that night. I fell into the fire that Najiya spoke of, except that I refused to be defeated by a boy who was months younger than me!

Who is God?! How is He God?! What does He look like? Is He really as big as the sky? Why would someone we don't see terrify us and throw us into the fire? And how can Omran claim to know His size?! Why not, though? He did steal the moon and hide it under his bed...

In the morning, I decided to venture this question at my dad. After all, he knew everything! I took him by surprise. He knit his brow a little, then decided to save me, perhaps himself too, by answering me with a passage from the Qur'an which I didn't understand. But he made me memorize it so that I would recite it to him three days later. I was exasperated with Omran more than ever for making me go to such lengths!

I sought out my mom as well. "How is He God? And where is He?" She confused me even more by saying, "God is big, and He dwells in the hearts of believers." I asked: "How?!" She put her hand on the left side of my chest. "God lives here in your heart." I slept in delight with my hand over the left side of my chest, feeling for my mom's gift. This is my heart and this is where God lives... I dreamed of Omran's defeat and couldn't wait till morning. "Tomorrow I will defeat you, Omran. I will call all our friends to have them witness my victory. I will tell you to ask me a question you won't be able to answer – 'Where does God live?' Only I know where!"

The next morning, I tried to wiggle my way out of breakfast, eager to join the gang. Suddenly, my excitement was replaced by mysterious gloom... I realized the problem: my heart was too small, much smaller than the sky and earth! What was my mom even saying? She must've made up any random answer. Exasperation gripped me as I imagined Omran hurling his laughter and mockery at me. My mom was brushing my hair, seeming sad, but I was busy feeling my left chest where God was supposed to live. I almost told her that I still didn't understand how this small heart of mine could fit He who is bigger than Ahmad's earth and Omran's sky. But she spoke first.

"You won't be going to school today."
"Why not?!" I asked in protest.
She took my little face in her hands, trying to keep from wailing. "No one will be going to school today."
"Even Ahmad and Najiya?"
"Yes, even Najiya and Ahmad."
"And Omran?!"
She sobbed through her response. "Omran went to another place, *ya binti…*"

"Where did he go?!"
"He went to meet God..."
"When will he be back?!"

I was dismayed, rendered defenseless. I thought, *He's gone to meet God, then! Ugh, he's going to get even more cocky now; he struck me with another fatal blow! He went stealthily. This selfish little show-off should've told me about his trip. If I were truly his friend he would've taken me with him!* I remembered the last time I saw his face engrossed in preparing his slingshot, indifferent to my bewilderment at the question he asked. He was already planning on going alone!

In the days that followed, spoiled Sayyida cried as she looked for Omran and couldn't find him. She sought refuge in her mother's chest once again. Peaceful Ahmad kept echoing what the grown-ups said: "Omran went to meet God!" Najiya corrected him as usual, saying: "No, no; he went to heaven and he's no longer like us... He's now one of the birds in heaven." That's what the grown-ups said too, but I no longer trusted them. Why would he turn into a bird when he knew what a slingshot could do to it?

The huge mulberry tree still carried the small slingshot Omran had left hanging from one of its branches. Every time I looked at it, I'd think that if Omran actually had become a bird, then the slingshot that got him must've been bigger. He wasn't coming back then! The realization filled me with anger and anguish. I felt a lump in my throat that wouldn't pass for a long time.

But now, every time I sit under a starry sky, like the one over our village, I look at our stars and imagine him playing among them, telling them about us and our fights over their twinkling lights. I can almost hear that memorable laugh of his. He's still bickering with me

from up there. I smile at him with joy, waving at the moon, the friend
he once hid under his bed.

Translated by Yasmine Haj

Saying Goodbye to Yuki

FATIMA BDEIR

From picture books to chapter books, I can spend days engrossed in reading. I remember borrowing seven books from the *Magic Tree House* series one morning from my local public library, and begging my mother to take me back to return them and borrow another pile that afternoon. I read more books than the library could keep up with. I reread my favorite ones and eyed those books labeled "Too Advanced for Third-Graders." I got through Monday mornings by anticipating what I would read on Friday afternoons.

My life was great until I was forced to socialize when my parents visited their friends, most of whom had kids in my school. Some of them had only girls who were much older than me, and some didn't have children at all, so I'd sit and chat with the adults. That's probably one of the reasons why I became mature at a young age. Of course, I'd instantly revert to a three-year-old if a kid's show, like *Dragon Tales*, came on TV. As you can tell, I lived on extremes: either I wouldn't see the light of day or I'd have morning coffee (hot chocolate or orange juice in my case) with the adults just to have my dose of social life. This worked well until we moved to Lebanon from the states. And as if that weren't enough, we moved to a small town in the South. I didn't get along with the adults or the neighbors' kids who played with sticks and acorns in the streets. It's not that the South was bad, it was just that I had been moved from the comfort of a four-story house to a place where if we wanted to take a shower, we had to inform the entire family, turn on the boiler, wait for an hour until the water was warm enough for a somewhat decent bath only to discover that it was still tepid. That's if the power didn't go out while we were waiting, either because the government cut the circuit or because too much power had blown out the fuse.

Then there was school. Without any books, it came close to being a hellish experience. I wasn't in hell, but I'm pretty sure I was somewhere in purgatory among people who cracked the spines of novels and others who didn't read. Way beneath us were the people who didn't even practice the effortless skill of watching fantasy shows and playing imaginary games with their siblings, because they'd rather play with Barbie dolls and soccer balls. I don't think anybody can completely understand how utterly miserable I was. Imagine this:

The Arabic teacher sat on the desk in front of me with her head hovering over my hand.

"Yes! Yes; excellent! Bravo! She's better than all of you put together!"

My lips couldn't help but curl into a shy smile.

"Miss Zahra," a student said, clearly annoyed at how long it was taking me. "What's the next word?"

"*Jibal.*[15] *Ji-baaaaaal!*" she beamed at me. I started writing it, letter by letter, erasing and rewriting when I got mixed up. The word was simple, even for a fifth grader like me. But in the states all we ever learned was the letters and how to read a few kindergarten-level texts in Arabic. When Miss Zahra learned that I barely knew the spoken language since it was my first year in Lebanon, she decided giving me seven times the attention was best. I detested it. My classmates grumbled at my incredibly slow writing speed. The teacher's smile was inhumanely large; her eyes grew to the size of ping-pong balls,

---

15 Mountains.

which was supposed to be comforting, but I just found it plain scary.

Dictation hour eventually ended, and the bell rang for recess. I sat in a corner of the gym, quietly eating my sandwich.

"Say *dovda'a!*"[16] said the coolest and, according to what I was told, sweetest girl in school. I tried my best to say it properly.
"*Dofda...*" I said shyly. The girls surrounding me laughed, clapping their hands around their mouths.
"How cute!" they squealed. It was the same thing every day.

I could have had a social life, if the tears hadn't stung my eyeballs and forced me to shun my classmates, move to a different corner, and then sulk as I watched the cobwebs and spiders. On good days, I'd find a fat round bug in my corner, and one day I found a dead bird to poke at as the ants marched over it.

It wasn't always like this. I did have a human friend at this school once, one who didn't laugh at my loose American tongue. Then things got complicated and we stopped talking. It wasn't complicated really. One day, she just said, "How about you sit with someone else from now on?" So no, I didn't have friends for the one year I spent in the South. I didn't have that many in America either, preferring to just count the seconds till I went home to enter the parallel universe in my mind. Only at this school, there was nothing to anticipate; no new material to read, no cable TV, just my bike on some days or a pen and paper on others. Nothing exciting. I desperately wanted a library. I'd read all the books at home an infinite number of times. I wanted a library at school more than anything in the entire universe. My cousin told me there was one at her school in Beirut, and my

---

16 Frog.

heart stopped. Could I make friends there? I decided I wanted to move. I thought it would solve everything.

It didn't. After I moved to Beirut, to a new school with an actual physical library, my social awkwardness was only amplified. I could now escape the reality of my out-of-place state through fiction, but it made my loneliness even worse.

Opting for a change of scenery from the stacks of books in the library, if you could call a room with two bookcases a library, I started reading in the playground among screaming and laughing children. Benches, I discovered, were more comfortable than the cold hard floor I sat on at my old school.

"See?" I told myself. "You're finally integrating into society." I told myself that despite the fact that I never spoke to anyone unless I really had to. Then one day while reading yet another abridged version of a book because the librarian wouldn't believe that I could actually read the 200-page original, I saw a girl from my grade holding something black and shiny, with red words on it. Was it... could it be... a book? Could a girl my age living in what I thought to be an illiterate country be performing the holy practice of reading? I got up and, without even thinking, walked up to her.

"Is that *Three Men in a Boat*? I've read it! It's so funny! But there isn't much of a plot." The words exploded out of me. Even though I was mostly speaking in English, she understood and replied, "Yeah! It's okay. But there's not too much to read in that library! I've already read most of the books." My eyes widened. Someone had read more than me? Suddenly, it became a challenge, I had to finish reading them all.

We'd sit together during recess and talk about books, while reading and fanning ourselves with them.

"My favorite is *Magic Tree House*. What's yours?"

"I don't really have a favorite... I like them all."

Her voice was low and shy; mine was loud and full of spirit. I'd get excited and chatter without pause, my sentences becoming impossible to understand. She was slow and deliberate with her movements; while mine were rash and quick. I'd bounce on my toes standing in line to go to class, hug and poke her nose.

Eventually, I realized the ruckus I was making in her quiet world and shrank back into mine. I could be as loud as I wanted in my head as I talked to myself and my fictional characters, so I returned to them. As you can tell, books didn't help. What made it even worse was my discovery of anime, Japanese animated movies and shows, which I became attached to. So much so, that I'd put aside reading a book for the fourth time to watch the images and complicated plotlines flashing on the screen.

I didn't feel like myself around real people. Strangely enough I could relate to fictional people more. It was as if I was meant to be born in another dimension, but accidently fell into this one on my way there. Years later, I made a friend at home.

You probably have the impression from the gloomy tone of this story that I'd befriended a doll I stitched together from a quilt and stuffed with cotton. If it had occurred to me, I probably would have done that at some point. But no, that's not what happened.

My sister Mariam and I never got along. I hated her and the way she thought she could have anything she wanted. I hated her stubbornness, her constant energy, her adorable face, her dimples, her perfect nose and the fact that she had more friends than I did... more *real* ones anyway.

I sat at the desk in the village house we visited every summer. I typed away furiously on my computer, trying to compress my anger into the "new thread" text box on a forum. "How dare she insult our Arty?" I wrote. "She thinks Harry Potter is better than Artemis Fowl. Her puny brains are incapable of comprehending the genius of our Artemis, the way he only needs three minutes to formulate an undefeatable plan, with counteractions for every single possible scenario that could happen. How are we even related?"

Holly Short hovered over me. Her wings snapped and buzzed, her crew-cut auburn hair bobbing in approval as I typed. She smiled at me, and I smiled back. Mariam lay on her bed behind me, her head sandwiched between the pages of the book she was reading. It had a shiny golden cover with the words "Artemis Fowl" printed on it. After much discussion, much debate, and much flinging of plastic pudding spoons at each others' faces, she'd finally decided to give it a chance. I didn't know why I wanted her to read it. It was my book to fantasize over, containing my fanfiction story, my copy to give to my children... but still, it'd be nice if there was someone else in this house to talk to about this...

"It doesn't have to be Mariam; if I had any *real* friends I would have made them read it," I said to myself. I was such a good liar.

"So," I thought, "how is Arty?"

Holly's voice echoed in my head. "His arm still hurts from the time you gave him a friendly punch."

I laughed.

"What are you laughing at?" Mariam asked. I could feel her voice piercing my fictional bubble. She just had to remind me of her existence, that she couldn't see Holly. Holly was only flickering in and out of my mind.

That night, the entire family sat under an oak tree, looking at the mountains before us that glowed a blurry yellow and stretched towards the night sky. We ate nuts and, as usual, my sister and I didn't talk much. She sat on a plastic chair, one leg tucked under her.

"This tree," my grandpa said pointing at its trunk, "is over a hundred years old." It didn't look that special to me; its trunk was strong and thick, its branches capable of carrying me and my three siblings when we climbed on it. But there was nothing special about it, except that it probably had more friends than I had, like the birds on its branches and the worms in its trunk. An inanimate being was more of a social butterfly than I was. Not that I wanted to be one.

Mariam jumped from her seat. "Fatima!" she squealed. "There's a well under the tree!"

Ten seconds of silence. Crickets chirped as my sister smiled manically at me, her fingers wrapped in fists under her chin.

"Yeah, so?" I said.

"There's running water!" she exclaimed.

Everyone looked at her, confused.

"What is it, Mariam?" My dad asked, rising from his seat. My grandpa took off his plastic slipper and braced himself for disaster in case she'd say that she saw a scorpion. My mom rushed towards her and put her hands on her shoulders. Mariam didn't pay any attention; she kept her eyes fixated on me.

"We can take an acorn from this tree and summon a fairy!"

I'd later scold myself for not having instantly noticed an *Artemis Fowl* reference that a newbie to the fandom made. I ran towards her, nearly shoving my mother aside as the excitement took over. We recited a chant we knew by heart as we held each other's elbows and jumped up and down. We ignored the adults who yelled at us for scaring them. We ignored the stones and sharp twigs under our bare feet. We ignored the fact that we'd caused a ruckus over what most of the world thought was nothing. To us it was everything.

It was the start of a friendship with the person I'd been living with for eleven years.

For those confused, yes, I was having a conversation with a fictional character in my head. No, I am not schizophrenic and I did not actually see Holly the fairy hovering over me. I was fourteen; I'd been in the country for three years. And still, I'd failed to get along with people at school or people in general. I compensated by talking to my fictional characters so I could feel that at least there was someone I could trust, even if that person was just someone inside of me.

Things almost got out of control and I actually started to dangerously favor fictional people over real ones. Sounds sad, I know. But eventually, I did finally accept reality and made some real friends. You'd think that after fifteen years, I would have gotten the hang of this "people thing" and would initiate some friendships. But being a failure at everything I'd done besides writing in Gnomish – a non-official language that wasn't used to communicate in the three-dimensional world except by yours truly – that did not happen.

Step One: Pour Some Guts

Her hand was extended. At first I wasn't sure why, then I looked up. She wasn't smiling, but she wasn't frowning either. What was her name again? Nour? Riham? Nourhan.

"Yuki, wait." I said in my head. "I think she's talking to us. I mean me. I think she's talking to me."

Yuki sighed but, as usual, I was the only one who could hear her. I was the only one who could see her long brown hair, her Cross Academy blazer and miniskirt, her cartoon eyes. Nourhan smiled, "Walk with us?" *Don't overthink. Actually, don't even think. Just use your brain to move your limbs.*

I took her hand and she pulled me out of my seat, leaving Yuki, one of my best friends, behind. Next to Nourhan stood Alex, the girl whom I sat next to the previous year and one of the only people who saw me drawing characters from anime and manga but didn't judge me for watching and reading them, and didn't call them cartoons. We walked.

Later during math class, I completely ignored Yuki. I ignored the sound of dragons and fairies fighting outside. Yuki wasn't happy with that. Harry probably wasn't either, since I didn't visit him in the village and stayed in the city to study, and the Room of Requirement in the meadow behind the house only opened to my touch. It wasn't fine.

Step Two: Commit to it; Mix Until Soft and Fluffy

I started talking with Nourhan and Alex more on MSN, and nobody liked that. "We're bored!" they said. "We need you! We need your help!"

Artemis once actually raised his head from his computer, and looked at me before ordering me around. "I need you to go undercover for me; you're the only one who can do it," he said, running his hand through his hair. He was surrounded by wires and monitors hanging above my bed, his chair levitated a few feet above the ground. Books and more books lined the walls.

Ciel wasn't someone to go after people; he put his dignity above everything. But even he would show me his soft side at night and ask me what was wrong when I was texting in bed. His hair would fall over his forehead and cover his right eye. I'd lift the black locks to reveal the demon star in his pupil, smile at him, open my mouth, and draw in a breath to say something... Then my phone would buzz and I'd pull the covers over my head to respond.

"I'm just inviting you and Nourhan. Don't tell anyone." Alex had sent on MSN.

Step Three: Boiling Point

I didn't even think about what to wear; Alex and Nourhan didn't care about such things, and neither did I. Yuki did care though; she was calling Lizzy over to help us pick out the best outfit when I chose a random dress from my closet. Lizzy gasped, "THAT?!" her blond curls bounced on her head and her cheeks turned a bright shade of pink, "You'll totally be judged!"

I waved her off and shrugged the dress over my shoulders. Yuki stood at the door with her hands folded. Lizzy stood in front of me with her hands on her thin waist, stamped her booted foot, and eyed me with unrealistically large pupils.

"What has gotten into you?!" she asked.

I just looked at the mirror to put on my veil. Ciel, who was reading a book on the floor looked up at us, "Why are you two fighting?" he asked. I paid no attention to him.

"I'm talking to you!" Lizzy said.

I walked right through her, stepped on Ciel, shoved Yuki aside, and left the house. Yuki didn't give up. She followed me outside where I waited for my ride. Yuki and I were alone, except for the invisible cars flying in the sky monitoring the actions of us muggles to make sure we didn't expose the wizarding world, and the hippogriffs and dragons playing together in the sky after their truce, and the train from Divergent and the factionless on it.

My back was turned to Yuki as I typed on my phone. "Be there in 15."

"I'm your best friend!" Yuki said.

I remained silent and didn't even turn around.

"I mean, who are they? They were never there for you before! Now they decide to be your friends and make nice after all this time?"

"They're nice to me... They don't care if I'm weird or hyper. And Nourhan reads too! And Alex might watch *Vampire Knight*! They sit with me at lunch. Just leave me alone." I said in my head.

"We're lonely!" she said.

"Well," I said out loud. "When I'm with you guys, so am I."

The train became my mom's mini-van. The hippogriffs and flying cars burst into silver and golden shaves and showered the world, and the dragons ate their tails and combusted. The lab Artemis and Ciel worked in became my pink and red bedroom, the way my parents designed it. I turned around. Yuki was gone.

Finally, I'd let go of a huge chunk of my life; I diluted the dose of how much I read and watched in order to make sure I wouldn't get as deep into the fandom as I had been. I started going out with my friends a lot more often and always texted them. I sat with them at school until the buses started leaving, just so we wouldn't miss a moment together. Actually, I'd become a generally sociable person who wanted to meet everyone, from classmates to janitors cleaning the street. That was how it was supposed to be, right?

But after putting aside my former obsessions, I felt a hole growing somewhere inside me. It needed to be filled. I had to obsess over something else, so I watched many TV shows and read fantasy series, none of which were as captivating as what I'd previously loved. It wasn't enough. At sixteen, I started filling that hole with rocks.

The Rocks: Politics and Religion

I moved from being consumed by the most ridiculously unrealistic things to the most real-life concerns. I don't think you understand what I mean by obsession. I read as much as I could about religion, attended religion classes, asked left and right about the philosophy of religion. Sometimes, I didn't find any answers. Other times, I found too many. Eventually, I discovered all the different theories and picked what seemed most fitting and logical.

It was time-consuming. But I still read fantasy and watched some American shows; they kept me grounded, like a balloon tied to a rock. I floated but not too far away. It had a calming effect on me. I made it my occupation to read the news. I woke up reading it, went to sleep scrolling through the stories... You'd think it was great, but it wasn't. The stress was, in one word, unmanageable. Living in a country with daily unpredictable political developments made it hard to keep up. It also made Lebanon seem like a lost boy in a dark room, trying to reach the door only to stub his toe on a chair and fall back. Then he'd get up and hit a wall. Move around it and hit another wall, and then another... Finally, he would trip over his own feet, something Lebanese people, being quite persistent and stubborn, managed to do quite often.

A year later, during my last year of high school, I found myself in the fictional world again. Yesterday was Monday, two of the Mangas, or Japanese comics, had been updated, and I still hadn't read them. I had ten minutes to get to class, just enough to finish a chapter. Nothing could be more satisfying.

The drama and effort of having to deal with real people pulled me back in. My fictional friends never gave me any trouble. I think the reason why I went back to this childish phase is because I'd grown. Yes, that sounds contradictory, but it's true. I came to know the world for what it is, and I'm not afraid to say that I'm deliberately ignoring a lot of it. Now, if you'll excuse me, I'd like to go back to reading my ninth comic this week.

Thank you for listening. Artemis and Yuki, thank you too.

Dry Sludge

HUDA AL-ATTAS

Alawiya tossed and turned beneath the summer blanket when a flash of heat surprised her between her thighs. Then came a strange stickiness, followed by a pungent smell. She plunged a trembling finger to explore what had happened, and it came back wet with moisture. She covered her face with a veil, lifting her finger to her nose. The smell made her dizzy for a moment; a mix of herbs, rusty metal, and elements she couldn't identify. A yeasty smell unlike any other she had smelled before billowed into the empty space under her veil.

Terror gripped her. She ran into the bathroom grabbing the dim lantern hanging on the wall as she went. Panting, she lifted her soiled brown finger. She wondered why no one had ever told her there was sludge hidden in her secret place. What was this sticky liquid? Her mother had told her nothing. Even Raqwan, her cousin and friend who was a few years older, had never mentioned it. Everyone had warned her about this soft, moist place in her body, against touching it or letting anyone else do so.

Her grandmother once caught her placing her hand there to scratch and instantly scolded her, "I will cut off your hand!" Alawiya froze in scandalized horror. Convinced her grandmother would really dismember her, she let the itch ravage her for the rest of the day, unable to tell anyone. Only the cool water from the bathroom jug brought relief from time to time.

She sniffed at the brown sludge again. What could she do? Breathing heavily with fear of discovery, she crept into the guest room. All she had to do was plug the hole where it was flowing. "*Akh!*" Alawiya tried to repress her cry as she wedged a piece of sponge into the place where sludge was oozing out. She had ripped off a small chunk from an old mattress propped up against the wall. She felt a deadly stinging between her thighs. She exhaled, hoping to ease the sharp pain, and returned to the room, throwing herself on the bed near her mother. Tears gushed down her cheeks, and she did not awake until morning. Her mother shook her violently, shouting under her breath in broken Arabic, "Alawiya! Alawiya! Get up! You've soiled the bed!"

Alawiya awoke in terror, searching everywhere for the piece of sponge. She found it soaked in blood at her feet. Her uncontrollable heartbeats were eased only by the quiet smile on her mother's face. It gave way to blessings and prayers to the Prophet as she repeated, "Don't be afraid; we must rejoice!"

Alawiya has become a woman, her mother thought. *Mother and daughter must prepare for this immense transformation announcing Alawiya's readiness for a man, for marriage, for intense housework, for the customs of the Wadi which prohibit her from inappropriate appearances in public.* Alawiya's mother told her she needed to prepare for *Al-Tabarrok* (The Blessing). She passed her a rag and taught her how to place and tie it. It was the 1940s, and no one in the Wadi then knew anything about underwear.

Her mother was determined to keep the incident a secret, as custom proscribed. She and Alawiya headed down to the store room, which was at the bottom of the seven-floor mud house. Taking Alawiya's hand, she directed her to rub it against every sack of grain, vat of dates, and basket of provisions, and then repeat the hymns and incantations. Holding Alawiya to her bosom, her instructions came out in broken Arabic and a smattering of Indonesian, "Praising be to God, our mercy, and obident, God over evil, mos powahful."

Alawiya giggled at the combination of her mother's earnestness and dialect, making her mother lash out at her in her language, "*Zam bal, zam bal*!! (Calm down!)." She explained to Alawiya that when a girl reached puberty and her springs poured forth, she must perform this ritual to bring abundant earnings and stores of food to the house and its people. Otherwise, the presence of a polluted pubescent girl would attract the devil's ire and the *jinns*,[17] who would have their way with the food and stores...

*

Crouched in front of the hearth, the old aunt was muttering to herself. Her eyes were clouded with tears and perpetually crusted with rheum. Perhaps because she spent most nights secretly grieving her fading years and fossilized femininity. She had never been touched by a man and her veiled face was invisible to all but unmarriageable kin. For over seventy years she had been living in the prison of tradition, barred from marrying anyone outside her social class. The awaited groom never arrived, nor would he. "The only man who'll have me is 'Azraël, the angel of death," she snarled. Her furious and sad muttering didn't impede her habitual taunting of Alawiya who had slipped into the kitchen. As she strolled, her face betrayed coyness, and she avoided eye contact. "Well hello, corn dolly!" the aunt sniped.

---

17 Evil spirits and demons (anglicized plural form).

She was referring to Alawiya's frame, which was as scrawny as the young corn stalk that little girls fashioned into dolls. They would peel away the skin and keep the pulp. From the bits of skin, they would mold an arm or leg or head and graft it back into the pulp. They then decided on the dolls' sex, marrying them off to one another and starting families.

As was her habit each morning, Alawiya grasped her eternally anxious aunt's hand with obsessive pity and kissed it. She sat in the corner of the kitchen floor designated for washing pots and pans and ignored the prattling old woman. Dazed, she recalled the morning ritual with her mother that announced her debut into womanhood.

The aunt continued her battery of jibes, shaking her head in the direction of the kitchen's small rooftop where Raqwan was looking downwards. "The Abyssinian's daughter (referring to the fact that Raqwan's mother came from Ethiopia) hasn't lifted a finger since this morning! She's too busy dangling from the rooftops!" she cried.

The palm tree in front of the house swayed to the sound of singing and beating drums which was growing closer and louder. Its fronds bowed with the wind, the loose strands dancing in ecstasy. Mesmerized, Raqwan rushed to the edge of a high roof and hung her head over to watch the wedding procession below, ignoring her aunt's commands to return at once to the chores she had abandoned. The beguiling melody of the reed pipe grew louder, and with it, heartbeats that sent shivers of pleasure through her limbs. She searched for the source of the music. Her pulse quickened when she saw Hussein's dark brown Qatifi[18] face and the swollen jugular veins

---

18 Qatif, or Al-Qatif, is an area in the eastern province of Saudi Arabia and one of the oldest settlements in East Arabia. Before the discovery of oil, its people worked as merchants, farmers, and fishermen.

on his neck. She whispered his name, and it seemed to slip off her tongue right into his ear. He lowered the reed pipe from his mouth and flashed his pearly smile. That very smile seduced its way into women's gossip circles. She wished he would lift his gaze and see her pining silhouette. "His sun-lit eyes are like dazzling orbs of honey," she murmured. But she knew he wouldn't look up to the rooftop. He had a reputation for bashfulness.

"Raqqqwaaaan!!" Alawiya teased as she scrubbed the ceramic jug clean. She playfully sang, "My eyes! I need medicine for what they've seen!"

Eventually, the procession reached the groom's house, and the reed pipes died out. Raqwan ran from the roof to the kitchen, turning to Alawiya with a reproachful look that warned her not to drop the ceramic pot which was trembling in her hands. Her look also hinted that Raqwan knew of Alawiya's pubescent secret. At that moment, Saadoun the servant entered. She was known for her foul-mouthed obscenities. "She needs to grab a donkey's (...) in order to stop breaking pots," she said about Alawiya as she leaned on Raqwan. She described the donkey's member exaggeratedly as if she held it in her hands. Raqwan laughed radiantly. She secretly awaited the day she would be wed to Hussein, her cousin and Alawiya's older brother...

✶

"Oh, my heart! My wealth! My earnings!" Alawiya's mother's screeches tore through the stillness at dawn. Her only son, Hussein, had drowned in the wild Harra[19] rapids. In the middle of the room a

---

19 An irrigation network connected to the main water canal. It gathers water from rainfall and snowmelt and channels it to the smaller aqueducts which feed the farms and palm beds.

bereft father cowered at the base of a casket. His limp body staggered one way and the next as he caressed the corpse with trembling hands, making his way from the green sheet embroidered with Qur'anic verses to the forehead, which he stroked. "Hussein, my son! I leave you in God's hands," he repeated between sobs.

When his bloodied palm emerged from the coffin, he could no longer control himself. He started butting the coffin with his head, choking on his sentences. Some of those present murmured the *Fātiha*[20] while others openly sobbed. Out of the room rose a blend of lamentations and consolations. Clouds of sadness spread through the courtyards. They crept through the windows, door cracks, and pipe ends until they reached the open sky over the town on the side of the mountain as it lay sleeping between fields of corn and palm.

Two of Hussein's friends who were with him on that moonless night helped free him from the clutches of the Harra, which had already crushed his arms, legs, and ribs. A witness said he had seen Hussein, his cousin Mustafa, and Mabrouk Badhawi, son of the reed player, out working the field that night. Two of them began to wrestle by the canal. He said he heard Hussein warn Mustafa and Mabrouk to be careful of falling in, and he urged them to carry the hoes and farming tools. "Let's clean the canals so the water can get to our farms," Hussein said.

In a sad voice, Mabrouk admitted that Mustafa picked on Hussein, saying his wimpy hands were only good for books, not real men's work. He said that's when Hussein grabbed Mustafa by the shirt, "See if you can get out of my wimpy grip now!" Aunt Fattoum, Hussein's Indonesian mother, wailed with a broken heart. She

---

20 The first *surah* of the Qur'an.

remained convinced until her dying days that Mustafa had pushed him into the canal.

In this sullen atmosphere, two people were teetering on the edge of despair. The first was Raqwan who was promised as a bride to her now dead cousin and whose body was consumed by fever at the news. The second was his grandfather, whom everyone called Abdullah the Beloved, as was custom. At that moment, his fingers fidgeted unconsciously. Some weeks ago, they had left their mark on the face of the heaven-bound young man.

Filled with regret, he recalled the look his grandson shot him when he had struck him that day. Mustafa had told on him to the grandfather, saying that Hussein had been reading a book for infidels.

"How do you know it's a book for atheists?" he asked Mustafa.
"The cover has a Christian name on it," Mustafa replied.
"That's not enough to accuse him of atheism," said the grandfather.
"But he said that religious leaders mislead people!" said Mustafa.
"He said that?" the grandfather asked.
"He said the clerics. And when I asked him what he meant, he said religious leaders," replied Mustafa.

The grandfather told him to fetch Hussein, and Mustafa respectfully exited the *majlis*[21] on his tip toes, as was custom.

When Hussein entered his grandfather's *majlis*, he kissed his hand before taking a seat on the ground. His grandfather gestured to the gilt cane leaning to his left, just below his turban and cloak. Abdallah the Beloved never left the house without his cane, turban,

---

21 A council, or gathering, among people with a common social, intellectual, political, or religious interest.

and cloak. The cane was not so much for leaning on as it was for looking grandiose, magnifying his height and punctuating the sharp looks he gave others. In between footsteps, he would draw circles with it in the air.

The grandfather stared at his grandson's bare head.

"Where is your *kuffiyah*?"[22] he asked sternly. "Didn't I order you to wear it and never take it off except when you sleep?"

Hussein didn't answer. It was a sign of respect not mutually exclusive from the self-confidence apparent in his features. The grandfather took note of his silence.

"What would you happen to be reading these days?" he asked.

The question jolted him. Hussein trembled with some remorse.

"A couple of different books," he answered.

"Would any of those books happen to be about atheism?" asked the grandfather, sure he had caught Hussein by surprise.

"That depends on how you think about it," Hussein responded.

That was all the grandfather needed to identify a hint of defiance in his presence. He slammed his palm on the ground and stood upright in a single sweep. The intensity of his anger was such that he forgot to speak in classical Arabic, a carefully maintained aspect of his ostentatious personality.

"Go get those books now," he said, pointing with unmistakable severity.

The grandson withdrew, fearful of an escalation. He heard his grandfather's footsteps behind him, and figured he was going to look around his room. It occurred to Abdallah the Beloved that

---

22 Arab cloth headdress.

this rebellious boy might also be hiding other things in his room. Several months ago, Hussein had frequented the youth's hangouts, turfs of a cast of juveniles who didn't hesitate to commit acts of vice and disgrace.

The grandfather rummaged through his things, remembering his grandson's disobedience and how he insolently ignored his commands: the way he would remain bareheaded, disregarding the *kuffiyah* which was meant to mark him as an aristocrat. The way he mixed too often with commoners and slave children. How he played hooky when he should have been attending ceremonies and sermons at the mosque.

Hussein remained at the threshold. As the grandfather peered through the shelves, Hussein suspected he was looking for something besides books. Maybe he thought he would find bottles of wine stashed away. He glanced at the jacketed books scattered across the floor, an arrangement which suggested that the reader was at once probing, comparing, and contemplating the substance between their covers. He lifted one up, reading its title aloud, *The Anthropology of Tyranny and the End of Slavery.* He picked up another, *The Iliad.* He was drawn to a book with a woman on its cover, *Romeo and Juliet.* He put the books down and picked up another. It was as if a snake had bitten him. *The Kingdom of God is Within You,* by Tolstoy. He threw it to the floor violently, scattering its jacket and rustling its pages. As his eyes caught another title, the muscles of his face began to twitch, *The Liberation of Women* by Qasim Amin. He no longer had the strength to persevere in his crusade through the literature strewn in his midst. How did these satanic tracts finagle their way back into his very own house without him noticing? He, who had cleansed his ancestors' library so that it was lined only with titles on jurisprudence, biography, astronomy, and medicine! He was sure he had buried the bulk of the books in the cellar away from the prying eyes of his grandchildren!

He heard a patter at the door and turned towards it. Raqwan stood in the doorway, paralyzed. She wasn't expecting to see the grandfather in her betrothed's room. The room, in whose air hung the portends of a coming explosion, was lit for a moment by her presence. Raqwan hurried to place her usual kiss on the back of his hand. He grabbed her violently and yelled, "What are you doing here?!" He spotted something bunched up beneath her head scarf, which was dangled all the way down to her middle, and he lifted it. "Paper and pen?" he demanded. He turned furiously to Hussein who was about to say something but was quickly cut off. "Women's liberation?!" he howled, cuffing Hussein on the face...

*

In the dark of night, Raqwan lay cowering in the hollow. It was a tiny chamber, no bigger than a meter-and-a-half, inside the main room with a lockable door that served as storage space. It was there that the flames of fever ripped through her and delirium propelled her into mysterious intervolving worlds. There, she saw her Abyssinian mother who had lost her mind months ago. She was wandering through corridors with hair grizzled well beyond her forty years. Raqwan saw tens of lanterns hanging from her mother's breast as she held Hussein's hand and led him away.

"*Mama*! Hussein!" she cried, but they continued on their way, and Hussein hummed a song as he went. She awoke with a start, shivering with fever. Raqwan saw Alawiya pressing her limbs to quell the shivering. Her eyes bore into her cousin's features which looked so much like her brother Hussein's. Raqwan brought her fingertips to Alawiya's cheeks. "Hussein," she called out unwittingly. Even the tears on Raqwan's burning fingertips began to evaporate from the heat. Alawiya shrieked out, shocked by their sting. "Dear God, have mercy!" she cried, pulling back her hand and running through the house looking for someone to save Raqwan from the fever that consumed her body...

The following morning, Raqwan listened to the whisper of palm trees coming from the fields outside the house, and the call of a mockingbird rising above them. It was a tender melody like the babbling of water in canals on lightless mornings. Again the mockingbird sang, "God is one, God is one." That's how the Wadi people heard the lullabies of this heavenly creature with its coat of shiny silver feathers.

She turned to Saadoun, who was busy chopping thick slabs of camel meat. Saadoun had raised her and Hussein, tying them both to her back when she did housework. She was reserved and didn't usually engage with the children. Hussein and Raqwan were her favorites, and for them, she made an exception. Saadoun was half farmer and half slave.[23] She had grown up in the house and taken on the mannerisms of the nobility who lived there. They, in turn, respected and feared her. She was a vault of everyone's secrets and Nour the Beloved, the old grandmother, confided in no one but her.

"Mama Saadoun!" Raqwan called out.

Saadoun glanced at her to signal she was listening.

"Do you hear the mockingbird? Hussein, God rest his soul, used

---

23 Slavery was practiced in the Hadramout community (in Yemen) until the mid-1940s. A decree agreed upon by the Sultans of Hadramout and the British High Commissioner to abolish it was passed in 1936. Ironically, the slaves rebelled against the decision. Their protests were rejected, however, and they were liberated by force.

to love its song," said Raqwan.

"May God compensate for your loss, my child," said Saadoun.

*

Five years had passed since Hussein's death, but Raqwan's whole body still seized up and shivered whenever she heard the torrent roaring through the Harra. It had swallowed up her love and pieces of her heart into its chasms. No one had cared about her heart that day. She ran after the casket only to be barred by the men, dragged back by the women, and given looks of condemnation by everyone. "A woman doesn't show grief over her man!" they warned.

She remembered it well; when just before dawn, the cries of Hussein's mother rang out. The night was at its cusp, and the cadaverous moon hid behind looming storm clouds. The rainy season was relentless that year. It was followed by a mammoth flood (The Zealot, as it was called by the townspeople) which left a trail of destruction that the Wadi people still talked about till this day.

Raqwan sat on a rock at the edge of the canal, scratching lines into the wet sludge. She felt a numbness creeping into her fingers. Her mind wandered back to the painful past. She remembered Hussein's warm fingertips as he pressed her thumb and forefinger onto the pencil, promising her that she would one day have the prettiest handwriting in the entire Wadi. She laughed at the time, glancing at her crooked lines and said, "It's chicken scratch!" Later, she repeated after him, as he read the squiggled words she had written...

Ayshoun, Raqwan's friend, called out for her to approach. The voice brought her back to the hateful gurgling sound of the water.

"Raqwan, Raqwan! Look at the Harra and conquer your fear of

it!" she said.

"Ayshoun, I can't. I just can't," cried Raqwan.

Ayshoun took her hand and gently guided her towards the edge of the canal. They looked into the deep waters with controlled contempt. The current was swirling into terrifying eddies. Ayshoun threw a metal can into it, which was quickly devoured and broken. Raqwan let out a scream, covered her face, and retreated...

Back at the house, Alawiya was filling the ceramic pitcher from the large amphora of water. She placed it at the window to cool, suddenly spotting her cousin Mustafa from afar. As usual, his gait was rickety and his head hung low, as if in direct combat with the wind. Secretly she was pleased that in the end arrangements had changed and he would not be hers. As cousins, it was expected they should marry. When the original marriage plans were made, and each male cousin was assigned a female cousin to wed, he was to be her lot. Mustafa, the Limper! With a mix of sorrow and relief, she whispered to herself, "Poor Raqwan..." Her favorite cousin was condemned to a life gripped by grief and would be married off to the Limper! Her family had decided he would take Hussein's place; Hussein, whose ribs were smashed in the dark, dark night.

Translated by Amahl Khouri

Silent Letters

Gabi Toufiq

Dear Diary,

Communication was never my family's strong point so all forms of it were banned at home. The favorite weapon of choice was to turn a situation around and blame me; the reasons were plenty: I am disrespectful, too loud, too emotional, and to add on all of that: I curse. My personal favorite is that I make a big deal out of things.

So, I chose to address my past through diary entries. That was the only way to stay silent. With time, silence was transformed from a haunting nightmare to a close friend.

*

August 21, 2010

Dear Dad,

I was supposed to go to school yesterday, remember? It was the first day of tenth grade—I was so excited, dad. I just wanted to leave the house—just for a few hours. I couldn't wait for my best friend to pick me up so we could walk to school together.

You never really liked her; you never liked Sarah. You thought she was bad news because she wore dark makeup and had tar-tinted fingernails. You hated the fact that I, too, had black nail polish on whenever I came back from her house.

I wasn't supposed to tell her to pick me up yesterday; I'm not allowed to be friends with her anymore. I didn't care, I just wanted to leave the house—I am so pale. Do you remember why I am so pale? You even noticed it yourself the other day. You said I might need some Vitamin D shots.

I finished ninth grade with high distinction, do you remember that? Do you remember how the principle called you that spring morning to say I was top of my class? Do you remember how happy you were; how proud of me you felt? Do you remember why you locked me in the house for months on end? Do you now remember why I am so pale?

*

August 20, 2010

Dear Mom,

I was wide awake when you came into my room this morning. I was really excited about going to school. I could hardly wait for the alarm to ring.

I was so eager to start the new school year that I prepared my uniform the night before. I got dressed in what seemed like no time and sat in front of the TV, staring blankly at the black screen. My thoughts drifted to a million places. I looked forward to seeing Rami at school—he gave me the attention you never did. My heart raced with both fear and excitement at the memory of his silhouette and I hated myself for it.

You interrupted my thoughts ever so alarmingly. You told me you didn't think I should go to school that day. I didn't understand what you meant; I thought you just didn't want me to walk to school with Sarah—which is something you've demanded before—but it was different this time. The look on your face was both stone cold and sorrowful. I'd never seen you look so conflicted.

I immediately became defensive; like I always did when I sensed I had done something wrong. I shouted at you, demanding an explanation. You kept your composure and repeated what you said that I couldn't go to school, not even in the future.

I knew what was going on. I knew it was something that had to do with the one thing I'd tried so very hard to hide from you. I knew it had to do with Rami.

At the thought of your reaction, my heart thumped so loud I could hear it. My stomach churned. We stared at each other for what seemed like the longest time. You demanded to see my phone—you'd always hated the fact that I had a cellphone. When I didn't respond, you rushed to my bedroom and began looking for it. I wanted to tell you it was under my pillow. I wanted to tell you to stop messing up my closet because it wasn't in there. I wanted to apologize more than anything; I wanted to sit at your feet and beg for your forgiveness. Instead, I asked why you wanted my phone. You told me that dad needed it.

✱

August 20, 2010

Dear Dad,

You left to work very early today—maybe you did it on purpose. Maybe you did it to give mom the chance to talk to me. She did. She called me into her room and blatantly asked who Rami is. Her voice echoed and in my ears. I looked down at my hands and saw them shivering. Soon my entire body started to tremble.

I stuttered a pathetic response—I didn't know how to answer. I asked her what she meant by the question. She was so robotic; she didn't sound like herself at all. It scared me. Her usually heavy-lidded green eyes were fully opened, staring into my soul, her short neck stiff with a readiness to attack, the veins on her forehead almost exploding. She looked very hostile. She didn't look like my mother. She asked me again about Rami. We were both quiet for what must have been an eternity and a day. My mind ran wild with thoughts.

Images of Rami came back to me and I pictured his bulging muscles pushing me against the cold wall. I felt his grip on my neck and his teeth tugging on my earlobes. For a moment, just a fleeting moment, I could feel his pungent cologne creeping up my nostrils as I began to fidget in my seat.

Do you know who Rami is, dad? Do you know what he's repeatedly done to your baby daughter? Rami is my rapist. I wish he didn't have a name, a face, or a body. I wish he didn't have the attributes of a human being because he isn't one.

He was there, day after day, for nearly three months, standing at the doorstep. There he was, saying goodbye, peaking left and right, stealing a kiss with lustful lips. Just minutes before, he had me pinned face down on the bed I grew up sleeping in, his massive body throbbing with ecstasy, sweating on the back of my neck. Just minutes ago, I was shouting at the top of my lungs calling out for help, begging him to stop. Just minutes ago, no one came to my rescue.

"How did you do it?" Mom's words echoed off the walls.

She interrupted my flashback, pulling me back to reality—a dark, frightening reality. When I didn't know how to respond, when I stuttered for the millionth time, she sharpened her tone and repeated her question. I knew I had to answer before she injured me.

"How did I do what, mom?" I attempted to compose a full sentence.

"Stop it!" She roared. "You're testing the limits of my patience."

"*Mama*, I just don't understand."

"What do you mean you don't understand? Do I need to draw you a picture?"

I lowered my head. I knew what she was talking about; I understood. I was so ashamed of myself, of what I had done, of what I allowed him to do. My heart didn't thump this time; I didn't feel a choking pain in my throat or a cloudy dizziness. Instead, I heard ringing in my ears and felt nothing else.

"Did he go inside?"

I slowly nodded. She paused for a moment to absorb my nod. I shivered.

"God!" So it's true." She was done absorbing.

"What's true?"

"What your cousin said last night," she blurted out. I don't think she meant to tell me this piece of information. She seemed to regret it instantly.

My cousin! My own flesh and blood. I find it difficult at times to refer to her as family. She is now engaged to my brother and is about to become "real" family. Rita and Ziad: the obnoxious, madly in love couple who told each other everything—sometimes too much. Rita was also my best friend. She was like an older sister. I confided in her; I was scared to tell anyone else and I thought she would be able to help me—perhaps I didn't say it right. Perhaps she didn't understand I was raped and thought it was consensual. Did I even know I was raped? I used the words "force" and "scream" several times, but maybe I didn't know what really happened.

I am yet to find out what Rita told you about me the other night, mom. And, knowing you, I probably never will. Knowing you, it will be buried deep in your subconscious only to resurface through your involuntary behavior. I can tell from your increasingly worsening treatment that she didn't get it right. But at least now you know, dad. At least you know what really happened.

Mom wasn't quite done with me yet. There was still room left for psychological scarring.

"You just shaved years off our lives with what you did, do you know that? Do you know what your father did when he heard the news?"

"What?" I dared not lift my eyes up to look at her.

"He took off his shoe and started beating himself on the head with it. He said this is not the daughter he raised. You are not his daughter."

Long pause. I choked. I couldn't breathe. I felt like someone shoved a cluster of gravel down my throat. I didn't cry—I was too shocked to cry.

"He wanted to disown you."

★

August 27, 2010

Dear Diary,

No one told me why I was taken to Lebanon. But I quickly figured it out: mom wanted me to see a doctor—a women's doctor. I don't understand why she wouldn't take me to one in Iraq. I suppose it would be too embarrassing to have a gynecologist check her daughter's virginity—especially since she'd befriended all the doctors in town.

I bet my brothers were wondering why mom was so nervous today, why I didn't mumble a word. Were they confused when she told them to take us to Zouk Mosbeh without providing an explanation? I'm sure they were. I bet they didn't understand why they were asked to wait outside for two hours—why we later came out and mom had a smile on her face. Did they suspect what happened in there?

Mom took me to see if I was still a virgin; to see if I had shamed and dishonored the family. The waiting room had black wallpaper, black leather couches, and a glass coffee table. It didn't seem like a medical clinic. It was more like a shady abortion place. The doctor's office was covered in luxurious mahogany wood; it was clear that the man made a lot of money. He could tell from our accents that we weren't Lebanese, so he started the conversation with small talk. Mom did most if not all of the talking. I sat quietly awaiting my inevitable doom. The doctor saw that I was getting uncomfortable and asked why we had come to see him. Mom told me it was okay; that I could trust him—that he was a doctor and doctors were to be trusted.

I told him many things. I don't remember what I said exactly; I choked at one point and broke down in tears. That was the first time I cried in front of mom. I told him all about that "friend" I had who wanted to be more than just friends; how I agreed to go out on a date with him because he was nice to me; how he raped me. The doctor asked me to elaborate on exactly how he raped me. I didn't want to, but mom pinched my thigh to make me speak.

"We were out," I mumbled, "and we came back." Pause.

"Keep going, dear." He said with a concerned expression.

Perhaps I should keep this part to myself, I thought, *or save it for a therapist.*

"I... I don't remember exactly what happened."

Mom sharply told me to try harder.

"He... He pushed me against the wall of my bedroom," I continued mumbling. "It hurt. He unzipped my pants. He was scared it wouldn't go in, so he put some lotion on it. I had moisturizer on my desk."

"Dear," the doctor interrupted. "Do you mean he was trying to... penetrate from behind?"

"I guess."

"So why are you here?" He cheerfully told my mother, "She's obviously still a virg—"

"Because he slipped." I was the one interrupting him this time. "He was nervous and in a hurry. He slipped. I bled. I don't know where it came from, but I bled."

Calmly, the doctor led me to the examination room next to his office. The florescent lights shone so brightly that he seemed not only to be examining my private parts but my soul as well. He asked me to lie down on the disturbingly white examination table and put my legs up. I didn't know I had to take my clothes off for him, too. He tried to unzip my jeans; I flinched. He said he needed to look "down there," to give mom an answer that would make her happy.

I got up, slowly took off my shoes, pants, and underwear and folded everything neatly on a chair nearby. The doctor seemed to be getting impatient. When I was finally done, he asked me to climb back on the table and put my legs up on the cold metal again. I struggled at first but, eventually, I was exposed to the eyes of this stranger—everything was visible to him.

He told me not to worry as he gently touched the outer part of my genitals; that this wouldn't hurt. I began trembling and crying again—he told me to relax my muscles, that he wouldn't be able to see anything if I didn't calm down. I couldn't relax. I couldn't calm down. How could I?

It was soon over.

"There's nothing," he said. "You're all good."

I was so confused; I didn't understand what he meant by that. I think I looked confused as well, because he seemed to have the urge to explain.

"There's nothing wrong with you; the hymen is perfectly intact. You're all good."

He left me to get dressed and went out to talk to mom. She seemed relieved. I came out of the examination room to find a huge smile on her face. She hugged and kissed me.

"*Mabrouk, habibti,*" she said, congratulating me. What for? She should've congratulated herself—her daughter had been medically declared a non-whore.

I wish I could remember the doctor's name. I would've called him to ask what he really saw. I could handle it; mom couldn't. I just wanted to hear the truth. I was sure what he said was a lie. He lied because he sensed how dire the situation was; how frightened I was and how desperate mom looked—he just wanted to spare my life.

I wish I could remember his name.

★

October 14, 2010

Dear Mom and Dad,

We just moved to a new house in Kurdistan. It's very small. I hate it. I hate everything about it. It smells too sterile and it looks too neat for my rebellious taste. The couches are unnervingly new. I don't like how American the kitchen looks. My room is pink. Why is my room pink?

I went to school for the first time today, dad. I went to take the entrance exam. Rita told me that this school is the most respected school in the city; that I would be lucky to be admitted. I failed the entrance exam on purpose. Did you know that? I wanted to tell you but you weren't home when I came back. I didn't want you to think that I'm too stupid to know the meaning of "circumstantial," "opaque," or "abysmal." I knew what those words meant; I also knew how to find the area under a slope. I just don't want to be here.

I slept clutching my guitar last night, dad. Do you know why? I bet it never crossed your mind. You robbed me of everything dear to me. You snatched me away from my school, my friends, and the town I grew accustomed to. You took away my computer and my phone and placed extra protection on the WIFI password, just in case I had any funny ideas. You disconnected me from the world, imprisoning me in a house that smells like carpet cleaner, in the hope of making our problem disappear. I slept next to my guitar because it's the last thing of value I have. I'm afraid you will decide to take it too, one day. I'm so afraid of what you are capable of doing.

*

November 3, 2010

Dear Mom and Dad,

Do you still love me? You used to say that I am your miracle child; you thought you would never have a baby girl to fill your home with love and laughter. Am I still that baby daughter? Whenever you'd tell the story of my birth, dad, you'd say you weren't sure you had enough love in you to have a third child. One day, a few weeks after I was born, you saw me sleeping in my crib on my fat, squeezed up cheek and I filled your heart with a new kind of love. Do you still love me?

You said some terrible things to me today, mom. You said that I ruined your life and that dealing with me makes you miserable; that you hate me. You hate me; your own daughter.

You said I ruined your life.

Do you know what happened to me? Did Rita tell you what Rami did to your daughter? Did she tell you all about how he pinned me against a wall and assaulted me until I could no longer scream? Or did you cover your ears during that part? I screamed, mom. I screamed and no one heard—I'm still screaming.

*

November 22, 2010

Dear Mom and Dad,

I feel so out of place. Why am I here? I don't feel like I belong anywhere anymore. They don't speak Arabic; I don't speak Kurdish. A girl in my class came up to me today and told me that she hates me because I'm Arab. I didn't do anything to her; I've never even spoken to her before. I hate myself.

Where are you, dad? Why haven't I seen you in over a month? Did you really beat yourself on the head that day? Did I really hurt you that much? I'm sorry. When will you come back home? Mom looks tired; she needs you.

Come drive me to school, dad. I don't like the bus driver. He always drops me off last. Come take mom grocery shopping; we're running out of food—I don't like cheap takeout anymore. Come back home, dad, mom is lonely without you; she cries all the time. Come fix the TV.

*

November 27, 2010

Dear Mom and Dad,

I'm sorry I came home late. The bus was a no-show today at school. I waited outside for over an hour but the driver never came. All the other kids called their parents and got picked up—no one offered me a ride. I couldn't call you because I don't have a phone. The security guard at school offered me his phone but I didn't have your numbers memorized.

I called Rami instead. I don't know why I did it; I felt like I had to call someone. His was the only number I could remember. He sounded happy to hear from me, like he truly missed me. I missed him too; he loved me—he still loves me. He asked when I was going to visit him. He said he wanted me to come back; he wanted to see me. I said I wanted to see him too but I couldn't. He told me he wanted to have sex with me again; that I'm allegedly his wife and it was his right. I hung up.

I walked home today, mom, that's why I'm late. I'm sorry. It took me more than two hours because I got lost. I've never walked home before.

*

December 8, 2010

Dear Mom and Dad,

I tried to kill myself today. I realized my presence was causing the family too much pain. I wanted to relieve you from the burden of my existence. Would you miss me if I slit my wrists right now?

I wanted to kill myself today. I know that your life would fall back in place if I disappeared. I know that sometimes you wish you had never prayed for the miracle daughter you told me about. I know I am no longer that miracle. I know I am nothing but a burden. I know it took every inch of will in you not to kill me for your honor, dad. I know the pride that comes with your theology degrees doesn't allow you to walk out on me, mom. I know you wish you could.

I didn't kill myself today. I told myself I was too scared to pierce my own flesh—I wasn't. I simply didn't want you to live with the guilt, to see the crimson stain on my pink carpet.

*

December 21, 2011

Dear Dad,

Today Mom caught me doing something I wasn't supposed to be doing. I was sitting on my bedroom floor holding a knife to my left wrist. I knew how to cut to make it lethal. I knew that cutting horizontally would not open the veins enough to make the blood gush out in large amounts, I had to cut vertically.

When mom took the knife away, I felt like I had lost my autonomy once again. I didn't like it. I was just glad that she walked out without saying or doing anything else—I expected a lecture and was pleased when one wasn't given.

✶

November 23, 2014

Dear Hope,[24]

Mom had an important meeting at the Ministry of Health, and Jamil, the driver, came to pick her up. She thought his car was not presentable enough, so they used dad's car.

Rami was watching from across the street, waiting for them to leave. After the door shut behind mom and Jamil, you heard him knocking. You knew his knock; he always tapped the door with his car keys three times, stopped, then tapped twice. That knock was the most fear-provoking sound you've ever heard in your life; more frightening than all the sirens, bombs, and gunshots you heard during the war in Baghdad. The sound pierced through your stomach and

---

24 Hope is the name I went by from age 13 through 17 because I hated the way my name was written in Arabic. I occasionally use it as a pseudonym or an alter ego. She is now a child of the past.

twisted it. You knew you had no choice but to open the door because Rami constantly threatened you. He threatened you with pictures, videos, and voice recordings. He said he would post them on social media or show them to mom and dad if you don't obey him. You believed him and never asked any questions.

You opened the door and he came in and kissed you on your neck right away. He told you he was hungry. You offered to heat up some leftover rice and chicken. He said he would rather eat you. You didn't respond—you just opened the fridge looking for that container of rice and chicken. The microwave was broken—dad hadn't fixed it—so you used the stove.

He snuck up from behind you and started moving his hands up and down, and all over your body. He stopped at your breasts and squeezed them a couple of times, then his hands ran wild again.

You stood there, as you did every time: stiff and speechless. You knew how this was going to end; you had the scenario memorized, visualized in your head. You tried pushing him away. You knew there was no escape; you tried your best to postpone it. You served him some food. You put it on the kitchen table. He devoured it.

Somehow, you ended up in your bedroom. He began kissing you softly. He slowly slid his lips down the side of your right cheek then down to your neck. You shook and shivered. He breathed heavily.

★

You heard tire screeches outside. You knew what dad's car sounded like. You thought mom and dad had come home and thought you were going to die. You felt a sharp, throbbing pain in your chest that was far more penetrating than the pain Rami caused you. You began hyperventilating and your vision blurred—your ears began to ring. That was the time you experienced your first severe panic attack.

Alarmed, Rami decided that hiding behind the door was a good idea. You called him an idiot and told him to leave through the back door and jump over the fence. Terrified, he cooperated. The two of you rushed to the white metal door at the back of the house. He jumped over the fence and ran away.

Your heartbeats slowed down a little. You thought it was over. You breathed again. You sat down on your favorite red couch in the living room trying to catch your breath; you knew you had to get up as soon as your knees allowed you to clean up any evidence he might have left behind. Your vision remained blurry. You felt light-headed and a little nauseous.

*

Knock, knock, knock; your thoughts were interrupted. You wondered if they saw him; wondered if he accidentally ran into them. You opened the door with shaky hands and, to your relief, Jamil was standing there. *It's just the driver*, you thought; *it's just Jamil.*

"Who was that?" He asked, his colorful eyes glistening with deceit.

You swallowed your words; you couldn't breathe and your heart beat a thousand times per minute.

"Who was that guy?" He asked again.

"Wha-What guy?" You stuttered.

"You see," he interrupted your stuttering. "If I weren't a decent guy, a perfect gentleman; if I didn't respect the status of your father and if I didn't care about your family, I would've forced you to go inside with me and make you do whatever the hell I want."

You froze.

"I could've grabbed you by the arm, or dragged you by the hair, and forced you to fulfill all the fantasies my wife wouldn't agree to. I would've fucked you to death."

No one has ever spoken to you like that before. *Who does he think he is*, one part of your mind said? Another part thought: *he's right; I should thank him.*

With a quick maneuver he grabbed your neck with his large hand, his fingers almost wrapping around its circumference, nearly lifting you off the ground. You choked, growled, snorted, grunted—you nearly lost consciousness. His callous hand left a red mark on your neck that lasted for days—you can still feel it sometimes.

"Bitch," he finally said, right before he spat on your face and slammed the door behind him. You were happy he let go of your neck. You were lucky you made it through that day alive. Yet again, maybe you didn't; you're still trying to find out.

✶

March 24, 2016

Dear Rami,

People expect me to be angry with you—I am not. Anger takes up a part of me far too large for your worth. I am not angry with you. No; I pity you.

I pity you because you, too, were a victim of a society that didn't know any better; because you are still trapped in that deadbeat town where nothing ever happens, where life doesn't thrive. I pity you because you have to live with yourself knowing what you did to an innocent girl; because you never found the motivation to finish high school. I pity you because you were forced into a marriage you never wanted; into having children you will never love. I do not pity myself.

I do not pity myself because, despite everything you put me

through, today I am stronger and braver than I ever would've been. I do not pity myself because, thanks to what you did, I am now able to deal with the world around me in ways I would never have imagined. I should probably thank you. But no, I won't thank you. I won't thank you because I loathe you.

I hate you, Rami, first and foremost because you robbed me of my innocence. You robbed me of my childhood; of the years I was supposed to be happy. But that's not the only reason I hate you.

I abhor you because you distorted reality for me; because you installed a veil over my vision that I've been trying so hard to remove. You twisted me into all the impurities I've become—pushing me into a spotlight of familial shame and sabotaged my perception of the world. But that's not why I abhor you.

I despise you because I can no longer feel physically safe with any man. Men represent one thing to me today, and that is danger. You distorted my image of what sex ought to be, of what love is. The concepts of love and lust have become so interchangeable in my head that I can rarely differentiate between the two. You took an adolescent who was absolutely clueless about the world around her and sexualized her in the most abusive and twisted way imaginable— then you called it love.

I have finally learned, Rami. I have learned how to bury you in the depths of my very own hell.

★

July 29, 2016

Dear Mom and Dad,

There are so many things I wish to tell you but I cannot find the words. Perhaps I can begin by telling you how wrong you were in misjudging the person I have become. I won't do that, however, because it seems useless to continue pointing fingers at each other.

I cannot blame you for the way you reacted because you didn't know any better; you were as lost and confused as I was, perhaps even more. You always put your work before your family: placing your careers before your parental responsibilities.

You both stopped living and gave your lives away to the service of others, and, in doing so the lives of your children were damaged. I have finally broken free from your hold over my life, from your threatening language and imposing beliefs. You must no longer think of me as the shameful and dishonorable daughter you are stuck with—I am not. You must no longer treat me like a child; like I am stuck in the past—I am not. For just as I have learned to let go of, and deal with the past, so should you.

Break free from the grasp of society, from what people think. Break free from your closed-mindedness and open your eyes to the world around you. Break free from the foul and mindless traditions handed down from your families. Break free, just as your miracle child has broken free.

The Lady in the Black Veil

ZEINAB AL-TAHAN

Through the folds of her black veil, she sees them before her, ghosts in black, colorlessly swaying. One tall quick-paced ghost almost bumps into her without giving her a second glance. Another examines her, taken aback, as if his eyes weren't accustomed to seeing a woman begging on the streets of Beirut. But that one coming from afar, a short ghost walking leisurely, looks at her with malice, making her outstretched hand quiver and expose parts of her skin. She retracts it instantly into the long veil that covers her face. The ghost man continues walking by, dragging his abhorred meagerness behind him.

She looks left and right, scoping the place she'd become familiar with many years ago. Time has trapped her here, but never embraced her stay on the street corners. On Hamra's main street, paved with marble tiles the color of the Lebanese sky, they park their luxurious cars, blocking pavements that swarm with pedestrians. She notices that City Café is crowded with customers this morning, and that he's alone, sitting there as usual, drinking his coffee and reading his newspaper. Every once in a while he peeks at her as if searching for a revelation... And her wonder grows every day, does he know her? The first time she saw him was in this café... no, elsewhere but she can't remember where and when... She takes her eyes off him and lets them haunt other ghosts.

He seems as stylish as the rest and just as pretentious. An old man in a grey suit adorns his wrist with a gold bracelet that sparkles in the sunlight, a gold watch on his other wrist. His colleague, or perhaps his friend, differs neither in dress nor appearance: a gold chain gilding his neck, grabbing the attention of passersby, the width shimmering across his chest. He shifts the beads of an embellished rosary through his fingers, as though he were the proud chief of some tribe.

She stretches her neck to see the lady in the fancy black coat, which she insists on wearing every day, even on sunny February days like this one, as if it were an inseparable part of her slender body. Her sighs deepen as she shuffles in her seat, a thick cigar tucked firmly between her rouged lips, turning the pages of her book with one hand, and sipping coffee with the other.

The aroma of hot coffee entices her every morning, and she dreams of tasting the expensive coffee of rich people, sitting with them at their table and telling them her story. If they knew her story, would they help her find a more appropriate job at her age? She misses her two sons and yearns for their childhood days. It's been a while since they've checked up on her. Perhaps they've forgotten about her. Najat is the only person who stayed. Will she leave as well when she gets her own life and world? She's now thirty, and some man has yet to ask for her hand in marriage.

Before the veil, there was her tall figure, reddish hair, and green eyes, which enflamed the hearts of many in her neighborhood, but it was only Najib whom she loved. His poverty did not stop her from marrying him. But she didn't know she was marrying into poverty forever. After Najib was killed, cleaning houses was the only way to survive.

Her children still blame her for choosing that lowly job. "You had other options, you've disgraced us…" That's how her eldest son would speak to her. When they grew up and their lives changed, they left and kept away from her. Perhaps they thought distance would wash their disgrace away. What would they say if they knew what she was doing now? She coughs violently to wash away her bad thoughts, drawing people's attention, particularly the stylish customer who resumes his examination of her. He adjusts his seat, puts his newspaper aside, and sips whatever's left of his coffee without taking his eyes off her… Suddenly, a fancy Range Rover passes by, blocking her view, deepening her sense of fragility and nothingness.

Suddenly a shadow looms over her body. The man before her stands tall and bends his slim body towards her. He whispers, "Uncover your mouth and I'll feed you." Astonished by his sudden presence, she watches him remove a rolled cigarette and light it for her, saying once more, "Come on, show me you're human." She stands up to walk away from this old man's nonsense, but he grabs her left arm. "You think I didn't recognize you? I recognized your walk and grand height. Come on, take off your veil, and I'll provide you with food."

When he notices how other people are staring, he takes a step back from the old woman and feigns a smile, motioning with his hand for her to pass in peace. Relieved, she walks away, her temperature rising to the extent where she imagined her black veil would catch fire. This doesn't at all resemble the mastery she'd shown on stage when she performed her first theatrical role about shame and submission. Now she realizes the difference between theater and reality. She recalls the night of the last rehearsal. After all the actors had gone, and she was rearranging her clothes, the director approached her, pulling her by the hair, demanding that they re-enact the rape scene together. Repulsed, she pushed him away, but he was too excited and physically stronger. She couldn't stop him from tearing her clothes off. The scene was brought to life, this time with real screaming and pain. She left the theater, dripping blood on the stage.

She arrives at the Turkish bath's wide entrance, tucked away from the main street, takes off her robe and veil to reveal another woman who had been raised with respect and dignity, a woman who once knew the innocence and sweetness of life. Today, only sorrow and sadness cast shadows over her eyes. And while the spark is still there, the pain breaks her, as though it were a real wound bleeding in her throat and voice. She says hello to the plump woman supervisor who gruffly mutters, "You're late, as usual... If it weren't for your old age and need of work, I would've fired you a long time ago... Go on, a stack of soft bodies need someone to pamper them in preparation for their big day."

She dons her service uniform and proceeds to the four young girls, their bodies swinging to the sound of music, whispering among themselves in laughter. With her little finger, one of them motions at her to approach. She complies, trying hard to avoid looking at their naked bodies. The girl hands her a pumice stone and says, "Rub my body softly and slowly." Taking the stone in her hand, she turns it in her palms, breathing deeply and commences with her task. Still dwelling on grotesque memories, she accidently scrubs the young girl harder than usual. Suddenly the girl starts shouting, "You've cut me!" The other girl runs to get the manager who hastens towards them, asking in confusion what happened. She sees the girl's back, something she was used to seeing, and says to the old lady, "You're back to your absent mindedness. I've warned you many times... This is it, stop what you are doing and leave. I won't need your services anymore." This time, the beggar doesn't beg. She collects her money and her bags, puts on her black robe without the veil and leaves. Still seeing people as black shadows, she walks among them indifferently. Days pass as she wanders, lost among the neighborhoods feeling trapped in disconnected dungeons that strangle her. This is Beirut's way, deceiving admirers with her ladylike looks, while gently cradling despair in her arms at night.

When she reaches home, an odd sound of loud laughter can be heard. Perhaps it's one of her sons, Jalal or Yehya. She could no longer remember their voices. She quickly takes out her key, turns it in the lock, and rushes into the living room, completely forgetting to disrobe. And there he was. Her pupils dilate, her face turns pale, her heartbeats accelerate, drowning out the sound of her daughter Najat's voice, who confusedly asks, "Mom, what're you wearing? Where were you?!" Her daughter asks again, shaking her mother by the arm. "Mom, this is Mr. Najdi. He's here to ask for my hand in marriage, and he wants to meet my brothers. Mom, say something!"

Mr. Najdi stands there, smiling maliciously, feeling vindicated, victoriously talking to Najat while looking at her mother. "Actually, I've come to meet your mother, and I have."

Najat looks at them astounded.
"I don't understand… what do you mean you came to see my mother?"
"I've seen your mother several times in this long black dress with a veil covering her face begging on the streets of Hamra."

Najat chuckles nervously at his accusation and tells him he is being impolite, but he continues speaking.

"When I saw you walking today I remembered you on stage and I suspected that perhaps it was you… when the wind lifted the veil off your face my suspicions grew, and then I heard your voice and glimpsed your eyes through the veil. Immediately I knew you were my old neighbor who used to drive men crazy... Your image has been imprinted in my mind ever since I was a boy..."

"Najat, stay quiet," says the lady in the black veil looking at her daughter and holding her hand to comfort her. She, then, turns to the man standing before her, smugly smoking his large cigar. Her hand swipes the cigar from his lips, puts it out in an ashtray, and she says, "In fact, I am a beggar and my job is not disgraceful... however, you... you are disgraceful. Get out."

Mr. Najdi walks towards the door turning to glance at mother and daughter once more. "Get out!" Najat screams.

The mother hurls her exhausted body onto the couch and smiles at her daughter.

"Calm down, my child... He's gone and won't come back."

"Yes, mother, he's gone and neither he nor any other man will ever want to marry me. The news will spread like wildfire, and I won't dare leave the house after today... I'll rot here between these four walls you've built for us with beggar's money... You, mom, are responsible for burying me alive, and I'll never forgive you..."

The mother's burden continues to grow until one day she makes a fateful decision that frees her daughter from disgrace.

Translated by Yasmine Haj

Amira's Mirror

Mishka Mojabber Mourani

The child glimpsed herself in the plate glass window that reflected the massive shopping mall under construction on the busy Achrafieh intersection. She was happy about the way her red skirt swayed, and how the sequins caught the sun. The nuns had brought the refugee children over to the big school and given them clothes for the winter. She got lucky this time, she thought. Last time, the ill-fitting pants and grey top looked like they belonged to *Teta* Umm Munif. She loved the clothes this time, even though the nun they called Ma Mère had reprimanded her prissiness. "Vanity will be your downfall if you're not careful, my child," she had said severely.

When the car slowed at the stoplight, she suppressed the urge to rush over. It was the lady again. The one with the dark eyes that stared blankly beyond the partially-open car window. The girl caught her reflection fleetingly; only the box of chewing gum and the green sweater appeared in the lower section of the window. She would look like this lady one day, and she, too, would ride in a car with windows designed to prevent outsiders from looking in.

*

Amira, a tall, slim, small-breasted woman with a graceful neck, liquid-black eyes and smooth chestnut hair, carries her head high. She had practiced her blank yet velvety look while still a little girl. People want to love her: men see in her the quintessential woman. Women want to emulate her. But, her husband, Sammy, dislikes her.

He cannot forgive her duplicity. The debacle with Ryan hangs heavily between them.

Since she married Sammy, who once dazzled her with his rugged good looks, his family background, and his promising future, she had become disinterested in sex. Still, she relished the power sex gave her. Any surrender to a lover came from the desire to own another person completely, to see that person slowly, to recklessly abandon other commitments.

When Ryan, suave and well-spoken, had wooed her, she at first hesitated though thrilled by his attentions, by his singleness of purpose, his impeccable French and English, his polished manners. Of course, from the start, she had not felt any physical passion for him.

Ryan was a challenge to her conservative background, for Amira was a model of traditional respectability: obedient daughter, amenable sister, dutiful wife, docile mother, loyal cousin, and respectful niece. Each of those relationships defined her, as they had her mother and sisters, and as they would define her daughter. Such ties ensured that she would be provided for; as long as she upheld appearances, she would never want.

Her husband attributed her lack of sexual interest to her inexperience as a young bride. She was barely out of her teens. He fancied himself as her teacher in the pleasures of the flesh. To her relief, she became pregnant almost immediately, pushing him away with the weight of hormonal changes heavy on her side. He waited for that phase to pass, but motherhood legitimately ensured his distance. She had three children in quick succession and was completely engrossed by them. Surely he could not expect her to cater to his crass needs.

Their youngest was eight when Sammy had an affair with a bubbly young girl he met while playing tennis. Mysterious phone calls, secret meetings, a boosted ego, but the pretty young thing soon left him for more permanent ties. He replaced her with another, while Amira assumed the role of wronged wife with quiet dignity. She did not like the situation but was determined to turn it to her advantage. Their friends shook their heads in surprise.

"How could he do that to her?!"
"... and such a beautiful and devoted wife!"
"Men are fickle!"
"... mid-life crisis..."

Her family found out. Her father pretended he knew nothing. Her mother commiserated with her and was proud of her daughter's composure and fortitude. She congratulated herself on having raised her daughter well. "I remember when your father lost his head over that Austrian secretary. I was beside myself! I ranted and raved and felt miserable, and then your paternal grandmother came over to say, 'Shame on you, daughter-in-law!' 'Enough of this carrying on. You seem to forget who you are and whom you have married! Men are weak. As long as they maintain their duties and responsibilities, they must be indulged. You, after all, are the mother of his children. I know my son. He knows his place. Go wash your face, fix yourself up... and grow up!'"

"What happened after that, *Mama*?"

"Well, your grandmother's scolding brought me to my senses. Contrite, I decided to weather the storm. Your father left his mistress a few months later, when the novelty had worn off, and she started to importune him. He came back to the marital bed invigorated and self-righteous. My mother-in-law had been right: men are weak, you learn to handle them and never reveal your feelings."

Although Amira followed her mother's advice, eventually her circumspection began to weigh on her. She was no longer praised for her magnanimity of spirit. Her acquiescence was taken for granted. The children were at school. Examining her face in the mirror, she imagined the tiny lines around her beautiful black eyes deepening perceptibly.

Amira had a degree in public administration and applied for a job at a government agency assuming that her family contacts would secure a position beyond her qualifications. She learned how to drive and was filled with a renewed sense of purpose. Soon after, a young employee at the office developed a crush on her. She strung him along and got rid of him easily enough when his amorousness became an imposition.

Another fling ended when her admirer, an official at the ministry, became frustrated by the impediments she put in his way, and quickly dropped her. She resigned and soon got another job at an NGO. This led to yet another relationship with a senior consultant.

She ended that affair abruptly when her husband's suspicion was aroused. "Why don't I drop and pick you up, darling? There's no point in both of us getting stuck in traffic every day," he unexpectedly volunteered one evening. She could not afford any hint of scandal and decided to limit her involvements to arousing but never fulfilling men's expectations, a game at which she became adept.

Then she met Ryan at a party. The intensity of his pursuit, with cards, poems, and dozens of red roses that graced her desk every

Monday, intrigued her. She luxuriated in his attention, but her coyness only made her more alluring to him. When, eventually, she gave in, they met infrequently and on her terms.

Ryan's ardor, after a few months of courting, turned to an all-consuming passion. He could no longer concentrate on his work, realizing with surprise, he was ready to give up everything for her. Ryan had spent his whole life working for his father, but he was nothing more than the boss's son. And he knew that. His father, a prominent industrialist with political aspirations, was an upright citizen, a pillar of his community with an unblemished reputation. He would certainly leave his son destitute.

Ryan had married very young, against the wishes of his father who had never forgiven him, never missing an opportunity to remind him of his poor judgement. Ryan never defied his father again, so, twenty years later, he remained married to uphold appearances and placate the old man. His villa in the Rabieh[25] hills was a cold but elegant monument to his father's financial status. But Ryan also kept a penthouse apartment in Beirut for when he was working late. His father indulged his expensive taste as long as he toed the line. Ryan had no qualms about leaving his wife, a spoiled, loud woman who had developed a taste for the company of other abrasive women. Their son was away at university in London. Ryan felt helpless whenever he thought of the boy who tired of his parents' foibles and eagerly escaped from the tensions of his miserable childhood. A bright, calculating, callous young man, he was already currying favor with his grandfather. Ryan did not worry about his son's future.

When Ryan met Amira, he was already bored after a series of

---

25 Upscale suburban area on the northern hills overlooking Beirut.

discreet affairs with worldly women. Amira brought him out of his lassitude; she disoriented him. With her soft-spoken grace, she seemed to be the embodiment of all that was pure and ingenuous. They met at his apartment, usually in the afternoon. She made him feel like an adolescent discovering the world for the first time. Even Amira relished their dream-like interludes together.

Ryan was well-read and would quote poetry to her. She luxuriated in the fantasies he created. "Let's just abandon everything and go away together. We can leave the country and start a new life. That project in Geneva could work. I'm sure of it. There's so much I want to show you, so much you haven't done! Let's do it while we're still young. This country has so many problems: a society of double standards, extreme wealth and poverty, massive infrastructure problems, corruption and clientelism, and now all these refugees flooding in. Your children no longer need you, and, anyway, they can always come visit us."

Amira dreamt along with him. They made plans, explored options. But she knew, of course, that none of those projects would ever come about. What surprised her most was his reaction when she told him that. Even now she finds herself thinking about the incident which prompted her to end the affair.

He used to drop her off at one of half a dozen different spots within walking distance of the garage where she parked her car in Achrafieh. She was very careful about being seen with him in public. Once when they stopped at a traffic light, she caught the reflection of a child in the side-view mirror urgently tapping at the partially-open car window. Turning around, she saw a little beggar girl with big, black, velvet eyes selling gum in her sun-browned, outstretched hand. The city was full of Syrian refugees who begged in the streets, congregating at traffic lights. The child wore torn, mismatched clothes, her face was smudged, her hands and nails dirty. But for all that, she was beautiful. Turning away from the child in disgust, Amira rolled up her window tightly. She urged Ryan to drive away. "Who takes care of these children," she wondered out loud, "Are they being coerced?"

Ryan was annoyed at her tone. "Perhaps they are abused," he said. "Who knows if she has parents, if her father is selling her services…"

The beggar girl put her palm flat on the rolled up window and banged the glass repeatedly. Amira glared at her and then turned away. A thought came to her mind; *Could I be her?* The child gave the car a violent kick just as the light turned green.

Her effrontery stayed with Amira. Her neediness. Her soiled outstretched hand. Her violent reaction. Amira felt she was being sucked out into the street. After that incident, she seemed to see the little girl's reflection every time she got into Ryan's car.

A few days later, she told Ryan they had to stop seeing each other. At first, he thought he had misunderstood. He made her repeat what she had said.

"What if it doesn't work out between us? I'll have nothing."

And then it struck him that she was serious. She had no intention of going away with him, of leaving everything just to be with him. His anger was as cold as it was deep. She had toyed with him and, for all his worldliness, he had not realized it. In a fit of fury, he sent two letters, one to Amira and one to Sammy.

"I need to see you one last time," he told her.

"Come see what your wife does on Tuesdays and Thursdays when she's working overtime," he wrote to Sammy…

Ryan hated himself for his deception, hated her for bringing it out in him, but he was determined to hurt her. Sammy had never had a liaison with a married woman. His code was clear: you don't destroy a family, ruin reputations, deprive children of their mother. That was not done.

For months after that, Sammy was distraught. He taunted Amira incessantly. With time his angry attacks were replaced by a cool and cynical disdain. She bore it silently, stoically. She avoided spending time at home. Sammy's pouting had driven her to seek the quiet of her room, but she tired of spending long hours staring at herself in the mirror. Amira resolved to throw herself into her work, putting in overtime and deriving satisfaction from accomplishing tasks assigned to her. Her NGO landed a big project involving refugees, and Amira was put in charge of it. She was as surprised as she was pleased when the manager announced her promotion. She didn't think he had noticed her.

Among her tasks, Amira was assigned to an after-school reading program for refugee children at the Karm El-Zaytoun Public School. She took the Achrafieh ring road, stopping at a red light. As usual, a gaggle of child beggars alighted on the stationary cars, offering boxes of gum, their grubby little hands outstretched. Amira scanned the children's faces, not sure what she was looking for. The light turned green and she continued toward the school.

Amira was met by the project coordinator who took her to a large room lined with bookshelves. Children were seated on a carpet in a circle. A young woman barely out of her teens was reading from a big children's book. Some other children were sitting in pairs or small groups, leafing through magazines or talking in a low hum.

Amira caught a glimpse of the green top and red skirt just as the little girl looked up. The coordinator introduced Amira to the children. She walked over to the girl in the red sequined skirt, knelt down, and asked her name.

"Amali," said the child confidently, her big dark eyes staring at Amira.

"How old are you, Amali?"

"Eight-and-a-half."

"Do you go to school here?"

"Now I do, yes."

"Why only now?"

"Because the Ma Mère in the other school said I am a clever girl, and that if I want to learn to read and write and count, I have to go to school."

"And why do you want to read and write and count?"

"So I can get a job and buy a car and have nice clothes," said Amali, and then added coyly, "Like you."

Amira laughed out loud for the first time in weeks. "I think the Ma Mère is right. You are a clever girl. Learn to read and write and count, Amali, and then decide who you want to be..."

The visit over, Amira left the school, got into her car and buckled her seat belt. Then she rolled down the windows as far as they could go, glanced quickly into the rear-view mirror, and slowly merged into the traffic.

MANTRA

NISREEN SANJAB

Eyes closed. Breathe. Repeat your mantra: *BABA NAM KEVALAM.*[26] Focus and inhale through your nose: one, two, three, four, five... hold. One, two... breathe out: one, two, three, four, five... hold. One, two... Focus on your breathing. *BABA NAM KEVALAM.* Inhale: one, two, three, four, five... hold... breathe out: one, two, three, four, five... hold. One, two. Repeat the process. Don't lose focus. I am on a planet in space. I can see all the stars and celestial spheres floating around me.

Breathe. *BABA NAM KEVALAM.* Inhale: one, two, three, four, five... hold. Breathe out: one, two, three, four, five... hold. One, two. They start to disappear, one star after another, one planet after another. No more specs to see. Breathe. *BABA NAM KEVALAM.* Inhale: one, two, three, four, five... hold. Breathe out: one, two, three, four, five... hold. One, two. All the stars have disappeared, all the planets including the one I am sitting on. I'm floating alone in a dark infinite space. All alone.

Breathe. *BABA NAM KEVALAM.* Inhale: one, two, three, four, five... hold. Breathe out: one, two, three, four, five... hold. One, two. *BABA NAM KEVALAM.* I am the universe and the universe is me. Breathe in: *BABA NAM.* Hold. Exhale: *KEVALAM.* Roll your eyes and focus on the spot between your eyebrows. Resist the temptation to slouch. Maybe if I focus hard on my posture and breathing I can detach myself from the physical space I occupy, from the sounds and

---

26 A Sanskrit mantra meaning "only the beloved's name."

odors, and from my body. Well that can't be too difficult. I can do it. *BABA NAM KEVALAM*. I cannot hear my daughter knocking on my door, asking for help with her math homework.

Breathe. *BABA NAM*. Hold. Exhale: *KEVALAM*. Good; she left. I wonder whether she will be able to manage her homework on her own. Of course she can. She's a tough girl. She traveled for twenty-five days at age eleven to a summer camp in Europe last year. She was on her own for the first time and she managed. I have done a good job raising her to be independent. With her, my second child, I managed not to be overprotective. I remember how her older brother used to give me a hard time. Well, they have two different personalities. Of course, I was anxious when I became a mother for the first time. Maybe some of my anxiety seeped into him. It's entirely my fault. I should have known better than to be so wound up. Besides missing sleep and rest, I mostly craved autonomy. I could not handle all that responsibility. First, the responsibility for my husband when I got married, and then the creature I birthed who was totally dependent on me. Responsibility has been my enemy ever since I got married at the age of twenty-three. I wonder why I ever got married. No, I do not. I love him, but I had my motives back then. I could not fulfill myself under the roof of my tyrannical father. I had independent thoughts, big dreams, and a free spirit larger than my parents' conservative circles. But, what's the use of brooding over the past, over the time I was forced to quit high school for ten days because of accusations of "negligence"? So what if the teapot was steaming and my mom had forgotten to take it off the stove? It was easier to take the blame for her; he might have divorced her and my siblings would have suffered. My punishment was just getting expelled from school. It seems funny now that I think back on all this. Why did it matter so much? Who wouldn't have welcomed a break from school, especially when your dad was forcing you not to go? Forcing.

That's it. I never liked to be forced. One firm principle I have is my independence, and education seemed like the perfect alibi to escape from my oppressive home. Education was my visa to distinction and self-worth. I knew early on that if I managed to be big-brained and distinguished at school, I could fight my way into a good university, and maybe, just maybe, leave home and travel abroad. It seemed like the perfect plan. Who could deny their child higher education? I tried to commit suicide by swallowing ten Panadol tablets. How histrionic that must have looked. Nobody dies from that! Focus. Focus! *BABA NAM KEVALAM.* What has passed is past. It's funny how our whole life centers around two defining thoughts: agonizing over the past or harboring anxious expectations for the future, when all we really have is the present. We never stop to appreciate the present even though it's all we can control. So focus on the present moment and meditate.

Breathe. *BABA NAM.* Hold. Exhale. *KEVALAM.* I wonder if she had breakfast. Did he do his math and physics homework? They have grown so fast. I coped better when she was born. With the first signs of post-partum depression, I called my counsellor. I became more alert after my previous three-year episode with depression. Seeking counselling was okay. It did not mean I was weak or crazy. I managed to delegate more responsibilities. I hired a house helper. I made sure I wore makeup to work. I reinforced my sense of sexiness when shopping for clothes. I resisted the feeling of guilt when enjoying a drink with my best friend. It was a victory to insist to my mother that "personal time" was all right and that I was not a bad mom if I claimed it. It was liberating to have such autonomy. This critical phase and the looming fear of relapse into a traumatic battle with depression lasted less than a year. By the time my daughter was six months old, and despite her being born with a hip displacement and wearing a brace, I had become stronger. Smack... come back! Focus.

Breathe. *BABA NAM*. Hold. Exhale. *KEVALAM*. Why is it so hard for me to focus? *BABA NAM KEVALAM*. Are the thirty minutes over? Focus. This is your personal time! Claim it. I have to take the laundry out of the drier and put another load in before the power goes out. Focus.

Breathe. *BABA NAM*. Hold. Exhale. *KEVALAM*. He says he misses me so much; that I'm not spending enough time with him. We have not had sex in a month, yet I don't seem to need it. I'm not as cold as he claims; I'm just too physically worn out and mentally preoccupied with all the chores. I still fantasize in my sleep about all those men desiring me. He's not one of them. Sometimes he watches, and I like it when he does. I become wet and I yearn for his touch. I don't want to wake up, fearing my drive will fizzle and be replaced with a whirlpool of reminders: having to wake up early for work; dozing off while commuting between three jobs; spending the whole night discussing his emotional needs and my lack of passion. Do not be distracted; *que sera sera*, whatever will be will be. You cannot control everything. Let go. *BABA NAM KEVALAM*. Why can't I trust that the world will function without me? Do I believe I am a goddess who needs to stay vigilant lest the universe collapses?

Breathe. *BABA NAM*. Hold. Exhale. *KEVALAM*. Maybe if I calm down, if I meditate, then I can better invest my time and be more available for my children, more emotionally supportive of my husband, and less sexually frustrated. I can perfect all my responsibilities. I can manage to finish grading exams that are already a month overdue, and maybe I can prepare my lecture for tomorrow. Then I must update my CV and email it as soon as possible... this was a good offer... Me, a school principal! I'm not there yet. I have to write this damn cover letter first and submit my CV. And this story! Why have I been dodging the offer to write a short story? You said you needed deadlines to keep you on track! You said you were more productive under pressure! It was a good challenge and you like challenges. Why accept another one when you have enough on your plate? I have always thought I was a good writer, but I never mustered the courage to write. What's my excuse now? What inspiration better than this thirty-minute introspection? Procrastination has become my motto, and I hate it when things never get done. It will happen. I will do it later. Focus now. Remember your mantra.

Breathe. *BABA NAM.* Hold. Exhale. *KEVALAM.* Breathe. And yes, I have to do my nails and leave the gym in time to pick up my children: my daughter from dance class and my son from his private tutor. What will I cook today? Just shut up and focus! We'll eat out. That's the solution. Now focus.

Breathe. *BABA NAM.* Hold. Exhale. *KEVALAM.* What if they don't ask me back for a second interview? What if I'm not good enough for the job? I didn't want it anyway. *BABA NAM KEVALAM.* The thirty minutes are not over. I fear they never will be! Calm down; you can do it. Focus on an image. *BABA NAM KEVALAM.* Distract your mind. Let go! Re-channel! Detach! I need an image that is immaterial, an image that triggers spontaneous detachment. But how can an image do that? It will definitely associate itself with something from my experience. Forget detachment! It can be an emotion. LOVE. They say that the concept and practice of love trigger inner harmony. Love universal, love particular, love total.

Breathe. *BABA NAM.* Hold. Exhale. *KEVALAM.* Love is my target, the focal point of my present attention. Love of my father. That's it. That was a victory. To learn to love him again. Truly and purely love him after endless hatred. To make amends and to forgive. I'm glad I was able to overcome his chauvinism. It was this paradoxical enigma that trapped me: the claims of openness and liberalism he bragged about when parading our intellectual achievements and his refusal to grant me a "liberal" life. My older brother had to chaperone me at parties; no male friend could call me at home. I was prevented from attending a "liberal" university and denied equal privileges with my bother. Breathe!

Breathe. *BABA NAM*. Hold. Exhale. *KEVALAM*. That's all history now. Maybe it's not! I can't erase it from my memory. I still recall painful episodes of injustice and oppression as though they were yesterday. Breathe in: *BABA NAM*. Hold. Exhale: *KEVALAM*. However, now I can forgive and move on. I have proven myself; I was able to marry a man of my choosing. I earned a degree from a "liberal" university despite my father forcing me to work several hours at his office, and doing countless chores like housework, driving my siblings, buying groceries, and having to prepare my dad's dinner right when I would go to wish him good night.

Breathe. *BABA NAM*. Hold. Exhale. *KEVALAM*. All that seemed a fair bargain for my autonomy as was earning pocket money through the student employment program at university. My resilience, though, did not pay off any time soon, yet I kept on pushing. I proved myself in the end; I became a trustworthy advisor to my mother, father, and siblings. I became my father's confidante, the person he relied on when he and my mom separated. I managed to get sympathy from him when I disagreed with my husband. We were equals and I was finally right. My opinions at thirty-three suddenly became valid. I made it happen, I held a central decision-making position. Ego, ego! Hold it back. Focus.

Breathe. *BABA NAM*. Hold. Exhale. *KEVALAM*. I picture my mind. I see her toying with my ego to circumvent my vain attempts at evading her. My thoughts run rampant exhausting my will which desperately seeks sanctuary from my mind's tyranny. *BABA NAM KEVALAM*. I try to focus. But it's a relentless thirty-minute combat I kamikaze into whenever I am alone with my thoughts. It's an open self-confrontation that forfeits nothing less than anarchy. My mind is unyielding. She distracts me by either creatively contriving thoughts to trap me in past episodes or by inflating my ego with the same episodes to quench my thirst for victory. I am stuck in the same narrative I masochistically enjoy repeating. However, my mind is I and I must not be my own enemy. Perhaps, like me, she is helplessly trying to claim her space. Maybe she is as insecure as I am now. Giving her the upper hand to plague me with anxiety over the future explains my fear of letting go, my fear of shedding my comfort zone as a victim of gender labeling and family prejudice. It's the inability to move on to the next level. I feel dizzy and my feet are numb. I have forgotten to breathe.

Breathe. *BABA NAM*. Hold. Exhale. *KEVALAM*. Keep going. It's just your mind fighting for breath. There, there, calm down. Breathe. *BABA NAM*. Hold. Exhale. *KEVALAM*. I relish the darkness behind closed eyelids. I entertain shadows that dance in my inner eye and I follow their motion. Specks, lines, and curves ebb and flow in mysterious patterns and I fall into a trance. There it is. I see it clearly and distinctly. Just like God's existence, I realize it. The tree stands furtively bright and luring. My childhood suddenly seems pure and happy. It's all the love in the world and the peace I am looking for. A sigh so deep and full finds its way into my lungs as I breathe in; it's the breath of my baby who dozes off while suckling on my nipple. The breath of my child after a heartfelt cry. A breath that stretches to infinity. And I try to hold on to it. A split-second of calm that feels like an eternity of harmony sweeps over my entire body and settles at that bright point between my eyebrows.

Breathe. *BABA NAM*. Hold. Exhale. *KEVALAM*. The music stops and I am ready to go back. I rub my hands and softly rest them over my closed eyelids. Slowly I open my eyes wide allowing my pupils to take in the burst of energy from the darkness I am peering into. One last breath and I am ready to stretch my legs and answer all the calls. I hesitate, hoping for one more moment of solitude. "Yes, come in." I'm ready to juggle my roles again: woman, working mother, wife, lover, daughter, decision-maker, and stubborn coward. I sit behind my desk and write it all down.

Grooming Rana

REEM RASHASH-SHAABAN

I love watching cartoons. They bring back memories of my childhood: frozen California orange juice, melted and stirred; a teaspoon of Nescafé in a glass of hot milk; the old lighthouse shining in the night; and Bugs Bunny – my favorite cartoon character. His seeming indifference and self-confidence in that slim long body gives him a power no other cartoon character has or will ever have, I find. Today I am watching TV and Bugs is still there, twenty years later. He hasn't aged a bit, but I have. I'm sitting on a couch, dolled up and waiting, hating myself, and hating the man I am waiting for even though I've never met him.

This morning, my mother walks into my room at 8:00 a.m., opens the shutters to let the warm Mediterranean sunlight in and declares, "Wake up Rana; I have great news!" The fact that she didn't address me as Rannoush, the nickname she and the family use for me should have alerted me. Licking her lips and smiling before proudly straightening her back, she announces, "Our neighbor, Umm Omar, has asked to see you. Her son, Amer, has just come back from the States after getting his PhD and is looking for a bride. He comes from a good family; it's a great honor! And besides, you're not getting any younger."

Visions of Umm Omar invade my sleepy consciousness. "*Ya habeebit albi,*" love of my heart, was the way she began every sentence. She would then grin stupidly, displaying a set of crooked teeth, and look me up and down while shaking her veiled head like a nodding rooster. I sat up.

"It's 2010! Who does that anymore?"

"We do; we cannot refuse to see him. Get up, habibti. You must prepare yourself. You're twenty-seven. You don't want to be a spinster, do you?"

When I didn't answer, she pretended not to notice.

"Why did you agree, *ya mama*? Do you think I will forget the man I love if I see someone else?"

"What? It's not that at all," she said, straightening the bottles on my dresser. "It's just that a lady has to receive all suitors. Refusing is out of the question; it's just not done by girls of good families!" She looks at me in surprise, hands on her hips.

"What would people say about us if we don't receive him? They'd hang us on the Snoubra tree[27] and our family's name would be tarnished forever!"

My mother continues to rearrange things in my room and as she makes her way to the door, she turns back and says, "Why don't you wear the beige dress you look so good in? And your high-heeled shoes, of course."

It's 5:30 in the afternoon. They would be here soon. I press the button on my phone and see the messages I had sent him this morning.

Me: Let's elope.
He: We can't do that!
Me: Why not?
He: We're not doing anything wrong. I want to marry you. I don't

---

27 A well-known Lebanese expression. Beirut used to be full of pine (snoubar) trees and the expression implies that everyone would find out because they would hang you on a pine tree on top of the hill and everyone would see you. Snoubra is also an area in Ras Beirut once considered the top of the hill.

ever want you to regret this. If we elope, you will lose your family.

Me: I don't care.

He: You're not thinking straight.

Me: She's bringing me prospective grooms.

He: What?

Me: She wants me to meet them.

He: Can't you just say no?

Me: Of course not. She would be shamed. (EMOJI). You can't say no to prospective grooms.

I throw my phone on the bed with a sigh. I think of my childhood, my father, my freedom. I think of the man I love. The man who has asked me to marry him. I came home a month ago and told my mother the good news. Instead of hugging me and jumping with joy, she said, "Marry someone with money. He will make life easier for you." I couldn't believe it. So that's what she thought? Is that why she divorced my father? So it was not his absence (he had to work abroad to support us) nor his bad temper (he could explode like a volcano then melt like ice-cream and be so sweet). It was because he was not filthy rich!

I snort.

"A young lady does not make noises like a workman. Is that what I taught you? And make sure you stand up straight. And hold your head high when you serve."

I kick the bed. No wonder my mother was never happy. She wears a perpetual scowl as often as her pale blue eye shadow and black eyeliner. She was from an old Beiruti family. "My father was one of the few people that owned a car!" she would always remind us. She had never even tried to meet the man I wanted to marry. She had taken me aside and whispered, "He is not from Beirut. He's not one of us."

What were we? I thought. *And what century was she living in?*
"Don't come in without makeup. We want him to find you beautiful," she added as she closed the bedroom door.

I kick the bed again, then run out to the balcony and gaze at the lighthouse, my eternal friend. At night it flashes every ten seconds, watching over me, reminding me that I am not alone. My father was gone and I missed him terribly. "It's alright," its rhythmic light says as it cradles me every night and eases my pain. Unfortunately, in the morning, the lighthouse is just a tall grey tower.

What should I do? What should I do? I walk back into the room and start to pace back and forth. What would Bugs Bunny do? He would usually pop out of a nearby rabbit hole and stand behind Elmer Fudd while munching on a carrot. Elmer would be looking for him, his gun pointed into the hole while Bugs would be standing behind him. To me, Elmer symbolized this stupid Lebanese society and all I wanted was for him to shoot himself in the face or disappear down a hole.

A few minutes later, I find myself staring at my reflection in the mirror. I laugh hysterically, tear my beige dress off, and grab an old pair of jeans. After removing my makeup, I mess up my neatly coiffed hair. *I am a human being, not a piece of meat!*

The doorbell rings and I take a deep breath, hoping no one enters my room before it's time. I hear the apartment door close as they walk in. Umm Omar starts with her customary *habeebit albi* and I imagine her shaking her head. I am sure my mother's smile is as big a *manousheh*[28] as she shakes hands with each of them and gives the mother three kisses on the cheek.

"*Ahlan wa sahlan, ya ahlan wa sahlan*; welcome."

I hide behind the door and wish I could vomit to get rid of the terrible taste of misery. In a few minutes I will be asked to appear, just like a cow for sale. They will parade me around like a contestant in a beauty pageant and it won't matter whether I have a brain or not. I just have to pass their test of "beauty." They will measure the size of my waist, my calves, my breasts. Then they'll start asking questions and I will have to say something socially acceptable to both the prospective groom and, more importantly, to his mother. I will also have to make and serve Turkish coffee. Perhaps so he can determine whether I'd be a good hostess or not. I hate myself. How could I have agreed to this? I think I hate my mother, too.

After ten minutes of mental torture, my brother comes in to get me. I march into the living room, avoiding my mother's glare and pretend to trip. I smile internally as the old pair of jeans that I'm wearing elicits gasps from both women. I shake hands with the guests, stand in front of Amer and say, "What's up, doc?"

Three pairs of eyes widen but I ignore them and take a seat. I keep my legs spread open and look at Amer from beneath my lashes. I have to admit that Elmer never looked as stupefied as he did at that moment. He sits there, brown pants strapped above his navel, a tight yellow shirt hugging his thin waistline, at a complete loss for words. But then, who could get a word in with Umm Omar in attendance?

---

28 A popular Levantine food consisting of baked dough topped with thyme and olive oil, or cheese, or ground meat.

I think they started talking. I don't know. My mind drifts to the man I want to marry and with every second, my anger turns into a stormy black cloud that threatens to break into rain.

"Rana?"
I jump.
"Rana, what is the matter with you?" says my mother.
I ignore her.
"*Ya habeebit albi*, Rana; why don't you sit in my seat?"
"Excuse me!"
Umm Omar repeats her suggestion and shows her crooked teeth.
"I'm fine."
"I insist."

Her old legs crack as she stands. I suppose she wants me to face her son so he can look at me at his leisure and maybe stare at my legs. Too bad for him; he can't see my calves. I get up grudgingly and take her seat. When I glance back at my mother, I notice her finger had started to twitch. She was really angry.

When it's time to make coffee, I make sure to fill the cups to the rim, hoping he stains his yellow shirt as he tries to sip it. I smile in satisfaction when he does. We sit in awkward silence that reminds me of the last time I went to a funeral.

"*Ya habeebit albi*," Umm Omar croons, "I hope you like flying." She adjusts her veil. "My son can pilot a plane, and anyone who marries him must learn to do the same." She smiles again, her yellow teeth hiding her lower lip. All I can do is imagine being forced to endure her stupidity and have children that could bear resemblance to her. I look at Amer and feel the remains of my lunch rising in my throat. Suddenly, I stand up.

"Where are you going?" shouts my mother.

"*Shu hayda*; what is this?" complains the rooster. Her knees crack as she gets up and gestures to her son.

"Amer; get up. Obviously this girl is not what I thought she was. She is not worthy of your foot!"[29]

"Oh yeah? Well maybe his foot has more balls than he does!"

"*Ya Lateef*! Oh my God; what is this? I have never been so insulted in my life!" Umm Omar's voice takes on an operatic tone as her head dances a jig.

"Neither have I."

"Wait, Umm Omar," begs my mother. "You, Rana; go to your room. I will deal with you later."

I take one last look at Amer, who is as confused as Elmer, and walk out.

✷

"You've embarrassed me and the family! This woman knows everyone in Beirut! You'll never find a decent groom!"

"What?" I screamed. "Have you forgotten? I already have someone, mom."

I look at her unfeeling eyes and say, "Don't you care about how I feel? I'm not going back in there. Come up with any excuse. I'm sick; I'm crazy. I never want to see that idiot again!"

✷

That night I dreamed he had come for me. In his white Peugeot. I stood by the lighthouse shivering in the cold. He got out and I clasped him to my chest, the warmth turning to heat as he closed the distance

---

29 A translated expression in colloquial Lebanese that indicates a lack of worth.

between us. I held onto him like a drowning person hangs onto a lifeline that is thrown at them. He was my entire world. I raised my head, opened my eyes and looked into his eyes. I love you, *I said.* I can't stand waiting. *He continued to look at me, but his lips did not move and suddenly I was standing on a deserted street, barefoot in the night. A strong wind rose from the sea causing my skirt to fly.*

I wake up. I decide that as soon as our cook, *Hajjeh*[30] Umm Nabil, arrives, I will ask her what the dream meant. I slowly swing my legs over the edge of the bed.

"Rana, Rana!" my mother calls.
"Hurry up. Get dressed. We're going shopping today."
"What for?"
"You need a new dress!"
"Why?"
"You have another suitor coming to see you tomorrow!"

---

30 A variation on the spelling of *hajjia*. See note 2.

The Way Back Home

YASMINA HATEM

I was on my way home. It's strange how despite not having lived here for the last ten years, it was still the only place I refer to as home. Stranger still, that coming here wasn't exciting. It wasn't something I ever looked forward to, and I never wanted to stay more than a few days. I did love how familiar everything was. How every time we drove from the airport to the house I grew up in, it only took a few minutes to feel like I'd never left. All of my senses recognized where I was. It became instinctively familiar; every corner, every building, the noises, the smells, even the shouting on the streets.

I was in my comfort zone, yet I was strangely uncomfortable. I always enjoyed the drive home, alone with my little brother. It was our chance to catch up, just the two of us, before I'd get sucked into the rush of being in Beirut for a few days. I kept my phone off until I reached the house. *A few more minutes of peace*, I thought, *before the flood of phone calls*. I'm lucky, of course, to have so many people to talk to – when I first moved to Dubai, I felt lonely. The only people I called were all in Lebanon. I was used to having long phone conversations on a daily basis and a full house bustling with activity. So when I moved into a little studio, all by myself, it felt like the quietest, loneliest place in the world. But I guess somewhere along the way, throughout the years, I got used to having my own space. My privacy. Anonymity.

As my brother was pulling up in front of our building on Sursock Street, I was struck by a mixture of nostalgia and nervousness. The doorman, Firas, spotted me trying to carry my luggage and, of course, he ran to my rescue despite my protests.

"*Ahlan wa sahlan!* Welcome back; welcome back!" he shouted for the entire neighborhood to hear. He had known me since I was ten years old, and on every trip back, he welcomed me with the same excitement.

That sure wouldn't happen in Dubai, I thought to myself; and I couldn't help but smile.

I rang the doorbell enthusiastically to signal my presence, and I could hear my father excitedly chanting "hello; hello; hello" as he hurried to open the door. When I was a little girl, it used to be me welcoming him home. He would travel for weeks at a time, sometimes even longer. My mom and I used to go meet him at the docks. It was during the war, and sometimes he could only return by boat. I remember waiting for him, trying to spot him through the crowd. When I'd finally see him, with his little mustache, carrying his big suitcase, I would run through the gate, between the crowds, like in a cheesy Egyptian soap opera, with my arms wide open, screaming at the top of my lungs... "Papa!"

I wish I could feel that kind of excitement now, the intense joy that reduced me to happy tears just because I was in my father's arms. Adulthood has a way of building walls around feelings.

Inside the house, nothing had changed. Not even in fifteen years... Except things were getting a little worn out; the colors of the cushions had started to fade. There were the same cracks in the wall, but the paint had chipped off a little bit more than the last time I was there. In the corridor I passed the picture table showcasing baby pictures and family photos. Beautiful moments that were captured to remind us of happy times.

In the living room, on the couch next to the television, I saw my mother. She sat in her spot looking as peaceful as ever. She looked up at me and smiled. She was never as grandly expressive as my father, but her love, though more discreet, was more complete. More protective. More demanding, too.

I crashed onto my bed, and I have to admit, it felt good. My room, despite having been turned into a dump for everything useless, was still my sanctuary. The walls I painted yellow when I was fourteen. The desk I scribbled on all throughout high school. My books! And my boxes, filled with letters and pictures and every memory I had collected during my life. This was the room I cast dreams in. It was the room where I awarded myself an Oscar, where I reported live from warzones, and where my imagination ran wild and life was full of incredible possibilities. *Maybe,* I told myself as I hugged my favorite pillow, *maybe I could build new dreams while I was here.*

"Show me the dress!" my mother's voice rang as she floated into my room the next morning carrying two cups of coffee. I was awake in bed, enjoying the fact that I didn't have to rush anywhere. And I really did enjoy being served coffee in bed. Mom knew I wouldn't utter a word before having my dose of morning caffeine...

"I told Souad to come do your nails at 11:30," she said.

Souad had been "coming to do our nails" pretty much since I was born. She must be in her mid-seventies by now, yet she still made the rounds, her back severely hunched from years of bending over. She wore thick glasses secured by a string around her neck and grinded and rattled her teeth while she worked. She was like an old aunt, always prying into every detail of my life, even when there wasn't much to tell.

"Why don't you come home? Enough with this living abroad!" she would insist. "Find a nice husband, have children! Nothing is more important than children." I knew she'd say this today too.

I showed mom the dress I had borrowed for the wedding. There had been so many weddings in the past few years that I decided to stop buying dresses and started borrowing them from friends instead... And this time, I had the most beautiful princess style high-waist purple skirt that would hide my ass and thighs perfectly! I tried it on for her. She said I looked "absolutely beautiful."

I skipped the whole hairdresser/makeup artist debacle because every time I dared to do it, I spent another hour removing most of the makeup and re-doing my hair. I wasn't very comfortable getting all dolled up, and my mother understood that. She remained the same with her short, funky-colored, stylish hair that she somehow managed to do all by herself. I used a curling iron and went for a more bohemian chic look.

By 2:00 p.m., I was ready to go. Physically ready at least. I stared at myself in the bathroom mirror, wondering if the black eyeliner contouring my eyes was enough. I hesitated adding rouge to my lips. I couldn't believe I was going to Tania's wedding. It had been almost twenty years since we'd first met, while sitting in a corner during gym class, acting "indisposed." And she was officially the last of my high school girlfriends to get married. That was it. I was now the only one left. Was thirty-four too old? Had I missed my chance? Were my eggs going to rot without ever fulfilling their purpose?

My father snapped me out of my thoughts. "Come out to the living room so I can take pictures of you!" he eagerly demanded. It was one of his favorite things to do – take pictures of his kids all dressed up before a party. They ended up looking awkward. The lighting was bad; the dining-room table a ridiculous background. I did it anyway; it was easier than arguing with him. And then of course, he said it. The phrase every single Lebanese girl dreads. I was prepared for it, I knew he would say it, but still, it made me cringe.

"'A'belik, hayete![31] When will I have the pleasure of dancing at your wedding?"

As if I could answer that question. As if there was any logical way to respond. Do people realize how awkward this makes a person feel, or do they actually believe their "good wishes" might bring good bearings?

I looked at my mother when he said it, grinding my teeth to stifle a snarky retort. She stared back, smiling, her eyes saying, "Calm down, you know he means well. Just take a deep breath." So I breathed.

The wedding was everything I expected it to be: grand, beautiful, traditional yet modern, personalized, generous, and overflowing with music, alcohol and dancing... Just like the parties Lebanese people are known for. I was, of course, a little nervous about attending on my own. It was awkward sitting at a table with no one I knew, but there were many people I hadn't seen in ages, and catching up distracted me.

"Did you hear Maya's pregnant? She's having a girl!"

---

31 'A'belik is an endearing expression meaning "here's to you." *Hayete* literally means "my life."

"What about you, are you thinking babies?"

I smiled and said, yes. I was now the proud aunty of three boys and two girls. I showed them their pictures, too.

"How's New York? Must be fabulous living there..."

I almost wanted to lie. To pretend I was still living an epic life in New York City, living the dream. Instead, I had to explain my move to Dubai two years ago. They were shocked, of course, never picturing me in Dubai. The truth was that I never pictured myself there either, but here I was, smiling and trying to convince them it wasn't that bad.

And then, there was Tarek. Tarek, whom I hadn't planned on seeing. But Lebanon is a tiny country and there's always a chance of running into an ex because he knows the same people. Still, I hadn't factored him in, and seeing him took me by surprise. It had been four years since he left me, and I had been single ever since.

"You look great," he said, and I decided to believe him.

"Thank you! I feel great!" I smiled as best I could.

"How have you been? Are you here with anyone?"

I had answered that question more than a dozen times that evening. It never fazed me to say, with a big bright smile, that I was happily there on my own. But my smile came out a little fake and the answer came out all wrong.

"I'm alone."

That was all I said, staring at him, not really knowing what I expected him to say. The instant pity in his eyes made me blush. Tarek had broken my heart. After three years together, he decided that he needed to be alone to find himself. He found the love of his life a month later and they've been together ever since.

"I'm getting married," he said.

I froze. It wasn't unexpected news. Not really. I was actually surprised it hadn't happened sooner. But for some reason, hearing it from him, at that moment, hit me hard. Not because I loved him or missed him. Nor because I wanted to be with him. But because he was happy. He wasn't alone.

"Oh, that's great news. I'm really happy for you," I lied. And then I mumbled something about refreshing my drink and dove straight towards the bar to top up my gin and tonic. I downed my drink and took the shot the bartender offered, trying to loosen up. That was when I heard two ladies, probably in their mid-seventies, gossiping about the bride and her sisters.

"*Al-hamdillah*[32] at least one of them is getting married!"

"Her older sister is still single; you know..."

I wondered for a moment if that's all that matters. If that's all we're measured by, as women. If that's all I measure myself by? Why did it bother me so much anyway? I'm a modern woman, a citizen of the world, living in the twenty-first century. I am independent. I pay every single one of my bills all by myself. I put myself through school. I've worked my butt off every day since, so why should I be ashamed? Why should I be cornered and embarrassed at being single? For not settling down. For being courageous enough do it all on my own.

"Stop judging!" I snapped at the ladies who weren't even aware of my presence. "It's so easy, isn't it, for you to sit here and judge! You think it's easy for her sister to be older and unmarried while everyone is watching her like she's some kind of freak? You think she likes it? Just shut up! Shut up!"

Suddenly aware of myself ranting, I walked away, my face burning

---

32 Thank God.

with shame. I left the wedding without looking back and somehow found my way back home.

Removing my painful heels at the door, I made the silent wish that everyone was asleep to avoid any more questions. I crashed onto the couch in my big puffy princess skirt and lit a cigarette.

"How was it?" I heard my mother's voice.

"It was fine," I said without looking at her.

"What's the matter?" she asked, because of course, a mother always knows when something's the matter.

"Nothing." *Just leave me alone*, I thought.

"Hey," she said, sitting next to me and taking my hand into hers. "I'm right here."

I shook my head. "You're not here..." I said. "You're not here, mom! You left me here all alone and I have no idea how to do this! I don't know if anything I've done is right. If any of my stupid choices ever made any sense! How can I know? I can't ask you! I can't tell you! I can just picture you, wherever you are up there, probably judging me, just like everybody else!"

"I don't judge you, Youmna... I never have. I think you're judging yourself."

"Every time I come here, I see you everywhere. I miss you all the time. And I ask myself a million questions I don't have the answers to. What would my mother say? What would my mother tell me to do? What would you tell me, if you were here right now, mom?"

"I would tell you that I love you."

I stared into the void in front of me. The empty space where she used to sit. The image of her fifteen years ago haunts me still: weak, bald, attached to a respirator, yet still telling silly jokes. *She never would've told me what to do*, I reminded myself. She was never that kind of mother.

I woke up the next morning, back stiff, with a terrible hangover. That, too, happens with age. I could smell the freshly brewed coffee. It was my sister. She came and lay down next to me, and I realized I was still in my big puffy princess skirt.

"Rough night?" she asked.

I nursed the coffee, trying to wipe out my dreadful memories of the wedding.

"You hate coming home, don't you?"

"I think... I don't like my life being judged. I feel like everybody is judging me here."

"Maybe you're just judging yourself."

"Hah! That's what mom said..."

"What do you mean?"

I smiled. I rested my head on her shoulder and closed my eyes.

HYPHENATION

NADIA TABBARA

Black Mary Jane shoes with green socks. The kind of socks with frills that call attention to the ankles. That's what Mom dressed her in. The rest of the outfit matched the socks: green shorts and a blouse with large, multicolored buttons.

She took a deep breath before walking into the school cafeteria. At seven years old, Sabah knew a thing or two about feeling self-conscious, even though she hadn't yet learned the words to express it. It's because she was different – no, that wasn't it. It's because she *felt* different and was reminded of it every single day. She wasn't great at speaking English, having only learned a year ago when she started school in this beautiful and God-awful country: America. She pronounced it like her parents did: *Am-mair-ka*, the place where everyone – Every. Single. Person – pronounced her name incorrectly. *Saba*. That's what they called her because their foreign tongues couldn't produce the sound made by the last letter of her name, a sound in between a breathy *haaa* and a guttural *khaaa*. Try explaining that to every single person you meet. Well, Sabah didn't. Not at seven years old and not for her entire life in *Amairka*, either. She just resigned herself to the fact that she had this name now, a sign of her American alter ego, a twin part of herself that she never asked for but was given anyway. Saba and Sabah; two names, one person.

Okay, Sabah, just choose a seat, sit there, and don't talk to anyone. In her mind, she pronounced her own name correctly. A few years later, though, even the voice inside her head would change it to *Saba*, depending on which twin she chose to lead with.

She inched further into the crowded cafeteria buzzing with other first graders. She only knew the ones in her class and she'd seen some of the others on the playground. They all called her "the new kid," even though this was her second year at their school. It's because in her first year, she didn't speak any English.

It was the first time Sabah ever went to school. Before that, she had begged her mother to let her tag along with her brother, Omar, but she was too young. When she was old enough to attend the local school, *oh happy day*, it would close again and her family would be on the move to some other village or country. Sabah had a small blue suitcase, always packed and stowed in the corner of the room she shared with Omar. His suitcase was green.

When they arrived at their new house in America, Sabah noticed both small suitcases were put away.

"Hey, Omar, where's our stuff?" She whispered as if it were a special secret.

He was carefully placing his collection of miniature boxcars in a drawer in their shared room, wondering how he could fit them all into such a small space. Back home, he had a whole closet and many drawers to himself.

"What stuff?" He said casually.

Sabah leaned in, insisting on whispering. "Our *suit*-cases."

"*Mama* put them away. Because we're staying here forever."

Her brother always said important things as if they were obvious and a matter of fact, like the existence of God and mermaids. Naturally, Sabah believed everything he said.

"We're staying..." It wasn't a question; it was more of an expression of shock and curiosity. Omar turned away from his boxcars and considered his little sister. He knew she needed good news.

"We're gonna go to school here." Sabah let out a tiny gasp of excitement. *School. Finally.* Omar shook his head, but Sabah didn't notice.

The first grade at Franklin Elementary School would hold many firsts for Sabah. On the first day, she entered a small classroom with a patched rug and colorful name-tagged cubbies, armed only with her wide-eyed expectations of triumph and, of course, her blue backpack.

When everyone was settled, the teacher began to speak. In English. Sabah hung on the strange sounds she made and the more she listened, the more she realized she couldn't understand anything. A feeling of incredible loneliness welled up inside her for the first time.

The sounds stopped and she watched as everyone stood up and placed their hands on their hearts. She did the same and when they started reciting, "I pledge allegiance to the flag…," she wondered how they all knew the words and why they were staring at the red, white, and blue flag in the front of the room. She mimed the same; she had no choice. After all, everyone was doing it, so she mouthed gibberish as best she could. It was the first time Sabah had followed anything or anyone blindly. The loneliness became heavier. In the months to come, Sabah would become that other version of herself; *Saba*, a girl who was mostly silent, always listening, and often writing.

Writing. Writing was her favorite thing to do. She listened a lot in those days and when she needed a word, she would say it in her head the way *they* would and then write it down. That's why there would be words spelled like *ak-shoo-ah-lee*. You had to read Sabah's stories out loud to understand them. The school psychologist, Dr. Karen, which come to think of it must have been her first name and not her last, especially liked Sabah's stories. She would ask questions about the curious way Sabah wrote and the drawings she made. At the time, Sabah thought Dr. Karen was her biggest fan, not having any idea who she was or why she was paying so much attention to her.

"Who are those people on the boat?" The doctor pointed to the crayon stick figures on the brown cardboard booklet Sabah had crafted herself. Dr. Karen looked like an awkward giant sitting in a kid-sized chair next to Sabah, who was beaming with pride at the makeshift storybook on her desk.

"Family," said Sabah.

"Is that how you came over here from Libya? In a boat?"

Sabah didn't understand the question. She looked around at the other kids, some coloring, some gluing cardboard shapes on top of each other. Whenever Sabah didn't understand something, she had a habit of looking around her, as if searching for an answer. She didn't find one.

"Boat?"

The doctor pointed to the hexagonal shape on top of squiggles of blue, the sea of course, that Sabah had drawn.

"No. Plane." Sabah made one of her hands into an airplane and flew it past the doctor's face. The doctor smiled.

"What is *Loobya*?" Sabah knew that *loobya* was green beans, because she hated them. Her mother would always make her eat them with rice. But why would Dr. Karen be asking her about that?

"Libya?" The doctor said.

Sabah nodded.

"The country you're from. COUNTRY."

Sometimes people spoke to Sabah in a louder voice so she would understand them. Sabah mimicked her the best she could, and it came out something like *cow-en-tree*. At that point, Dr. Karen had taken out an atlas and pointed to Libya. Sabah stared; at first she was mesmerized by the woman's red nail polish, because it reminded her of her mother's. Then her eyes went all the way down to the edge of Dr. Karen's red painted nail to the word LIBYA inside the borders of the North African country. Sabah was confused to say the least; she peered at the map in front of her, searching for the boot-shape. When she found it, she placed her tiny finger there and took a sharp right until her finger stopped just past a small island. Dr. Karen edged closer to where Sabah was pointing.

"Lebanon..." Dr. Karen considered Sabah. "Yes, of course, honey, my mistake. You're from Lebanon."

✶

"Are you a lesbian?"

Sabah had just unpacked her lunch from the small paper bag. It took some effort, but she had found part of an empty table and sat on the edge of it, as far away from the group of seven-year-old girls as she could. As much as she tried to go unnoticed, somehow, it never worked.

"You're a lesbian!" This was the blonde who at that moment turned to the rest of her friends. "She told me she was!"

"What is lesbian?" asked Sabah. It was an innocent question. Hurt contorted her face and for little girls who would grow up to be the type of insecure women who always blamed and attacked others for their own incompetence, that hurt face, that was their bread and butter, their way in, their closing kill shot.

"She's Lesban-ese!" squealed the redhead with freckles. *What the hell were freckles anyway?* Sabah wondered.

She turned her face towards her lunch and focused on unwrapping the cellophane off her tiny sandwiches. *Just ignore them;*

just ignore them; just ignore them – she repeated the mantra with each unwrapping of the *za'tar* and tomatoes soft baguette sandwich. The truth was, she didn't want to ignore them; she wanted to talk to someone, or rather, she wanted to be talked to.

"What is that?" The blonde again. She talked with her mouth full of peanut butter and jelly.

Sabah had just taken a bite and noticed the green of the *za'tar* and olive oil had soaked into the bread. She looked at the girls just to make sure they were talking to her. They were. She finished chewing, swallowed, bought some more time before answering.

"It's *za'tar*," she said.

"It looks like mushed up frogs!"

"Eeewwwwww," the girls broke out in unison.

Sabah didn't finish her second baguette that day; instead, she waited until the mean girls got distracted, got up, and went to the bathroom, not to use it, just to sit there. She swung her feet, black Mary Janes and green frilly socks, back and forth and cried softly. She had gotten used to it.

✶

Now that Sabah was seventeen, her feet were flat on the ground, and this time, she wasn't hiding; she was sneaking a cigarette in between classes. She sat on the toilet seat as her friend Emily stood up. She was neither a blonde nor a redhead; her hair was a shade of light brown that Sabah couldn't place. Saba, at this point.

"My mom is *such* a bitch. I'm going anyway; fuck her." Emily was always using words like that and Sabah wanted to agree or support her, but she couldn't find it in herself to ever think that kind of thing about her Mom, let alone say it. The guilt would crush her. Sabah dragged her cigarette and let out the smoke.

"I can't go."

"Why not? Just sneak out, who cares," Emily said.

Sabah knew there was no way that was going to happen.

"What's going on in there?" came an adult's voice.

The girls threw their cigarettes into the toilet and held their breath, hoping that this would pass. Sabah lifted her legs so that they wouldn't be seen from the opening of the stall. A loud KNOCK. "Come out here right now, both of you. Right now."

"It's not my fault you moved us here. It was your decision!"

Sabah stood in front of her parents, arms folded, leaning heavily on one leg, the stance of an angst-filled teenager ready for the fight.

"What does that have anything to do with smoking?"

Her Mom turned to her Dad. "I just don't know what to do anymore." She threw her hands up in exasperation.

"All my friends are going; I don't see why you can't trust me."

"How can we trust you when you're smoking on school grounds and getting in trouble?"

"That's beside the point." She had just learned this phrase and was using it as often as she could.

"My seventeen-year-old daughter does not go out to concerts. We don't do that. We don't have girls that do that. Or ones that smoke for that matter. I just can't believe it."

She recognized the hurt tone in her mom's voice and went in for the kill. "You chose to move here; you have to deal with the consequences of us being American."

"Hey. That's enough," her father interrupted.

That was her cue to storm off. She stomped past her parents, leaving them in the fluorescent light of the kitchen, her mother leaning on the counter, too exhausted to fight back. Her husband put an arm on her shoulder and when she looked at him, her face said only one thing: *Did we do the right thing?*

*

"*Yi habibteh*,[33] that is so sweet," said the woman sitting next to Sabah on the plane. "There aren't many young people like you who decide to come back to Lebanon."

Sabah smiled.

"If you ask me, I don't understand it," the woman took out the stack of items from the back pouch of the seat in front of her. Sabah noticed the veins on her hands and how they danced with her movements. Her nails were long and painted a pastel purple, which wouldn't have been that strange if it wasn't for her matching lipstick.

"Don't get me wrong, I love this country, I just love it." She fidgeted with the lock on the tray table, her nails too long to grasp it. Sabah leaned over and opened it. The woman looked straight at her and then a quick flutter of her artificial eyelashes, up and down, as she scanned Sabah's body.

"Of course, the food is the best in the world, who can say Lebanese food isn't the best in the world? I dare you to find better food. Italian food? Forget it. Japanese? What's with the raw fish, but I guess we're not ones to talk, right? I mean, we eat raw meat for God's sake." She sighed deeply as if recalling a memory. "The weather too, the gorgeous weather." Snapping out of it, she turned her attention back to Sabah, another quick flutter of lashes, up and down. "But especially the food."

Sabah couldn't tell if this woman was somehow calling her fat.

---

33 An endearing expression meaning, "Oh, my dear."

The Lebanese dialect is mysterious in that way. Unlike any other dialect of Arabic, it is rooted in context, so this woman could either be genuine about her obsession with Lebanese food, or she could indeed be making a backhanded comment about Sabah's weight. Most likely, it was a mixture of both.

"But honey, what it does, what the country really does, is beat you down. It beats your dreams down. It just does, I'm sorry to say it. I really am. But the food, my God the food."

"It's my home," Sabah said, mostly to convince herself. "At least, I think so."

But the woman had already stopped listening and was flipping through the inventory placed on the tray table in front of her: duty free magazine, safety card, puke bag.

Home is where the heart is, read the sign that hung in Sabah's childhood house in *Am-mair-ka*.

"You need to go back into the foreigner line," an army officer reached across the counter with her passport in hand.

"But I'm Lebanese," Sabah said.

"This is an American passport. Get into the foreigner line, please."

"It says I'm born in Beirut," she said. "Just look at the first page. Born in Beirut."

He didn't budge, still reaching across the counter. "The foreigner line, please."

Sabah sighed and looked at the foreigner line. It was long.

"*Yalla*," he barked.

Sabah snatched her passport back and lifted her chin, hoping he would notice. He didn't. She walked away, the wheels of her suitcase making a high-pitched squeak with every full revolution. She looked back at him, but he had already moved on to the next arriving passenger. She heard the THUD and CLACK of his stamp on their passports.

Sabah *squeak-squeaked* past Duty-Free towards the exit. She smelled *baklava* and cigarettes, even though this had become a non-smoking airport, the air was heavy with stale second-hand smoke. It wasn't romantic, but still nostalgic.

She had collected her bags and was now pushing a trolley down an airport hallway until it opened up into a wide exit at the gate. Hordes of people were pushed up to the railings, some holding flowers and gifts, others carrying signs with handwritten names on them. Spurts of excitement in the form of "there she is," and "hey, over here!" came at her. She craned her neck in an attempt to see past the chaos until finally, she heard familiar voices calling out: "Sabah, Sabah! Over here!" Two uncles, three aunts, husbands, wives and a gaggle of children, all there to greet her. She waved enthusiastically and quickened her step.

This is my choice. I choose to return. I choose you. Her thoughts came in random, imperfect fragments.

Her long-lost family engulfed her with hugs, an entourage of love. Between the exclamations of, "look how you've grown," and, "is it true you're staying?" she thought she heard a faint "she *looks* American," whispered between two of her cousins.

"She obviously moved here to find a husband," said *Khalto* Yasmine. Sabah had always loved the distinction the Arabic language gave to aunts: your mother's sister was *Khalto*; your father's was *'Amto*. "Why else would she move here?"

"I'm sitting right here, *Khalto*," said Sabah.

They were in the living room and Sabah's *Teta* and two *Khaltos* were sipping Turkish coffee, waiting to turn the cup upside-down into the saucer so they could read their fortunes in the maze the dried grounds made on the cup's inner rim.

Yasmine, the youngest, picked up the silver *rakweh*[34] and poured a tiny amount into a tiny cup and handed it to Sabah. "Just take a sip and turn it over."

"I don't like coffee," Sabah said.

"What do you mean you don't like coffee?" This time, it was her other aunt, Lamis.

"Just take a small sip so we can read your fortune. It's not going to kill you. We just want to find out when you'll meet your husband."

It seemed as though all the women in the room leaned forward in a collective edge-of-your-seat moment.

"What makes you think I want to get married?" said Sabah.

They retreated in their seats; a resounding gasp filled the room.

"Don't be so American. Of course you're getting married," Yasmine said.

"And having children too, *inshallah*,"[35] said *Teta*, with a smile on her wizened face.

Sabah loved her grandma more than she knew how to express. Her smile would always make her feel like she was getting a warm hug. Then she turned back to her aunt: "I'm not American, *Khalto*."

"She's not," her grandma shot a knowing look at her daughters. "*Habibteh*, born here and raised with my eternal love. I don't care that they moved you halfway across the world, I knew you'd always come home to your *Teta*."

✳

"You even walk like an American."

---

34 Levantine Arabic name for a small pot used to make Turkish coffee.
35 God-willing; hopefully.

"What does that mean?" said Sabah.

She was sitting in a smoky Beirut pub with Nayla, an old friend whom she had looked up when she first arrived. Nayla thought of herself as Sabah's unofficial guide.

"You can't claim to be Lebanese without visiting Jbeil," Nayla told her when they sat on the steps of the ancient Roman amphitheater. Sabah was admiring the shimmering sea and resented the fact that Nayla had interrupted her.

"You walk in a way that makes you look like you own the place," Nayla said in between sips of her cocktail.

"I do not."

"It's not a bad thing," Nayla said. "It's just who you are."

Who I am... Who am I?

"That's just not true. It's not who I am. I'm more than how I walk or my accent or my passport or..." When she looked at Nayla who was checking out a guy at the bar, she realized that she hadn't actually said any of those things out loud.

Sabah stood on her Grandma's balcony and could see slivers of the sea between the new buildings. It whispered loudly that day, because the wind was heavy.

Who I am... Who am I? Who I am... Who am I?

Waves have a rhythm that is precise, regardless of how randomly the wind moves. Sabah closed her eyes and felt the warmth of the sun on her face. The longer she stood there, the louder the whispers of the waves became. When she opened her eyes – *was it a few minutes or a few years later* – she had the beginning of an answer.

She touched her cheek and was surprised that it was wet with salty tears. An image flashed in her mind, a fragment of thought, only this time, she held on to it, she needed to hold on to it for some reason. *Just a little bit longer, just to bring it into focus...*

Black Mary Janes with green frilly socks.
Sabah walked into the school cafeteria and sat down at a table. She turned to the girls on the other side of the bench.
"I'm Lebanese. And this is za'tar. And it's delicious."

She lifted her chin just as a tear spilled down. For a moment, she wondered if this was her imagination or an actual memory and then decided she didn't care.

The waves continued to whisper.

I am... I am... I am...

Come Back Home

SIMA QUNSOL

The 13th of June was the day I left Beirut forever. Exactly one week before my departure, I spent my day crying in a hotel room under the big looming words: "The more I find myself, the more people I lose." In a failed artistic endeavor, each bedroom of the hotel had a different trite saying painted in black on the wall.

"I wish they had hired me for that," I told my friend when I first checked in a few days prior. "These quotes are stupid."

But at that moment mine spoke the gospel truth. Although I hadn't even left Beirut yet, I felt I had lost a lot already. The reasons were many, the main culprit being what I had self-diagnosed as Premenstrual Dysphoric Disorder, which punctured each healthy month with a brief interval of mental instability. It came and went, but on the days it hit me, I would spiral into temporary bouts of anxiety and depression, feeling entirely dysfunctional. The second reason was that a week earlier I had graduated from university. But instead of feeling accomplished, I felt nothingness like a slap in the face. I also no longer had a place of my own. Before the hotel with the quotes, I had been living in the same dorm building for four years. The rooms were small and perpetually dirty by virtue of being old, but I loved them nevertheless. There was a period of ten days between moving out of the dorms and flying back home to Jordan in which I had planned to stay between friends' places.

"I am going to couch surf," I declared, "to spend quality time with all the friends I am going to leave."

But when the moment came, I could not do it; I could not reconcile with the idea that I was going to spend my last ten days in Beirut as a guest instead of a resident. So I got the hotel room in one final attempt to feel grounded somewhere, and have a space of my own. The fourth day in the room was the day I cried. I had packed all my belongings and was ready to leave. Ten minutes before check-out time, I called the reception and extended for a night, after which I stayed in bed for six miserable hours. I felt prematurely, helplessly detached from Beirut.

∗

Not once in my eighteen years of living in Amman was I allowed to linger purposelessly on my street. "Come inside the house," my parents would insist, even if my friend's car was going to pick me up in a few minutes. "Wait inside the building!" My family, like many others in Amman, had one ultimate domestic goal: privacy. Domestic discourse focused on raising fences and expressions of neighborly distrust. Every time I returned from Beirut, I argued with my mother because she preferred the curtains down and I preferred them up. I never lower my curtains in Beirut, I would tell her. My tiny box of a bedroom in Hamra is a part of the street. *I am not afraid of visibility.*

∗

Every time I flew back home, I was greeted by comments about how I'd become a *Lubnāniye*. Older relatives and acquaintances would summon their pseudo-Lebanese accents and outdated perceptions of Lebanese life and give me a knowing smile I could not identify with. "Lebaneseness" to them was synonymous with pleasure, style, and food. But if there was one thing I exercised that made me feel quintessentially Lebanese, it was lounging on my balcony in Hamra.

I spent more time on that balcony than inside my room. On my balcony, I would smoke a cigarette, make a call, drink coffee after a heavy lunch or, in the mornings, sing, tan, watch the rain and lightning. I would lean against the railing or – after wiping away a thin layer of dust – sit and watch life unfold on Sidani Street. Eventually my roommate, Farah, would pull up a chair, and when the season was right, bring a bowl of fresh *jaranek*[36] sprinkled generously with salt.

The street was a space of fascination. Over the years I became familiar with the interiors of every slice of apartment my balcony allowed me to see. I knew the residents, especially the ones who spent as much time on their balconies as I did on mine. Often Farah and I would make up stories about them. If I saw any of them on the street, I would probably not recognize them, but on my balcony they were the people I lived with, as if our common balcony time was some sort of communal activity. I found comfort in the proximity and consistency of their presence. Every morning, the housekeeper in the penthouse of the building facing mine would clean the terrace, even on rainy days. The old owner of that apartment would make a brief appearance, crack open a window, light a cigarette, take one or two puffs, then shut the window and disappear inside with her cigarette still in hand. Two floors down, a young man would always help his mother air out the carpets and mop the balcony floor. Above them was an apartment bustling with life. Every night, the wide-

---

36 Sour plums.

open window to the left radiated with light that changed colors. Some days it was red, other days yellow, or purple. The television was perpetually on. One afternoon, when I was sitting out, in my pajamas, with a bowl of strawberries in my lap, three men came out on their balcony and set up an *argeeleh*. For a while we kept glancing at each other. One of them raised his hand and waved at me. The other two followed suit. I waved back before we returned to our separate balcony lives.

✶

The only distance I crossed on foot in Amman was between my school and my house, a seven-minute walk. On days when the weather was dead and an unmoving cloud of dust hung in the air, I felt like I was living inside a giant artificial dome. Amman had that effect on me. I would be crossing a strip of empty land right in front my building, and my eyes would sneak a look up at the grey sky. Then a car or two would drive by me, reminding me that I was not alone.

I might not have been alone, but after living in Beirut I often felt isolated from everything around me back home. My bedroom had not been used in years: a rigid bed, a chair-less desk, dusty shelves of old books. The closet doors hid bare clothes hangers, a couple of outdated dresses and some worn out t-shirts I had stolen from my brother's closet. On the top shelf was our Christmas tree, packed lazily in a carton and stored there without my consent. The room was scattered with memorabilia dating back from childhood through my high school years. The floral curtains no longer matched my taste, nor did my purple bed sheets or the turquoise-striped paint on the walls. But I never bothered to change them. I had become a stranger to my own room. During my longer breaks, it would take me two weeks to unpack. Like a passive guest during a short stay at a hotel, I found it unnecessary to invest time in unpacking when I was leaving soon.

My entire house felt too big a space, with too much clutter. I found myself obsessively organizing; I emptied out the kitchen cupboards and rearranged the utensils and tableware, disposed of old shampoo bottles in the shower and dry pencils in the office. I filled up bags of unwanted clothes and shoes.

On each visit, I picked my own niche in the house – but never in my bedroom. Sometimes it was the corner of the faintly-stained orange couch in the TV room, where both my parents spent their evenings. Other times it was the far end of the glass dining table, where the Wi-Fi was bad but the sunlight could reach my skin through the large balcony doors. I utilized the space for the length of my visit. Eating, working, and doing my nails there. I picked a favorite fork, a favorite mug, and used them ritualistically. I became unable to have my meals unless served in specific plates and bowls exactly the right size. The excess of space and belongings made me uncomfortable. I found myself longing for my dorm room, for a small private space filled only with manageable amounts of everything over which I had complete control.

*

I fell in love with Beirut more and more the closer I came to leaving it. In my third year, on a cold March evening, I attended the final session of a condensed course I had only grown to appreciate as it was ending. Others did not share my sentiment – I later found out – but I felt very moved by the minutes leading up to our final departure. I suddenly felt the weight of transience; the same group of people will never gather in the same setting again. I left the class overwhelmed with a lack of closure, like there was so much more to be said, questioned, and discussed than our limited time had allowed.

As I walked out of the Main Gate of the American University of Beirut (AUB) and up Jeanne D'Arc Street to my building, my melancholic mood draped itself all over the city of Beirut in the cold and darkness. I looked around me, *really* looked, and for the first time truly comprehended the street's density. There was movement on every street corner, people and cars and neon store signs and the wind and my beating heart overwhelmed me. I had to stop walking. I felt burdened with guilt. The bustling Beirut I had come to love so belatedly was slipping through my fingers and I was now experiencing the end of things, traces of the life I could have built, the aftertaste of missed opportunity and wasted potential. Beirut became simultaneously what I had and what I could have had.

✶

In my house in Amman I would always wake up to unsettling silence. In a sleepy haze, I'd walk from room to room, searching for Beirut through the windows, but would never find it.

✶

"I don't know where my roots lie," I once told my friend Zaina as we strolled down Clemenceau. "I feel like I have deeper roots in Beirut than I do back home. Is that possible?"
"I think roots lie in people," Zaina replied. "Not places."

We walked silently as we pondered that sentence.

"I think I agree," I concluded. But a week later I changed my mind. It was midday and I was drinking coffee on my balcony. It was the first time the sun was out after a long series of gloomy days. I was staring at the tattered buildings facing mine, at the faded paint and shabby shutters, and was suddenly gripped by the sad realization that in a few months this view will be replaced by the cold, square structures of my street in Amman. I became increasingly aware that the moment I was living in would soon become a memory. I panicked and called my father.

"I don't think I want to go back to Amman after I graduate," I told him.

"You really should," he replied. "You'll come back and work for a year, and then work on an M.A. You need experience."

"I'm scared I'll go back and never leave." My voice cracked. "I'm scared you won't let me leave." In my head, I could already see the hanging dust and permanent dreamy sky.

"Why would we ever do that to you, Sima?" he asked. Because of money, I thought to myself. Because of circumstances, convenience, health. *Because you went back and never left again.* "We want what's best for you. We want you to do your MA and your PhD, and to travel and explore. But for now, we just want you to come back home."

But as I spiraled into an emotional mess, home didn't mean anything to me that day. The people I called home in Amman had scattered around the world. Some, like my parents and relatives and good friends, remained there. But my brother was in London, my other friends in Brighton or Boston or Montreal, exploring their own concept of home. The people left were not a strong enough incentive for me to return to Amman. The people in Beirut were not an incentive for me to stay, either. It wasn't just about the people. It was the experiences we all shared living in the dense urban fabric of Beirut. It was the way our roots intertwined and twisted around each other.

✳

I was once on the twenty-first floor of a hotel one summer evening in Amman, as the sunset washed the city in gold. For a brief moment, the scene moved me. I tried to take many photographs but none of them turned out right. The grey blocks of buildings looked too square and rigid. The streets were too wide and empty. The horizon was too low. Something was missing, but what was it?

Later that night, I remembered my brother's visit to Beirut. He and I were strolling along the Corniche when he told me, "You know what I think? The people in Amman are miserable not because of Amman itself, but because there is no sea."

I suddenly remembered my friend Rami, who once took me to his favorite spot by the sea in Raouché. We sat on the giant rocks at 3:00 a.m. bombarded by the crushing sound of waves in the horizon, and the faint cacophony of late-night urban life behind us. The sea was vast, continuous, harmonious. The city was compact, incongruent, inconsistent. I felt at the point of collision, and the juxtaposition exhilarated me.

✳

The last time I flew from Amman to Beirut, after the Easter holiday had ended, I knew the coming month and a half would be exhausting. In a hazy blur I had to juggle overdue papers, final exams, visiting guests, graduation, moving out, and saying final goodbyes. For a brief moment, I wished I could fast-forward and find myself on my purple bed in my turquoise-striped bedroom at home. Many nights I fell asleep anxious, or unable to sleep at all; I could not feel comfortable anymore. My dorm room became suffocating. The sockets by my bed always hummed, and every night I imagined getting electrocuted in my sleep. I tossed and turned until I found a position tolerable enough to allow me to doze off, but my mattress creaked and squeaked, and always woke Farah up. I wanted to be transported somewhere where the bed was bigger and the water truck did not wake me up every morning at six. Day by day I grew tired, and one evening on my balcony, I felt the wind blow all the way from Amman, carrying with it a fondness for home that I had forgotten. In that fleeting moment I could almost smell my house. I could smell the bed covers I clung to during summer nights when an unexpected breeze blew in through the open windows. I could smell the jasmine that lined the steps up to my grandmother's house. I could smell the wet soil as I stood, ten years old again, behind my father, who was watering our garden. I could smell the box of spinach pastries we ordered every Friday lunch at my great grandmother's house, and I could smell the freshly-washed bed sheets that hung in her backyard, where my cousins and I would hide, staining them with our dirty hands. I could smell warmth, familiarity, serenity.

✳

I was walking down Jeanne D'Arc Street with Nour when she stopped me at the crossroads and said, "I never thought I'd have a place to call my own, where I can walk down the streets and say hi and good morning to people, and have interactions and relationships that are truly *mine*."

The most mundane incident had elicited this epiphany. We were in the supermarket, and the cashier had greeted her warmly.

"How is your sister doing?" he asked, "Why haven't we seen you recently?"

"We've moved out of Hamra," Nour replied, and they fell into conversation like old friends. It was so easy to fall into conversation with people in Hamra. Everybody felt like an old friend. When my brother came to visit during my last semester, he mocked me about this. As a Londoner, he found it amusing that during the three-minute walk from his hotel to Bliss Street, I could very easily run into five people and start conversations. I could not explain to him how natural this was, how at home I felt on the streets of Hamra.

I never thought I would call Beirut my city. But in the days following my departure, I received calls and letters and e-mails from friends in Beirut telling me to come back home. Every time I read or heard the word "home," something stirred within me and made me cry. If Amman was the home I was given, Beirut was the place I made my home. "I don't know whether it will be a year or ten years," I said to all my friends, "but if there's one thing I know, it's that I will go back to stay."

I said that to make myself, and my friends, feel better about my departure. But more importantly, I said it because it was an unshakeable feeling that had blossomed within me since the day I moved to Beirut. I said it because I wanted to make a promise to the city I loved that I would not leave it behind for too long.

Nour's words reverberated throughout my remaining months in Beirut. Not once had I realized how intricately my identity was tied to the city until she blurted out her thoughts. We were, at that point, turning into Sidani Street, *my* street. To the right was a towering, bland white building, my building, shops – old and new – pedestrians, idle workers, the cacophony of traffic and construction, the smell of fresh *mana'eesh*[37], fried onions, cigarette smoke and trash, they were all mine. The shining sun was mine, and the rays of Mediterranean gold that bathed the city were mine. Beirut was mine.

---

37 Plural form of *man'ousheh*. See note 28.

Skin Map

CYRENE BADER

"Fine gal! Marry me!"

The scrawny Nigerian boy's voice rang in my ears, echoing from some twenty-five years ago in my head. The one pick-up line every Nigerian man would use irrespective of social, educational background, or age group for that matter. We were driving past Sabra, a route taking us from the main Airport Road through where the Embassy of Kuwait is located, leading to the Assad Highway. A route I would have never dared take alone. We were heading towards his family residence in the Dahyeh area. Another very obscure area in my mind's eye. The various cramped stalls of goods in the crowded marketplace transported me back to my teenage years in Lagos, Nigeria. In the exposed safety of the car, I pulled down my long sleeves, absentmindedly trying to cover up my tattoos. Watching the majority of women dressed in traditional Muslim attire made me feel naked. Tattooed women are not looked upon kindly. It was quite a shock for me when I deduced from a conversation with a devout Muslim dressed in a burka that these women feel equally exposed outside their own neighborhoods. They feel vulnerable, almost targeted, as curious eyes follow them, just as I do in conservative areas.

When I used to walk home from school every day, I learned to adopt a brisk walk and a dead stare fixed only a few feet ahead. I was a specter of sorts. Expatriates were perceived as privileged, and a young girl overprotected, never left to walk unattended, always escorted with a driver in the safety of a car. It was the feeling of not blending in, I guess, that reminded me of the countless times I was accosted by children and adults alike trying to draw my attention in various ways. Unlike now, I felt safer then walking the mile-and-a-half lugging my school bag that weighed almost as much as I did.

The market women were larger than life to my thirteen-year-old eyes. "Commort[38] for road, useless boy!" They would yell at anyone rudely attempting to block my path or touch my arm. I felt safe surrounded by the big women who didn't know me. They would bat at the boys like they would at an irritating fly hovering over their goods.

I unconsciously touch the tattoo over my left forearm through the fabric: "Hiraeth," a homesickness for a home to which you cannot return, a home that maybe never was; the nostalgia, the yearning, the grief for the lost places of your past. A Welsh word. In the overpopulated metropolitan city of Lagos, I never felt I belonged. When I was asked in a friendly manner where I came from, I would reply, "Palestine." They would grin with beautiful white teeth that illuminated their brown faces and cry out excitedly, "PLO?! Yasser Arafat!" before making a high gesture of the victory sign above their heads, their eyes sparkling with good will. It's strange that people from all walks of life are familiar with the Palestinian Liberation Organization and its leader. Here in Beirut, the city I was born in, people generally show curiosity towards my origins due to my awkward, untraceable Arabic accent. When I announce I am Palestinian, expressions change, and I am often told in protest, "but you don't look Palestinian!" which leaves me with a furrowed brow asking myself if that was supposed to be a compliment or an insult. This brings me to the third tattoo on my left upper arm. It is a map

---

38 A pigeon English term meaning to remove oneself from a place or situation.

of Palestine with an Arabic inscription that means, "I am the birth right." Part of me had it done in loving memory of my father; another part was in rebellion to the "You don't look Palestinian!" comments. I always felt the need to be branded with an identity of sorts.

We are stuck in traffic at an intersection under a bridge. I have no idea where we are by now. I am enjoying being able to look out the window and soak in my surroundings. Usually I am the one driving, anxiously lost with no sense of direction, desperately looking for road signs, any sign in fact that would anchor me. I see peddlers and wares on display; kitchen utensils, colorful clothes in a blinding variety, and street food side by side with cheap electronics and jewelry knock-offs. The smells of human sweat and burning garbage overwhelm me. I close my eyes and sink back into my seat, slipping into a fond memory of my late father in a place very similar to the one I find myself in now. Occasionally he would take me on a trip to the market to buy books. We would hide from the sun under a bridge very much like this one in Lagos. There would be mats spread on the ground stacked high with used books. He would patiently wait hours at a time for me as I foraged among textbooks, manuals, novels, classics and a seemingly endless array of nonfiction, never rushing or showing outward signs of impatience.

"Did you find anything you like?" He would ask going through the books I'd collected. "Ah, you found a copy of Neitszche's *Beyond Good and Evil*." A smile crinkled his eyes. "I read that years ago. Mmm Tom Clancy; this I would like to read myself." My father was not an even-tempered person by nature. He was unpredictable, passionate, and sometimes even volatile, which makes those memories of our book scavenges very precious to me indeed. I was in awe of his intellect as much as I was terrified of his temper. If any of the men present attempted to start a conversation with me, a fight would break out and I would lose my chance at purchasing new books. Books were the only thing that made my life bearable.

I don't remember a time I did not read. As a toddler, the youngest in a family comprising four older siblings, I would demand they read me a story. I had a meagre selection of children's books, well-worn and tattered, and I could recite them by heart by learning to recognize the shapes of the words. On the inside of my right forearm, the words "I have lived a thousand lives" are etched. They are part of the words George R.R. Martin wrote, "I have lived a thousand lives and I've loved a thousand loves. I've walked on distant worlds and seen the end of time. Because I read." Apart from being an avid reader, I had been uprooted and reinvented so many times in my life that I honestly felt I'd lived several lifetimes.

My family left the city of my birth, Beirut, when I was barely eighteen months old due to the Civil War and moved to Lagos until I was four. Then we spent a year in London before moving to Limassol. At the age of ten we moved for six months to London again, then stayed for six months in Cairo before returning to Lagos. At twenty-one I moved to Johannesburg for a year-and-a-half. By the time I was twenty-six, I was married with a child shuttling between two states: Nigeria and Lebanon. I got divorced at thirty-three and started struggling from scratch in a society that could not accept a divorced single mother, all the while adjusting to new climates, languages, and accents, changing schools, meeting and parting with friends. I would barely start to settle or find my bearings before it came time to move again with each construction project my father was working on at the time. That sense of growing up with the same kids, at school, cousins, or neighbors, was never familiar. I had to accept that wherever I was, it would be temporary. And it became a feeling I could never quite shake off as an adult, until I met him a year ago.

He looks across at me in the car. Puzzled by my silence, he asks if I am alright. I reach out and hold his hand. He smiles and apologizes about the traffic as if it were his fault. I tell him it's alright. His endearing attentiveness never fails to warm my heart, especially knowing that his family never forgave him for marrying a divorcée and bringing up a son that was not biologically his. Not to mention that I am not a practicing Muslim. It was a bitter pill for them to swallow.

He came into my life a few months before my ex-husband finally lost his battle against cancer. Needless to say, he was a huge comfort. In spite of all my struggles to give my son, Ryan, a sense of home, it remained a seemingly insurmountable challenge in Lebanese society, where religion, sect, and gender play major roles in one's life. My ex-husband, Salah, was Druze, and since I was not, it made our lives complicated when we moved to Beirut. As if divorce was not enough, I was ostracized by Salah's family in much the same way as I am by my new family.

Suddenly, a thought flashes in my mind. "Naguib Mahfouz," I say. He slides a glance at me and says, "What about him?"

I feel my throat and lips are parched. I attempt to make sense of the jumbled emotions I am feeling. "Home is not where you were born; home is where all your attempts to escape cease."

He smiles in recognition of the quote. It finally dawns at me that it doesn't matter. My nationality, passport, culture, where I was raised, or where I was headed suddenly seem totally unimportant. We remain in amiable silence for a few minutes.

"That's how I feel when I am with you," I say. "I will always find home when we're together."

Body as Home

ZEINA ABI ASSY

Three days before my twenty-eighth birthday, I sat in a coffee shop in Brooklyn and cried. It was 8:00 a.m. on a Monday. But it was President's Day, so most of Brooklyn was still sleeping. And after the baffling 2016 election cycle, Brooklyn was also probably too heartbroken to start the day. The sun's rays were beaming through the windows, warming my face, a rare phenomenon in February, especially in a city known for its winter wrath. I had intended to write, but whenever I started a sentence, flashes of my life boiled up to the surface, and it hit me, as it had many times before, just how loveless my life was. I was unsure when it had started, when I began to abandon love relationships. The more I thought about the past, the angrier I became. Angry because of how I now see myself after all these years, still battling against a Lebanon obsessed with a singular idea of beauty. And I was angry because this led to the uneasy, forever obscure ways my body had been handled by men.

✶

Beauty has always been the main interest of women in Lebanon. Beauty means being thin, first and foremost. Most girls start removing excess hair on their arms, legs, body, and face at a very young age. Mothers tell their daughters to be hair-free, beautiful, and skinny at all times. Banks offer loans for plastic surgery. From the forehead all the way down to the ankles and toes.

I was eleven when I first went to the dietician. My family was concerned with my weight and wanted to start me on a diet early. I remember thinking it must be easy to do this, to cut down on food in order to lose the fat. I also remember hoping that no one would find out I was on a diet. I was too young to understand willpower but old enough to know there was something wrong that I needed to fix. I don't remember much about the visits to the dietician – and there would be many doctors, many diets, many terrifying offices with threatening scales along the way – except for always feeling scared, as if I was on trial, and declared guilty every time. Guilty of not abiding by the laws of beauty that had – and still have – a powerful command on culture and society in Lebanon.

I was raised in the small town of Jbeil in a family of five. I was the youngest and only daughter with one of the biggest bodies in the neighborhood. I grew up in a world where everyone was slim, slender, and elongated. All my neighbors were thin; most of my friends at school were thin; and even my mother was thin. My father's sisters were big with wide hips, full thighs, round stomachs, and generous breasts. From an early age, my mother had warned me not to become like them: fat, undesirable, and husbandless. This was when I decided, barely ten at that time, to take up as little space in the world as possible. I wanted to minimize the possibilities of my body standing out, of revealing just how large it was. But in the process, I later realized, I was minimizing myself.

It did not help that I was a ballerina. I went to ballet school for ten years from the age of two, and in the earlier days, I was happiest when I put on my tutu and headed to dance class. But the older I became, the more my weight felt like an obstacle. The act of dancing freed me, but the act of dancing ballet as a full-bodied girl in the nineties, in Jbeil, horrified me. So a few years into my dance lessons,

I would go into ballet class, already defeated, aware that my size was a *problem*, and find a place at the very back, usually in one of the corners. I would pick the spot farthest away from the mirror, behind rows of skinny and graceful girls, hoping that if I couldn't see myself, then maybe no one else would. With every *jeté, chassé,* and *pirouette,* I would will my body to land softer, to defy gravity, to come back into position without making a scene.

It was not only in ballet class that I hid myself in an effort to hide my body. In school, I made sure to be as quiet as possible, speak only when spoken to, and train my movements to be less obvious, less loud. I was relying on my capacity for silence to protect myself. And though my classmates were kind, we were kids, and there were things we did not understand about our differences. I found it hardest on days when we had P.E., when I would hear whispers in class whenever I lagged behind: "fatty," "cow," and, the harshest slur, "lazy." I heard it at home, in school, and at family gatherings. My family was well-meaning, but they wondered why I was not losing weight and thought I was lazy. I heard it in their whispers, saw it in their eyes when I went for seconds at family dinners. I hated that word because of all the effort I was putting into changing my body. At the time, I lacked the right thinking and resources to lose weight: I hated my body, so it was hard to find the will to change it. I was married to the idea of dieting and cheated on it secretly. As a result, the weight of my failure loomed large, a heavy load to shoulder on top of feeling ugly, fat, and most of all, lazy.

★

Back in Brooklyn, the coffee shop was filling up with post-workout meetups, catch-up sessions, and coffee dates. I had stopped crying. I spread out my books across two tables, put my winter gear on the four surrounding chairs, completely oblivious to how much space I occupied. In the midst of all this morning activity, I took sips of my chamomile tea and calmed myself with thoughts of how I had changed since moving to New York.

Though the strictures of beauty, society, and family no longer affected me in the same way, I continued to mourn the sadness I felt growing up, the hate towards my body and the invisible space I boxed myself in. But mostly, I mourned the need to break out of it all. Suddenly, I realized the complexity of change, and how despite growing up and moving on, these memories had a lasting effect. I still struggled with the inability to invite love into my life.

*

Before New York, there was insatiable Beirut. I moved there at eighteen to attend the American University of Beirut. I lived on the smallest street in Hamra, in the heart of Beirut, where the smell of Turkish coffee wafted into my room every morning, and old voices filled the neighborhood with a nostalgic symphony. Moving there was the first of many instants in which I finally felt some freedom to clearly see myself.

It was uncommon for a girl to leave her parents' home before she married, but my parents did not always subscribe to social norms. They had both moved to Beirut to attend university – my mother from Marje'youn[39] and my father from Chikhane[40] – and so they realized the value of living independently, creating the opportunity

39 A town and district in the Nabatieh area of Southern Lebanon.
40 A town in the Jbeil District located in Mount Lebanon north of Beirut.

for me and my brothers to do the same.

Moving out meant valuable time alone, and I was excited about the prospect of aloneness. I wanted to test my own rules, build my own empire of individuality. To walk and sleep naked, to have trouble sleeping in an empty house. I wanted to stay out all night, to feel the thrill of Beirut. It was always comforting to know that Jbeil was close, that my family was close. During that time, I decided to formulate my own definition of what it meant to be beautiful. I filled my days with things I wanted to explore: writing, art, activism. Coupled with my hunger for Beirut, a resilient, powerful, and beautiful city in spite of her flaws. Moving led to discovering and redefining things on my own terms.

While studying graphic design at the AUB, I met a group of girls who became my little family in this new city. We all came from different backgrounds and areas in Lebanon, and looked very different from one another. One was a short blonde with the biggest blue eyes who hailed from Syria but had grown up in Ramlet El-Bayda; another was a quirky brunette with light brown hair and a fit body; there was a French-y duo who were both petite, with long brown hair and curvy bodies; one had the biggest fountain of curls and a boyish, nonchalant demeanor; and me, full and rounded. We became an ecosystem of support to one another. It was despite, or rather, because of our differences that we were able to reject societal expectations. When together, I felt the barricades around my body slowly breaking down. And when my body did slip into its largeness, it went unnoticed.

We set out to navigate Beirut through our own intellectual and creative development, trying to understand ourselves within the context of Lebanon in the early 2000s, a time of persistent bomb attacks, a time when our womanhood was emerging in a city afraid of a free woman. Maybe in comparison to the region, Lebanon seemed a tad too liberal and open to women's rights; yet, patriarchal strictures remained deeply nestled in the system. To this day, a Lebanese woman does not have the right to pass on her nationality to her children; very few occupy parliamentary positions or are involved in policymaking; they must remain well-behaved virgins until marriage.

But we wanted to fight the system. The six of us leaned on each other and encouraged one another to grow, change, and reject everything that held us back. We grew angry with society and fell in love with our own version of Beirut. We went on 4:00 a.m. road trips – to safe and unsafe places – and tried to see the other side of things while the rest of the country was fast asleep. We marveled at the beauty of Lebanon and mourned its dying potential. We pulled all-nighters to work on deadlines but spent the night singing and dancing and living instead. We spent our nights partying, dancing, kissing strangers, but always found our way back to each other the morning after. We recorded almost everything we did together; everything was hilarious and exciting and fun. We wanted this time in our lives to last forever. We spent weekends by the sea and felt a rare sense of freedom when the six of us were together. It was a revolutionary moment for us, abandoning the given path of how a woman should behave in order to experience the thrills of living. And in the midst of the random bombings, we tried to keep Beirut alive with us, through our own little lives. And when the Arab Spring erupted, we were too busy with our own revolution – a six-girl uprising in the streets of Beirut.

*

During that time, my mother was diagnosed with stage-four liver cancer. With the fear of losing her, I began to excuse and understand my family's concerns with my health while growing up. My mother often sat me down when I was ten or twelve to explain that she just wanted me to be healthy, that she was more concerned with my health than my weight. And though her pursuits were honorable, all I heard at the time was that I was fat. My family provided me with all the love and support I needed growing up; however, teaching me to love my body was far beyond their reach. It worried my mother that I was growing up with a large body, one more prone to developing illnesses, one less like hers and more like my father's side of the family. So when she received the devastating news, she was thankful my body was not built like hers, yet still scared that I would suffer. And when she got sick, I understood and felt that fear.

For my entire life, my mother was an everlasting force of nature. She was never human. Her flesh and bones were vehicles for this force to have a form. She never got younger or older. She remained my mother, a phenomenon. And the tensions we faced were almost entirely related to my body. I fostered resentment towards her; it felt like we were enemies on opposite sides waging a war over my body. But when she got sick, I understood that *she* was not the enemy.

It suddenly occurred to me that all the external forces I grew up with were not what I had been fighting against; I was fighting against myself. My mother researched ways and food habits to strengthen her body and cope with chemotherapy. The way her body responded with admirable strength and grace later became the most profound lesson I ever learned from my mother: if I could do right by my body, it would stay healthy. But there were other factors that affected how I saw my body, namely men and power, and I would be unable to embark on a peacemaking journey for many years.

Along with family and society came the danger of desire. The first march I ever took part in made me aware of my political nature at the age of sixteen. After Prime Minister Rafic Hariri was assassinated in 2005, thousands of Lebanese took a united stand, gathering in Martyr's Square in Beirut to demand the exit of Syrian troops and celebrate the unity of our country. The sun was strong and its heat infused us with energy. It was a glorious day for Lebanon. There were deafening crowds demonstrating, but the second I lost sight of my friends, I was quickly felt up by a man who figured his actions would be lost in the shuffle. It was at that moment that I began a complicated relationship with my body and men. I felt a violation that I couldn't describe, so I opted for silence. When I saw the look in his eyes, a weird feeling of relief came over me as his hands traveled over my body, telling me I was desirable despite my body's flaws.

After that incident, I went from hating my body to seeking hungry hands in order to rectify the way I saw myself. And living in a city like Beirut made it easy to seek power in the hedonistic pleasures of the flesh. My girls and I went to a pub in Hamra a week after my mother was diagnosed, and there he was, the sexy bartender. He looked attractive, with his thick dark curls and dim brown eyes. We were ordering shots, and he was dropping bombs on me. Rounds and rounds of "Blow Jobs," "Condoms," and "B-52's." It was as though he was summoning my hormones, and summoned they were. We stayed long enough to leave with the bartender. I rode behind him on his black motorcycle... At his place, those shots took their toll, and we did rounds of them in his bedroom. He had a perfect body. As he hovered over me, with so much alcohol in my body and so much heat, I was in absolute ecstasy. It felt good to be united with a stranger. I left his place that night, or the next day, and went home to change before going to class. Everything trapped inside me had come out in my orgasms, and it was freeing.

There would be men that I wanted, and men that I hated, but the touch of their hands, with or without consent, translated into a twisted idea of bodily power. So whenever I felt powerless in the face of my mother's illness, powerless in the confines of a hostile political climate, I sought redemption in the rush of sexual adrenaline, drinking, and smoking.

*

Over the past year in New York, I developed a hiatal hernia, which obliged me to completely change my lifestyle. I blamed New York and the fast pace of life in the city for my condition. I had a full-time job in a demanding and toxic work environment; I was establishing an art organization with three other writers; working on my O1 Visa application to stay in the U.S. and work; and trying to carve out time to write. I found it nearly impossible to balance everything while tending to the demands of everyday life. I was stressed all the time. My eating habits were odd: sometimes one meal a day, sometimes a diet of coffee, water, and bananas, followed by a few days of healthy eating, overshadowed by more days of late-night meals and morning fasts. It was all disruptive, and my body reacted.

When I found out about the hernia, I decided to help my body heal. I bought a book about acid reflux reduction and learned about all the food I should eat and how to cut out everything that damaged my body. My life was still just as busy, but I was able to shift my eating habits to healthy meals within a healthy schedule. And then I joined a gym. I told the personal trainer on the first day that my goal was to be healthy, to feel strong, and be able to kick some ass. I wanted to feel my body's power. I was, after all, an Arab woman living in Trump's America, and I needed to take care of myself.

I took serious strides in New York to create a relationship with my body, and that meant reflecting on how I treated it growing up. New York was telling me I was sexy and beautiful, but the more I heard it, the more I thought I was being lied to. My friends told me to see myself the way they saw me. However, I couldn't see myself through other people's eyes, even if it meant seeing myself in a better light. It all stemmed from the inside, these overbearing feelings of defeat, and once that became clear to me, I started to reevaluate myself. When I took responsibility for the hate, I was able to take direct action to turn it into love. I continued the journey of dieting, or rather different eating routines, habits, and lifestyles, but now I was doing it to feel better inside. Now, unlike my time in Jbeil and Beirut, I wanted to be good to myself.

When I arrived in New York in 2013, I was mostly overcome by how large the city was in comparison to Beirut, and how tiny I felt in relation to it. I enjoyed the feeling of being small in an enormous environment. When I left Lebanon and immersed myself in New York there were things I had to leave behind and things I decided to keep. I struggled to keep Lebanon close enough while freeing myself of the constraints of life there. I missed my family and the gentle breeze of early mornings in Chikhane. I missed my girls and the way life felt glorious with them in the midst of a bleeding city. I missed the angry streets and our rotten causes. I missed being close to death and thinking that life couldn't possibly be this profane. I missed the anxiety rushing underneath my skin and the lethal vibrations of bombs. I missed the simultaneous security and danger of the familiar and the mundane. I missed being home.

Though I yearned for Beirut and her intensity, I was free in Brooklyn. And once I realized that, I started looking at leaving Lebanon differently. Leaving gave me the chance to exist outside the strictures of my culture and family. The thought of going back put pressure on my heart, pressure that I would go back to hating myself and my body if I returned, and I could not bear the thought of that.

✳

I stayed in the coffee shop until it had emptied out again. And by that time, I was no longer crying or sad or angry. I laughed when I realized how much space I had occupied but felt happy about it. On the subway the previous Friday, during rush hour, I caught myself manspreading but I didn't care. I loved noticing small daily gestures that allowed my body to expand again into places and spaces I had avoided. Being an Arab woman in America demands certain loudness, one that can stand in the face of false narratives about the Arab world in general, and the Arab woman in particular. This loudness, once suffocating, was now finding purpose.

Since I left home, I have come to negotiate new ways of seeing myself as a reaction to being away from my natural habitat. Though my religion mattered and didn't matter in intricate ways in Beirut, being from Lebanon makes my religion a focal point in New York. I never noticed my Arabism in Beirut. Just like breathing, it was simultaneously insignificant and necessary for me to stay alive. In New York, it is a force, like a concave lens, one that I have to defend, explain, justify, and hide from on a daily basis. In New York, I love the sound of Lebanon on my lips and the way I sometimes see Beirut on my skin. In Lebanon, my womanhood was an act of defiance, my nakedness a protest against the country. In New York, my womanhood mimics Beirut; it is a statement made for Beirut and her rebellion, a city unlike any other in the Middle East or the world. She is curved, delirious, and lustful.

And one day, when the love in me solidifies, I hope to make my way back to Beirut and be able to exist with love – and in love – in the place that I call home, the place that runs inside me like a gushing river of wounds, the place that has given me the most exhilarating feeling of being alive.

The Half-life t$_{1/2}$ of the Body

HIND SHOUFANI

"A half-life is a mathematical and scientific description of exponential or gradual decay.

It is constant over the lifetime of an exponentially decaying quantity, and it is a characteristic unit for the exponential decay equation. The half-life (t$_{1/2}$) of a radioactive isotope describes the amount of time that it takes half of the isotope in a sample to decay. In the case of radiocarbon dating, the half-life of carbon is 5,730 years. In the case of the female body, no one knows."

The only book you made into a film, at the quarter-life of the self, was entitled *Written on the Body*. Back then, the decay of a carcass riddled with cancer was a family portrait you remembered well.

And, here you are again, at the half-life of the body, observing how your own natural composition grows weeds.

Start with your feet.

Your feet, adorned for decades with glittered anklet kisses, have been hurting for the last few years now and won't stop.

They ache on the mountain in Kyoto where you journeyed far and left nothing behind. In Paris, where you crossed these homelands you blame for pin-needles pricking into each sole.

Your feet, making you sob in the *medina*[41] of Tunis, from the hungry eyes of men left to their fates, and the fault lines of agony digging into your heels.

Kneeling on wide Manhattan avenues searching for a brighter

---

41 An old Arab or non-European quarter of a North African town.

past, you, now needing to stop, lift your bones, sit, take a pill, smoke.

Are these the same feet that star-flowered into cartwheels on the northern beaches of Batroun? That ran giggling in teenage years through Damascene alleyways? How could these be the feet that climbed the Dragoon mountains in Arizona? The ones that exclaimed loudly as they sank into the boiling beach of Muscat, jumping *hot hot*, hopping *ow ow*, find your sandals, *quick*!

Are these the same feet that danced in London, the same inebriated tap steps of high-flying Berlin, the same ballerina arches of a perfectly poised baby girl in Amman, scented only with jasmine?

You question the flogging you have bequeathed to your feet.

Perhaps they inherited the weight of a country with a whip, smacking.

Your feet have carried this theft for thirty-nine years/ no wonder

no wonder *you wonder*
that your feet protest this luggage.

You once wanted to write a poem for the man you love, to tell him he is like your feet, ever there, still carrying. That those before him poured concrete around your heels, going nowhere – how his love treaded lightly, took you to the far-flung edges of worlds inviting, traveled you back to hearth and nighttime surrender, never twisted, never tore, as ethereal as it was, as low voiced as it was; this love put one foot in front of another, the one trick the body first learns.

You never wrote that poem, occupied as you were by nerves inflamed, their weight bearing you down. You wish you had.

Your high heels, now abandoned in unreachable closet spaces.
Your sexy-ass nine-inch strut.

Your seven variations of colored fishnets.

The stares encircling sleek thighs.

Dainty sandals in rhinestones.

Delicate straps, tanned skin, shimmer, shine.

Running. Running. Running.

Gone.

Handstands on the streets of Beirut, feet pucker-pecking the clouds, singing

"*Estrela, Estrela, que brilha no céu da Bahia que brilha no céu da Bahia, me guia...*"

Gone.

Belly-dancing on wooden tables, the clink of glasses tinkling as you drank like it was of no consequence, no morning-after acid bile, no pounding in the Achilles, like it was no small feat to sprint to the finish line of a long night laughing.

Gone.

You wear boots with insoles, solid comfort, big strides, a thick cushioned, even-keeled harness that says – here, support, stand, sturdy –

here run/ hike/ stomp

the ground with your insistence on journey.

You love a man born of oak, who awakens in the morning to smile at the thought of you, who does not close his arms. Who means the words forming on his tongue, and forgets to argue when you try. You live with a man who does not complain when you limp and stumble, who does not ask the difficult questions until you are ready, who holds your hand across couches, turbulent flights, and storms.

It takes all of the leather and plastic and iron and lace you can find to protect your feet at the half-life of your body.

Having come so far, you can no longer be naked.

Having stuffed yourself full of loss, your feet demand this shield.

On the news, a man yesterday, or last year, or five years ago, picked up the ligaments of his dead child in Gaza; placed bone and muscle and cartilage in a plastic bag, carried them in streets now lost to all the maps.

You try not to think of little feet, once pitter-pattering in the sun, toes warm and splayed like baked flatbread left out in the Mediterranean heat.

What is forever now taken from us all?

The sun is setting in the bay. You look down at your own bare feet, in yet another hotel room over a dirty Beirut sea. Your toes are painstakingly painted aluminum silver matte. Your feet are a magic charm. The sun bends, rubs them, and the horizon says, *Stretch those tired thoughts of yours, love, point those toes like a torch, hobble out and kiss these Beirut streets.*

At half-life, you no longer have the best legs on campus.

Someone said this to you a long time ago, walking the cobblestones of literary education in a short woolen green dress. *You have the best legs on campus*, he said.

You believed, walked further, took those boots to stairwells and catwalks, to gyrate in the furthest corners of what was left unbombed in Beirut, to carry cameras in what was not dangerous in beautiful Brooklyn. And once, a long time ago, you took these legs to the Carmel mountains, walked on the same sands that tornadoed your father's Galilean face, your mother's Nazarene name, your brown-eyed grandmother's travels to give birth in lands foreign and unkind.

Now, at the body in half-life, those legs want to sink.

How the veins in them remind you of the water draining to the edge of clay pots holding beloved plants, turning the paint to fine powder crumbling, then obvious rends and gaping striations in the surface, then figments of time on the floor.

But your legs still swing over fences when necessary, squeeze into ever tightening clothes, show up for the meeting, the dinner, the kitchen sink, the necessity to crouch over a public toilet bowl, not touching anything.

Perhaps you ought to bare these bones, bitter or not, bloody or bloated, brown or bleached. Declare – these legs have kicked up a shit storm, booted out interlopers and banged such drums belting beauty.

What are legs but vines wrapped around your tall, lithe lover? If your thighs could encircle his horizon, are they not then the most perfect of all legs?
The most hardworking calves/
the sweetest inner slopes/

If these legs contain all his language, spoken and not, can cross over the river of this bed and stay the course, if they can stretch into star shapes, point at the moon, cajole the dawn into reading poetry, are they not also the line at the center of saying grace?
Bow down, light a candle between them.

But never mind the quarter-life perfection you remember; you know you have always hated the deposits around your knees.
Patient, too, they refuse to budge.
Sitting, standing – *the worst.*

Your squat knees do not evoke the subtlety of the Empty Quarter.

They don't give your thighs the length of a Liwa dune.

Dimples appear where you wanted bone and nothing but edges. You can pinch them easily, and even that, hurts.

Knees. You feel sharp tremors when on them, tired of the push from behind in which you have sought meaning for years. Now, pressure and relief when the throbbing is done. On your knees, you are no longer comfortable. No longer giving in with élan to the mattresses ululating this act. But, you know the push can remain relentless, a masculine belief in the sturdiness of round creatures.

Somehow, this reminds you of Syria. Of an entire nation now on its knees.

Hands clasped behind heads, necks buried in mounds of dust, a twinge of all that has been lost spiraling through knees always bent, tied, beaten, and bereaved.

Is this the connected joint we have built, meniscus shredded, cap overflowing with blood? Sinking, the body crashes into knees whipped by time, arrogance, and all that running you took for granted, that hustle you revered.

A decade ago, a doctor nonchalantly told you that you were entirely sick, mostly because of your brain. Your knees could not stand the city aflame in smoke and assassinations and car metal exposed. Strengthen yourself, said another doctor. Take a walk in the evening sun, buy some vitamins.

Your almond-eyed friend told you to visit an old man with a white beard instead, go up the mountain, find him tucked away, minimalist and uninterested in money.

There was so much you wanted to tell him. His strong, veined hands. The little office with sinew diagrams on display, chakras counted and recounted, the lucidity in his sad eyes.

I am in awful pain, all over.
Lie down. Stop eating wheat. Don't drink dairy. Breathe.
What's wrong with my body?
The city. The sounds.
Why do my knees hurt so much?
Oh, that. That's fear.

He aligns his hands silently above your kneecaps. All is still, and your words extinguish. Tibia, you breathe. Fibula, you pray. He stands there, hands pulling at the infected air around your knees. He sucks and sucks and sucks the light out till it turns golden. You let him. He keeps pulling out shell-shocked debris until a small pop of release is freed, as pale as the coldest light. Pure virgin maps are now your articular cartilage. And it ends. In the cells of synovial fluid, the waves have ceased.

The man with the white beard removes his hands. This is all I can do for today, he says.
I know, you think. *I knew when it ended.*
The willow tree in your stance shakes off the snow and yawns.

What is it about you, Beirut, you with your witchcraft everywhere?

Such blooming, always.
But you, you are still only one.
Regardless of the degree of decrepit decay the body may or may not succumb to at half-life, the hips are firm about the notion that you could push, breathe, freak out, squeeze and eject something the size of a living watermelon. *No, no thanks, no sir, hell no, nuh-uh, as in a headshaking no, not having it, nope, niet, la'.*

This is a womb that loves its life alone. Sheds walls and rebuilds its fortifications unbothered. It reads late at night, drinks Jameson on the rocks and smokes. It sleeps in late, tumbling easily into coffee and emails. It feeds only itself, when it wants to. Bears the needy cries of no one. Laughs loudly and does not apologize for not answering the phone.

But the womb does not forget. In its half-idle days, it still lights incense at the temple in the face of all the babies held aloft in arms elsewhere.

You visit the home of old friends on a fine Ras Beirut afternoon; their babies hug you for years. The body shrugs off stagnation, rises in an unbridled *dabkeh* to meet those ribs, that nose, those ears, those little feet on tiptoe, never ever tired.

Gold-spun baby boy of my spirit, you are barely three years old, younger than the death of my father.

Young baby boy, you, with amber and the alphabet, you with the eyelashes of a dervish, little boy with melon, with nectarines, with peaches, little alabaster boy drinking water through the gurgling bubble of a crescent-shaped mouth, shaped the volume of a heart that constricts and leaves room in its ventricles for you, only you – little baby boy of our bougainvillea balconies, our creeper plants hugging the whole street in desire, our boy of lessons, of music sought out and abandoned to, our subtle child of nuance in language rising, fingers greedy at the slippery sweetness in the burst of a peach plunged into, little boy of wonder and your mama's dreams – how wonderful it is that a body made you in secret. How much of you is not mine, and never will be, and yet, here are words to evermore thank the soil for you.

But then, there is also Beirut, later.

Crippled child on the beggar streets of last night's Hamra, eyes like empty cupped palms, arms and knees bent in wrong angles, staring above, unmoving. Child with heart unloved, muscles splayed on a hard floor –

Forgive us, forgive our impotence, forgive our failures and our feet that walk on. Forgive our voices.

The man you love turns his kind face away. He cannot look or linger. You understand. You know that he fears his foreign love of your homeland will combust in an instant; his lungs will waste away at the sight of a crooked child and her crook government.

Crippled child on the beggar streets of last night's Hamra, what did your mother feed you from those breasts she hides so carefully?

How do you face the day, not knowing what face is, what sunlight does to plants?

What mothers smothered their breasts in their arms and begged for your forgiveness?

I look at breasts, all the time.

One violent day amongst others, half-a-life ago, your mother tells you of her secret trip to a clinic where strangers in rubber gloves first started to list the descent of her family.

I have a small lump in my breast. Going tomorrow to get it removed, she says. *Don't cry, habibti. Please.*

Who knew that one fatty tissue lump could unleash such destruction?

You cry, unaware in your fear of how long the death of a breast could be mourned.

What books have not been written, what kisses did we not dive into because one woman was left bare?

Mastectomy. A word that holds in it the curves of sorrow, not dwindling.

What abusive love affairs would we have been spared if this breast remained perfect?

What bad habits, dizzy spells, poems of vomit would we have left unturned had this breast stayed the course?

What altered generations picked up Molotov instead of clementine in the absence of this breast?

Why would a breast accrue so much hatred from those it gave nothing but sweetness?

If our cells have learned the lesson of centuries, and evolved, and stored the trauma of layered insults in families refugeed and bereft, why would these cells not cull the overspill of mitosis gone rogue, gone evil, gone maniacal?

Malignant, the name hardly describing this invasion by multiplication.

The new cells refuse to keep the charter, navigate in the waters beloved and fresh. Mud banks with worms grow around your nucleus. A generation of rabid cells baring fangs drip pus and forgetfulness. Why are breasts so beautiful, so weak?

Your breasts at half-life are unimportant to you. Not given the life they would have chosen to nourish, left for display, accosted by dust and fog.

You have been told they were still young, alert.

As young as you were when a singular particular breast first tore the front page of a book you had started writing, inked in gratitude. Took this verse and burned it.

And now at half-life, you cultivate much more tenderness. You remember the life before, the faith before the witch-hunt, the day before the doctor's appointment.

At half-life, you know all the advice, have seen what could befall wanderers, those with no progeny or prayer. You still refuse to listen, because this is also what you have inherited – this will, this trauma festering in self-punishment, this resistance. You write of a breast, now turned Kali, destroyer of the world and giver of life, all meat without stitches. A duality nestled into the essence of a breast, one whose assault heralds the storm, barrels the frozen gale into the face of children open-eyed, silences the tongue of the man, their father, standing, wondering how to.

Would it now take 5,730 years to stop mourning? What carbon is this that invaded your breast? Could that be the full-life of a small lump of fat tissue? Could our voices have said the right words to make it stay?

You have been told your voice was a lullaby, its evenness boring your fraught senses into the shutdown they desperately needed. A voice as salvation in the vicious Beirut night, to those who stayed throughout her war.

Screw that, you think. Nah. No thanks. My voice is not a lullaby for someone's comfort. My voice is a foghorn, a bellow in the afternoon glare. You want to speak for all the crumbled heaps of bodies in dungeons and late night bars, almost shuttered.

All you ever knew of your voice was the loudness of a stage where you often fool yourself into believing that you are doing the good work of poets, revered throughout the centuries as prophets and mad(wo)men.

Outside the stage, the world crashes around you in camps and airports and subway stations in the news and you keep speaking, ranting, yelling on that pulpit you built for yourself, with poisoned memories and letters in unreliable ink.

We can only suffocate on our own feebleness under pillows of words propped up.

Our wrists at keyboards are abraised and beat; we pop pills and crack our shoulders hoping our elbows will cajole grace into another day of writing.

We read and read and travel and get paid to read and make old ladies in the south of France weep. We enchant men who sit in the back of a giant concert hall in Pittsburgh, a knife twisted in their gut, who speak of nothing and leave right after. We hug and hug the calm wet faces in New Orleans, and touch the hair of youngsters in Iowa City who want to electrify our bodies with this love our words rammed into them, and it is never enough. You cannot speak for the voiceless; they remain in camps, in cold tents shuddering, scraping the sides of a can with a spoon that grates on the spirit. They remain bent over sidewalks, ignored. They remain raped and shivering. They remain giving birth on the street at the entrances of local hospitals that won't let them in because of a wallet unworthy.

Can you smell them? Wrapping one puny plastic blanket in Libya over the child draped on a lap in a boat bobbing into hell, orange mixed with black, mixed with lungs flooding in panic and regret. Your poems are nowhere to be seen at the bottom of the Mediterranean. Can you see them?

Please.
Please get some sleep.
Turn off that light, brush those teeth, take out those itching

contact lenses, wash this made-up face and don't look at the pores, apply cream to the half-life of the skin. Avoid the mirror. Get to bed. Pop those earplugs in.

Yawn.

Did you send that invoice? No, you didn't.

Send that invoice. You have to mail a physical copy. How tedious. You forgot to buy ink for the printer. Why is it so expensive?

You really must buy a house.

But where?

Anywhere, you are free.

Ah, a passport that can take you everywhere, even back home to the Galilee.

Ooh, buy a house in the stolen Galilee.

How to un-name a mountain, a sea, to reclaim it as your own.

Um, are you allowed to buy one house back from thieves?

Apparently, you have to decide these days if you are still Arab. What a strange thought to question. You love how your occupied family plants flowers throughout their village, this invisible village you never thought would ever speak your name.

This is the most beautiful gene you inherited from your father. The love of plants. And roots.

Drink water, sit up, scratch your misbehaving scalp.

I love you, fingers.

Lying down, what a terrible way to live, you watch too much (awesome) TV, girl. That's not going to get you that house in the Carmel mountains, nor the next big project, nor the flat belly you really could do with.

No, not by lying down, reading trash.

I love you, shoulders.

Your big belly feels comfy.

You like hugging your belly, having it spill into your hands.

I love you, jelly belly.

Okay, stretch your back, curl to the other side. Lift your arms over your head, high.

Bedtime yoga, how cool is that, eh. That's practically exercise, that is.

I love you, spine.

Don't knock the books over, the ones by your bed, the ones you don't read because the Internet is so full of anger and breaking horror and people you deeply love.

Check your phone. Maybe the next big thing landed in your inbox today.

You are hungry. Corn cake with *labneh*[42] and *makdous*?[43]

No, no point; it's past 2:00 a.m. Try to sleep.

Okay, one last check. Hey, someone still thinks you are pretty. Nice comment that.

I love you, face.

Why are your stardust friends all in other countries, tripping on magic?

That's a really cute baby.

Ha, good gif.

Oh, someone smashed another truck into people, they're dealing with it as terrorism, more terrorism, you really shouldn't yawn, but it's almost 3:00 a.m., and your eyes are burning.

I love you, almond eyes.

You did read a research about electronic light not enabling sleep. Lie down again, please.

I love you, heart.

Don't auto-play the video of sarin killing babies in Idlib. How are you supposed to sleep now, how could they look so peaceful, why are they grey?

Why are all the men in the video not moving but topless?

---

42 Soft cheese made by straining yogurt in Lebanese cuisine.
43 Small oil-cured eggplants stuffed with walnuts, red peppers, and garlic.

Thank God you don't have babies.

I love you, hips.

Bombs, Istanbul. Bombs, Kabul. Bombs, Brussels. Bombs, Beirut. Bombs, Amman. Bombs, Cairo. Bombs, Kuwait. Bombs, Tehran. Bombs, London. Bombs, Gaza. Bombs, Damascus. Bombs, Aleppo. Bombs, Homs. Bombs, Baghdad. Bombs, Mosul. Bombs, Sanaa.

Thank God your parents aren't old and far away and alive and trapped in rubble.

You selfish bitch.

I love you, wrists.

Stop scrolling though, its 3:30 a.m. Drink some more water.

You love water.

You must have been made of water in your previous life.

Your earplug is hurting. Do you really need to shut out sound so much?

I love you, lungs.

Yes, yes you do.

How cute was dad when he eloquently explained how the class struggle also exists in how often the subjugated neighbors scraped and dragged furniture around at midnight and let their kids scream into the late night, hopped up on sugar and the lack of books. He always found Marx in everything.

You miss your dad.

You are an elitist pig, brain.

Well, at least you can laugh at yourself. You giant cliché, you.

I love you, grey matter.

It's nice to think of your brain as squiggly squishy substance you can poke at and squelch.

Ok, drink more water.

I love you, neck.

Sit up, lean forward, grab your toes, breathe and stretch.

Mmm, nice hip pull there, feel the lightening in your lower waist,

must be good.
   Must be good.
   I love you, feet.
   Sleep.

HERE AND THERE IN A TIME OF TERROR

RIMA RANTISI

Thanksgiving, 2015

I found out I was pregnant with my first child on Thanksgiving day. The night moon was low, giant, and golden-orange. I took photos of it and learned, through an Internet search, that it was the second night in a row it had been on display. Two full moons, two lives in one.

I have held Thanksgiving dinner at my house since moving to Beirut in 2007, inviting both Lebanese and American friends and new acquaintances to join in a hodgepodge of dishes that we cook up: cranberry-orange sauce, garlic mashed potatoes, spiced pumpkin soup, spinach-feta puffs, corn bread, mulled wine or cider, and a Michigan-style butter-injected turkey surrounded by Lebanese-style rice garnished with almonds, walnuts, and chestnuts. Rami, my husband, always makes pumpkin and pecan pies for dessert. Thanksgiving dinner is an event that friends begin asking about in October. We sit at a long table, sometimes two. Somehow we had formed an extended family. It was fitting that the news of a new member would come on this day.

No one knew I was pregnant – we had only learned a few hours before dinner. I had sat on the sixties' style dark blue tiles of the bathroom floor, the pregnancy test almost touching my nose as I stared at the two lines, my breath heavy. When I found Rami in the kitchen, I showed him the test, and all he could say in similar disbelief was, "What's that?" We embraced in a giggly hug, squeezing away the fears of the last year spent trying to conceive.

I had to tell my friend Lina, who sat right next to me at the dinner table. She and Rami had been friends since the fourth grade. When she introduced me to him, we had been friends for a few years since our exchange in the English department bathroom about our love lives.

"How are you?" she had asked.

"Depressed. I recently went through a bad breakup." I was wearing my heart on my sleeve since an ill-devised engagement had ended.

"Oh! I just broke up with my boyfriend, too!" Here she broke out into a huge smile.

I invited her to share my office where we smoked cigarettes and started a long-lasting friendship. My baby would know her as the person who urged his appearance on earth.

At the table, I texted her: "I'm pregnant. Found out today." I watched her read the text, and her eyes grew white. She mouthed, "How could you do this to me?" I laughed and whispered that I couldn't believe it, either. It was real: I was now eating and breathing for two. I took a small sip of wine that night, but ate heartily.

A Beirut Café, 2016

I asked a few friends if they knew the science of a suicide bombing. I had just come back home from South Africa, was eight months pregnant, and had some *things* on my mind.

"You mean you're wondering how you can survive it?"

"I mean, how will a bystander die if she sits here and a suicide bomber is at that door," I pointed about twenty feet away, "and he blows himself up?"

"Shrapnel."

"Pressure. The shockwaves can pulverize your insides."

"What about the fire? How does it spread so far?" I asked.

"Depends on the size of the bomb."

"You wouldn't survive it."

"I could hide under the table," I said.

"Yeah, that might help, if you hide in time."

Watching the Lebanon War from Chicago

I was in Chicago in 2006 when leaflets announcing impending war dropped from the hell-heavens of the Lebanese sky. Israeli warplanes had invaded Lebanese airspace where they stayed for thirty-three days, bombing it backwards in time. The walls of the Chicago bungalow that I lived in were goldenrod yellow. The room glowed when the sun shone through the long row of windows, painted shut by the previous owners "for security purposes." I sat on my hand-me-down couch where I could look out at my quiet residential street when I received the call from my mom.

"Things are not calm in Lebanon," she said evenly in the middle of the phone call from Peoria, Illinois. "The airport was hit." She was three hours away, and so I could not see her face that day or even for the next thirty-three, but I imagined the worry line between her eyebrows, which always betrayed her feelings. My grandmother, who still lived in Lebanon, has the same line.

I was working at a Middle Eastern fusion restaurant called Souk, where every weekend Thurayya, the belly dancer, and a three-piece Oriental band behind her stirred the mixed crowd of high-heeled Arabs and Chicagoans into a frenzy. Most of the regulars were transplants from the Middle East. Souk was a place where they could feel at home with others like themselves, people who needed a taste of home, to converse in Arabic, to dance to the rhythms of Lebanon, Iraq, Jordan, Syria, and Egypt. They indulged in green apple martinis, *arak*,[44] cigarettes and hookahs, *mezze*,[45] deep drums. The singer belted nostalgic Arabic songs he repeated every week as he strutted in his suit and tie while Thurayya undulated between tables, her tanned skin and toned arms glowing under the lights.

I would go downstairs to take breaks and deep breaths of cigarettes, lean against a wall, and sometimes think about how I came to find myself crisscrossing a dance floor, carrying colorful martinis through pillows of smoke. I had just received my master's degree and was exhausted from teaching (starting a career) and waiting tables (paying bills). I was attracted to working at Souk for the same reason the others went. It was a place where I could get my dose of the "mother country," even if later I realized that our ethnic identity – which, it turns out, can be a shallow reason – was the main thing that brought us together.

In 2006, when Israeli air forces systematically destroyed Lebanon's highways, main roads, and factories, and turned homes in southern Lebanon into towers of broken stone, as civilians pulled children from the rubble, people extended their condolences to me at the restaurant. One regular, a young woman, approached me and mentioned that her family was originally from Bint Jbeil, where more than eight-hundred homes would be completely destroyed by the end of the thirty-three-day war. She grimaced and then returned to her table where her friends awaited. The restaurant was packed, the lights dimmed and ready for show time. The singer struck up a tune

---

44 A clear alcoholic liquor distilled from grapes, raisins, or dates, flavored with anise.
45 A selection of small dishes served as appetizers in Middle Eastern cuisine.

popular during Lebanon's 1990 post-war days, the chorus of which translates to a rambunctious and repetitive "Lebanon is being built again" as the young woman from Bint Jbeil interlaced hands with the others and joined in a circle for the *dabkeh*. Despite all attempts to express our connection with what was happening in Lebanon, we were disconnected – safe – distant and dancing to a song that promises the country's return from the depths of hell (yet again). We, too, were distanced from the reality that when a place is destroyed, or left behind, it cannot return to what it once was.

Lebanon, at the time, meant grandparents who spoiled me and my siblings as kids and teenagers – hell, even as adults. It tasted like pan-fried eggs in butter *and* olive oil, handpicked cherries, figs, loquats, paper-thin *markouk* bread, Nescafé made with fresh milk delivered to the door. It was hot summers that smelled like sea, sweat, and that particular mixture of car exhaust and village that I would get a whiff of on the streets of Chicago. It was kindness and love. It was where I learned to no longer be ashamed of my heritage. It was where I lost the discomfort of speaking Arabic or referring to my father as *Baba* in front of my American friends. The trips we took to Lebanon taught me that it was okay to be "different" in America. I did not have to be blond or blue-eyed or wear Abercrombie and Fitch. My mom did not have to make meatloaf for dinner or go out for beers with my friends' parents. Before my visits, I had experienced Lebanon through my parents' filtration, and through the media.

When I arrived home at 3:00 a.m. that night, I turned the news to CNN as Anderson Cooper and others stood in northern Israel where ambulances could be seen in the distance. By the end of the war, fifty-five Israelis would be killed and over a hundred injured. The other half of the split screen showed a live reel of those dead and injured in southern Lebanon being whisked away on stretchers by neighbors or the Red Cross. By the end of the war, all the major Lebanese bridges would be destroyed, leaving chasms into which passing cars would unwittingly fall; one million people would be displaced, sleeping in schools, parks, convents, and relatives' homes all over the country; over one thousand people would lose their lives, not one of whom I know by name; over four thousand would be injured during the war, and hundreds after it in fields where cluster bombs were mistaken for toys. I would know all of this information later, but not from CNN. I cried in front of the television each night I watched the footage, for a place I would – though I didn't know it then – call home just one year later.

South Africa, Thirty-Three Weeks Pregnant

During my pregnancy, I collaborated with two teachers, in Michigan and Slovakia, on a course we entitled "Narratives of Peace and Conflict." The course was meant to open a discussion between students of three countries, focusing on conflicts in the world and the peace processes (or lack thereof) that followed. We won a grant that sponsored a trip at the end of the course for all the students and faculty involved. We chose to focus on post-apartheid South Africa. The reading list we compiled comprised an unhealthy dose of apartheid and post-apartheid literature, which recounted the worst atrocities I have ever read about. Reading about them while pregnant, and knowing I would soon be in South Africa, sparked an unchartered brand of fear in me.

One character who haunted me was "Hammerman" from the book *My Traitor's Heart* by South African journalist Rian Malan. Hammerman's moniker came from his ritual of sneaking into white people's homes and smashing their heads with a hammer. He would spare the children in the house; if they woke up, he would gently walk them back to their rooms as their parents' heads lay in pools of their own blood.

Malan investigates the life and trials of Simon Mpungose, Hammerman's real name, describing him as a "potentially good manmade monster by apartheid." Mpungose inherits his grandparents' "sin" and excommunication from their Zulu village because they bore a child together despite being first cousins. This truth follows him through his childhood and after his abandonment by his drunkard parents. He lives in the bush, survived by stealing, and finds himself in and out of prison for most of his adult life in apartheid South Africa. During one stint in prison, he suffers punishments such as "ring-o-roses" where naked black convicts are made to run round and round in a circle as they gasp for air and are beaten with hosepipes and lashed. One such episode leaves Mpungose unable to walk for a month. His time breaking rocks in the prison quarry "under whips and guns" of the white warders, brings him to say, "You hold [the rocks] in one hand ... and break them easily. It is not long before the rocks are the white man's head." According to Malan, Mpungose was *never*, from birth, treated as a human.

At thirty-three weeks, I found myself in South Africa. At this point, if the baby was born, he would be a full being. When I began creating the course with my colleagues two years earlier, I had not sketched a pregnancy into the plan. I had always come and gone as I pleased: sleeping on a train from Bordeaux to Cannes, hiking for seven hours in the Barcelona countryside, crossing the border to Syria before the current war ravaged it, moving to Lebanon on my own at twenty-eight. I traveled without fear, only caution. In South Africa, as my belly protruded before me, I could not do as I pleased, and I did not travel without fear. The first thing I heard from a local in Johannesburg, our taxi driver from the airport, Ronaldo, was:

"This place is crazy. Be very careful. Watch your things." He gave me a purposeful look.

Chicago and Beirut, the two major cities I have lived in, are segregated according to race and religion, respectively. But they are also segregated by safety (read: class). In Chicago, you knew that Humboldt Park was rougher than Logan Square, even though separated by only a street. Or when you saw on the news that a four-year-old girl was shot by a stray bullet inside her home, you knew before they said "South Side" that it wasn't in your Northside neighborhood. In Beirut, depending on the political climate, you understand that crime is not random, but targeted – whether it's a car bomb awaiting a politician or a suicide bomber detonating himself in the middle of a residential Shiite neighborhood described as a "Hezballah stronghold" in the foreign press rather than a neighborhood full of people, minding their business, walking home at rush hour, killed for nothing. If you are killed by a bomb in Lebanon, you are the victim of a combination of your luck and your identity. As we rolled into the fancy hotel on the outskirts of Johannesburg, I was struck by the privilege of safety I often enjoy – due to my luck and identity.

Later that day, after lunch, my American colleague warned our group of twenty-four that a "poor man from a township might stab you in the heart with a bicycle spoke" and flee with their expensive cameras if they walked as nonchalantly as they had that afternoon from the Johannesburg development of Newtown to the surrounding shabby blocks. We had spent the semester grappling with race relations, predeterminations, stereotypes, post-conflict contexts, and reconciliations. Her warning, and our resulting fear, somehow negated the fuzzy feelings we had conjured in the classroom – those self-satisfied feelings derived from the idea that as proponents of peace and harmony between peoples, we understood prejudice and how to avoid it. The strange streets of Johannesburg quickly proved that being a warrior for peace relations in the classroom was not being a warrior in the world.

Four days after our arrival, the news announced: "The State Department on Saturday warned American citizens in South Africa of the imminent threat of terrorist attacks" and these attacks would be "indiscriminate, including in places visited by foreigners such as shopping areas." The South African government denied the claims, but the U.S. embassy confirmed the warning. My American counterpart was solemn when she mentioned the alert to me and our Slovakian peer. How should we discuss this with our students, she wanted to know?

"Let's not mention it," I said, "We get these warnings all the time in Lebanon." I knew this wasn't the case for her in the U.S., but I didn't feel like abiding by her as a point of reference.

"Yes, but if they hear about it before we bring it up, they may panic. We need to be prepared with a response."

We did not agree on a response. I had become weary of Western terror alerts. In Beirut, I'll just have had a perfect summer day, my beach-skin toasty, a watermelon in the fridge, and I'll check my inbox to find: "The Department of State warns U.S. citizens to avoid travel to Lebanon because of threats of terrorism, armed clashes, kidnapping, and outbreaks of violence near Lebanon's borders with Syria and Israel." When I first moved to Beirut, I would closely read the entire email and forward it to friends. But I noticed that the emails seemed to come a few times a year, like protocol, and they sounded eerily alike. (Since I moved to Beirut, the embassy has not warned me of the four car bombs that claimed several lives in different corners of the city. Nor did it warn me that a war would rage in my neighborhood in my first year there.)

My colleagues and I brought up the topic to students later in the evening, over pizza. We gathered in one of the adjoining townhouses where the students stayed. Although the security warning employed that old familiar general, speculative, fear-mongering language, South Africa was not my country – I did not know how my luck and identity would fare there – and I was responsible for these students and this small human inside of me. I was in a foreign place in the middle of a bloody summer, with ISIS targeting civilians in tourist areas around the world. How could I run if a gunman was on the loose? What if the fear made me go into early labor? How could I have put myself in such a situation so far along into my pregnancy? Protecting myself now meant protecting someone else.

One of my students nonchalantly echoed my sentiment: "We live in Lebanon. We're used to these alerts – and then nothing happens." A few asked questions, illuminating the fact that we could do very little about this. And despite the threat on malls and tourist areas, we did not change our itinerary, which included these destinations. The shelter of safety and comfort that we perpetually inhabited could not easily be destroyed.

But a few days later, I sat at an outdoor café, eating a bowl of pasta and daydreamed about my death, right there on that sidewalk. My privilege no longer mattered. It was now just luck. We could find war-like violence in a nightclub in Miami, in a Bastille Day parade in Nice, in major airports, in a tourist café in Burkina Faso. Had the men who committed these acts of violence experienced the brand of hatred that Hammerman did? Were they too not loved as babies, as growing children? Were they not treated as humans? Can we ever know what drives them to kill, kill, kill?

As I walked through stalls selling tribal masks and colorful necklaces and dresses in Cape Town, I was stiff imagining men in black masks with machine guns appearing in the aisles. My students roamed wide-eyed, enamored of their surroundings, venturing to eat fried caterpillars at dinner and asking the locals questions about South African society. I couldn't even be happy that their discussions reflected so much of what we had examined in the course. I was envious of my younger self in them. Traveling had always given me new eyes. But today travel took on a new meaning as I expected to bring a human from the tight safety of the womb – which, too, could not be protected from today's brand of terror – into this sprawling, unpredictably violent world.

Our tour guide, an ex-prisoner at Robben Island, where Nelson Mandela spent twenty-six years in prison, told us that after serving twelve years, the first place he found himself was back in his mother's kitchen. He said that was one of his greatest moments. In carrying a child to term, I had only been thinking of how to keep a healthy environment in the womb for him, but I had not thought much about what it meant to be a mother, or like my child would be, a son. Two hours after he was born, he clamped down on my breast to eat, as I gasped from the surprising pain of it. To be the source of sustenance for your baby means that you cannot stop. You cannot decide to skip a meal or leave your baby behind when you want. You must continue to be vigilant about keeping your baby alive, and in turn, your child will see you as their greatest protection.

Robben Island drifted further behind us as we ferried off into the crisp, clean air toward the mainland. Its sordid past, with its small cells, gave way to the vibrant and sprawling Victoria and Alfred

Waterfront, displaying live African music, five-star restaurants, hotels, boutiques, and a mall. As we stepped off the ferry, I became conscious of the security warning, as we were at one of the most popular tourist destinations in South Africa. The waterfront's jubilant atmosphere was surreal after the prison tour. The transition from memorialization and history to commercial indulgence urged us to forget what we had just seen.

When I went inside the elegant mall, I imagined a mass shooting. I began living it in my mind. I sat down on a bench while my eyes scanned my surroundings until eventually all I could see were pieces of flesh and puddles of blood, as one of my students sifted through Nike clothes for her sister.

Now, eight months later, I sit in my warm home in front of my computer as my baby sleeps soundly in the next room. I cannot conjure that fear anymore, but I know it derived from the specter of responsibility that I suddenly embodied, wrapped up with the realization that I had very little control over the things I worried about. You cannot protect your womb from a bomb; you cannot make another person see past your color; you cannot contain people's fear when they have been warned of the worst; and you cannot control the rage of a person who has set out to kill.

Homecoming

The baby kicked and pushed in rhythm with my anxiety. I was on a flight back to Beirut from Montpelier, Vermont, which felt like the safest place on earth, where strangers said hello along quiet sidewalks lined with tall evergreens and Victorian houses, there in that far corner of the country. It was a world away from South Africa, but only a few weeks separated the trips. While I was further along in the pregnancy, it wasn't until I was on the plane to go back home that the anxiety crept up.

Istanbul was on my mind, where forty-nine people had been killed a week earlier in an attack at the airport. I watched a video in which the airport entrance lit up in flashes of orange and black: a suicide bombing. I took deep breaths to relax as I imagined telling Rami not to wait for me in the arrival lounge at the Beirut airport. I was convinced of its danger. But I never did tell him. He doesn't believe in this way of life – theoretically dodging danger. He, too, never heeds security warnings in Lebanon but for different reasons than I. He lived through the Lebanese Civil War during his childhood, which left him at age four with no appetite, no energy, and no outdoors. Today, his mother says it was her own crushing anxiety that cast gloom onto him. On an especially violent day during the war, as rockets hailed into their neighborhood of Ras Beirut, she decided it was time to leave the country on a short flight to Cyprus to live for a while. That day she had held him close to her and rolled down the stairs of their apartment building, to dodge any flying glass or debris in the event a rocket hit their building. Today, he remembers Cyprus as a place where he rode his bike all day.

When I arrived, the lounge was as I have always known it: a long line of people with crowds behind them waiting with flowers at the railing, leaning over to kiss their loved ones who were pushing carts of luggage, prepared to stay for weeks or maybe months or even just returning, like me. I have always anticipated these images, knowing how many families are split among continents. I have been on both sides of this railing. Rami, coincidentally, was waiting for me outside because we arrived at the same time. Nonetheless, the familiarity of the airport had already made me forget my fears. Imagining a suicide bombing in the Beirut airport as I stood in it became impossible –

this place was home.

In 1992, when I was thirteen, I landed in Lebanon for the first time I can remember (there were two other times at one and four years old, which I can only remember through pictures, like the one of me riding on my grandpa's back at just a year old with an unlit cigarette squeezed between my teeth). As with most of the passengers on the plane that July, it was the first time my parents had been to Lebanon in nine years, due to the heavy fighting and instability of the Civil War in the eighties. On our descent, I looked down from the plane window and noticed the square white houses, so different from the ones in Illinois. As the babies' air-pressure screams subsided, applause filled the plane and tears trickled down the sides of passengers' faces, including my mom's. And somehow, the plane's wheels touched the runway, and two words swept across my mind: *I'm home.*

This was before satellite television spilled out the open windows of everyone's village home, and I was part of the first wave of the diaspora to "come back" after the war; in other words, my siblings and I, the *Amairkaan*, were somewhat of a spectacle. Walking through the village provoked unapologetic stares (can you see curious old skirted women on their porches?). It's not that we looked different, except for our smooth-lined American clothes. I learned that people were not necessarily interested in who we were (besides what family we were from). Instead, questions seemed to derive from a curiosity about how we saw Lebanon – and what was it like *b'Amairka? Which is better: here or there? Do you have this kind of traffic there? Do you eat mlukhiyyeh*[46] *there? Would you ever live in Lebanon?*

---

46 A traditional Arab dish made of cooked jute leaves with chicken, broth, and a side of rice.

When I was a kid in elementary school, I distinctly remember being infinitely grateful that I never had to switch schools and be away from my friends, and that I didn't have to grow up in Lebanon, where there was war. When I looked at the ultrasound images of my son's fingers and toes, I thought about how one day he will be required to stamp his fingerprints onto foreign documents. He will be asked questions at borders. When customs officers ask him where he is from, will his answer be "America"? "Lebanon"? Will his American passport dictate his identity? Or will where he grew up? Will he, too, be happy in the place he grows up? Will he, like my mom and dad, leave his country because it is too violent to stay in? Or will he be like me, and move across continents to discover the other side of things just because he can.

After Birth

Bringing life into this world is not a very different act than living within it. You walk right into its utterly painful and beautiful arms, suffer moments of hesitation, and doubt that you can go on. You cannot see the way ahead. The only way to make it through, to the other side of pain, is to breathe. That's all you can do: breathe into its escalating madness, because when you bring life, you are accepting all of it. You are saying, I have to do this so that life goes on. You will puke, shit, cry, scream, and spill pools of blood after you have pushed so hard that your face melts into the back of your head, into the hospital bed. You will shiver in a sterile room with strangers disposing of your insides, the afterbirth. It is terrifying. But then, what is more terrifying is keeping that life which you have brought into the world alive. When he leaves the sterility of the hospital, at just under seven pounds, his hands as delicate as butterfly wings, and he is suddenly one with the chaos of honking cars, the smog, dusty vendors selling crunchy bread, the dark, dark coffee, and beggars asking "please" for a little change, for something to eat; and then a car ride later he sits, small as can be, in your home for the first time, you will look over at him and wonder: How will I protect you from life?

An Article

ZAINA ERHAIM

It's six in the morning. The cold air blows through a window covered with blue plastic bags, into the small crowded room, but fails to cleanse it from the thick smell of farting, mixed with heavy snoring and smoke fumes wafting from the garbage burning in a small metal bin for warmth.

It was a quiet night; only two mortars and a missile hit nearby, so all are enjoying good uninterrupted sleep, except for Nisreen. She is lying on an old flowery mattress along with her five children and their father. On the other side of the room are the mattresses of her mother-in-law and sisters-in-law. She finally decides to get up, steps over her two boys and pokes Fatimah, her eldest daughter. "Wake up! Your father will be up in ten minutes and you're still asleep! *Yalla*; get yourself up and prepare the warm water for his *wudoo*."[47]

Fatimah rubs the sleep from her eyes and hurries to the kitchen while Nisreen quietly prepares breakfast, covers the metal tray with a thin white cloth, and disappears into a room where she puts on a long, bright purple dress and matching high-heel shoes. She steals a quick glance to make sure she can escape. Fatimah enters the room interrupting her.

"Where are you going, *mama*?"
"I am going training today."
"What training? It's still early. Did you get *baba*'s permission for

---

47 Ablutions performed before prayer.

that? Who is going to make lunch for him? What training?

"A woman journalist came to our village yesterday and is giving a journalism course at our center," Nisreen whispers. "So I'm going to see what that is and what the outsider looks like."

"*Joor-nalism...* What? What you are talking about, *mama*; wake up!" yells Fatimah, her surprise turning into shock.

"Shush. This is between the two of us, your father will beat the hell out of me if he finds out," she glares at Fatimah. "Shut your mouth and tell him I'm in my hair-dressing class when he asks," Nisreen orders her firmly.

"What if he discovers the truth? He will kill us both! You are ruining our reputation. Where is your honor? Are you also going to go on TV, act shamelessly, laugh loudly, and mingle with men? What's happening to you, mother?"

Nisreen slaps Fatimah across her face. "It's just training, and I won't be going further than 100 meters from our home. I just want to see what other women do, and how this one came to our town on her own! I certainly won't be a TV presenter. Your father would not only divorce me, but also marry two other women and bring them to my room to punish me."

"I don't understand why you are taking this risk," Fatimah says rubbing her stinging cheek. "Go quickly now and I will try to cover for you."

Nisreen quickens her step to avoid being asked by any of her nosy neighbors about her comings and goings. She murmurs all the Qur'anic verses she memorized for protection and help. Finally, she arrives to a dark basement where fourteen other women are anxiously awaiting the mysterious outsider.

"Did you know that the journalist doesn't wear a headscarf despite being from our province?"

"Maybe she's Christian!"

"No, she is not!"

"I heard she was living abroad; maybe her family was too, so they allowed her to go scarf-less."

The trainer walks in. Everyone stares at her in silence. Abeer, the oldest trainee among them and mother of ten, elbows her friend: "I told you she is a woman like us; there is such a thing as a Syrian woman journalist."

All the women take off their colorful shoes and sit on a dull carpet in an "open box" position looking up at the trainer.

"I am Zaina; I come from a town nearby. I've studied journalism in Damascus and completed my master's degree in Britain." The women are astounded. "Before we move on to proper introductions, let's all please agree on a security plan: if there is bombing or shelling, that room (she points to the adjoining room) is the safest, please grab your children and run there. If our center gets raided yet again, we'll claim to be involved in illiteracy training, so I am an Arabic teacher and my name is Ruba. If one of your husbands brings an armed group to take revenge on any of you participating without his permission, we'll claim to have permission and he's violating their ruling. By the time they discover what's happening, we'll all be gone."

Training starts and Nisreen thinks it complete gibberish for the first couple of hours, until she begins getting the hang of it and becomes actively involved. She's the first to ask questions. By lunchtime, she realizes she's completely forgotten about her household chores, and becomes part of something larger for the first time in her life.

At the end of the first day, Nisreen heads over to the hairdresser nearby. She rubs some hair dye on her fingers and puts spray on her clothes before returning home. Her husband, Abou Ahmad, is sitting on a small armless chair in front of the house, smoking.

"You're late. Where were you?" He asks stiffly.

"I was in the women's center as usual; we had two ugly brides today with awful hair. They had dark skin too, so I put more than three layers of whitening cream. Their grooms should thank me for the magic I worked on them."

"Hmmmph," he grunts.

He bought it, Nisreen thinks to herself when she sees the hint of a smile on Abou Ahmad's mouth. Her sense of humor, skill at changing the subject, and the day have passed safely. On the morning of the third day, Fatimah wakes her mother up. "*Mama*, please don't go today. I'm afraid we might get hit by a bomb and die while you're away, please stay. Stay *yam*."[48]

Nisreen ponders her options for a few minutes before asking Fatimah to wake up all her siblings. The training center is safer than their house since it's underground. She decides to take her children with her, for she has been eagerly awaiting this day to learn about planning how to write an article. She doesn't want to miss this important lesson.

"What about *baba*?" Fatimah protests.

"God doesn't take evil men; he won't be harmed," says Nisreen while getting the sleepy little boys dressed.

---

48 A shortened form of *ya mama*.

All six family members head to the women's center, moving as stealthily as possible, staying close to the still-standing stone walls for protection. When they arrive, they see that five other women have also brought their children along. The children create such commotion that Nisreen finds it nearly impossible to focus. But she makes sure to write down every single point the trainer mentions. She'll work on it later that night when everybody is asleep. She will write a story and hide it from her husband and the extended family.

By 9:00 p.m., Nisreen finishes cleaning the house and scrubbing a mound of dirty laundry. She also makes up the mattresses with some help from Fatimah. Though exhausted, she sets to work on her assignment. She squats in the corner of the room next to the window, and writes:

The topic: Domestic violence increases after the revolution.

Interviews needed:

Umm Ali claims that the bruises on her forehead were caused by shrapnel but that's an absolute lie. The whole town knows her story. Even my little boy heard in school how her husband whipped her hours after she gave birth to another baby girl. He was furious that the baby wasn't a boy who would inherent the family name. After punishing her for giving birth to a girl, he left the house and married his cousin the next day.

And then there's Marwa, whose husband crushed her thighs because she was bleeding for three months after getting married; he accused her father of 'selling him ruined goods.'

I need to speak with Dr. Rasha, the town gynecologist, about the cases she knows of, how the number of abused women changed after the revolution... Hopefully she can give me some statistics, because no one else is keeping track of this...

Then I can interview Ms. Hala, who runs the local women's center. She can tell me the reasons behind the rise in domestic violence rates over the last six years, and how the organization is trying to help victims...

Ms. Rawan who used to be a lawyer, can give me information about the Syrian laws on domestic violence.

Around midnight, Nisreen succumbs to exhaustion. Abou Ahmad wakes her up in the morning and asking why she didn't sleep on their mattress.

"I was waiting for the electricity to come at dawn to iron your socks because you don't have a clean pair to wear to the mosque prayer," she answers. When he gives her the "good wife" pat, she suddenly realizes her ability to make up stories quickly and flawlessly. But journalism is about facts, not lies, she reminds herself while getting ready for the fourth day of training.

Nisreen puts on her special orange dress under her black coat, takes her new notebook and heads with renewed vigor to the training center. But her enthusiasm just as quickly fades when the trainer tells her there is one thing missing from her plan.

"You need to interview an Imam, Sheikh, or a local religious leader, to add the Islamic point of view on domestic violence and the *Shari'a's*[49] interpretation."

"Yes I know, but you're an outsider. You don't know..."

"I don't know what, Nisreen? Tell me? What's the matter?"

"I can't even visit my male cousins, let alone meet and interview an Imam! It will cause a scandal in our town!"

"Even if you cover your head?"

"Yes, I will still be a woman meeting a strange man! And where

---

49 Islamic law or jurisprudence that governs the way of life.

can I meet him? In the men's quarters of the mosque where he gives his speeches? In the butcher shop where only widows go?"

"Can't you do it over Skype?"

"What is that? A new organization in town?"

"Hmm, I am sorry Nisreen, but it's an important interview."

Overwhelmed by her impossible new task, Nisreen drags herself back home.

"You're too busy to cook *yabrak*[50] for me today, too?" asks Abou Ahmad as soon as he sees her approaching.

"Oh, look at you thinking about your stomach while I am thinking about my big important article! May God have mercy on my parents' souls for putting me in your bed," Nisreen whispers. "I will make it for you tomorrow," she promises with a forced smile.

She buys his silence for a few hours to focus on her dilemma. While mopping the floor before arranging the mattresses, an idea lights up her eyes. "Why didn't I think of this earlier?" she exclaims.

She stays up all night writing down questions to ask the Imam. The next morning, she accompanies her older son, Ahmad, to the Imam's house, has coffee with his wife, and tells her she urgently needs answers from the Imam the next morning.

For Abou Ahmad, her visit was a waste of time, women chatting, useless; while for her, it was the beginning of an article, a dream come true! Her instructor's encouraging comments make Nisreen even more keen on improving her writing.

---

50 Grapevine leaves stuffed with rice.

She writes about Umm Hadi who ran out of face powder but isn't planning to replace it because there won't be dark scars to cover up. Her plan was successful. Last week, she wore a black dress and white headscarf. Then she asked her husband to remove some metal from the balcony. She knew it was the remnants of a cluster bomb that had fallen during a Russian airstrike. And so, she chose to become a widow because no one could protect her from daily beatings and humiliation.

Publishing her story under the name of Al-Sham'a Al-Modee'a[51] on a website with the help of her trainer, brought Nisreen money for the first time in her life. It was a large sum. She made $100 on just one story. It was actually twice as much as her husband made every month.

She was able to hide her name, her new career, and her new personality but she knew she couldn't hide her money. So she decides to confront her husband. She goes to the second-hand market and buys new shoes for her five children and for Abou Ahmad.

On her way back, she also buys vegetables and fruits from the local market. The shopkeeper sarcastically asks her, "Has your husband found gold coins under your house?" She smiles and replies, "No, I found the treasure in me."

---

51 Lit candle.

To Myself

HAFSA BOUHEDDOU

Despite the look in your eyes, it would be unfair to assume that you don't love life. You are passionate about it – those who love it the most are also the most impatient. For a long time now, you have been searching for a loophole in your fate. The obsession has grown into an avalanche inside of you, snowballing and hurtling you toward the darkest point.

You sleep thinking morning will bring an end to the frenzy, lift the feeling and silence the commotion inside, but it only becomes more pronounced. When you glance in the mirror, you hate yourself even more, with your disheveled hair and baggy, rumpled shirt. What do you hate the most? Your unkempt eyebrows, which have hairs so long they can reach the top of your forehead? Or your round body, which looks even bigger in your floppy shirt? You pull it back tightly, scrutinizing your curves, feeling even heavier than you already are with the weight you recently gained.

Drowning in the shadows of your memories, you manage to retrieve a few snippets. *Wouldn't it be wonderful*, you ask yourself in the mirror, *if when I sleep, I could control what I dream? I could be a flurry of winter's first snow, frolicking in the December wind and gleaming in the light like a pearly spark.* You're terrified that monotony is now bound to you like a ghost, unwilling to let go until it's robbed you of all reason to live. But luckily enough, you have a reservoir of patience. *Give life a chance to surprise you.* You recall engraving the words a wise person once said, which you framed and hung near the Christmas tree. You want to write something more, but you can't figure out how to make the sentence – "Sometimes all you need to do is stay alive and take care of your soul for the sake of days to come" – briefer.

A sudden desire to turn on the Christmas tree lights early sneaks up on you, and a renewed desire for life creeps in. You feel like dancing. Through the window, you can see the heavy fall of snowflakes swaying and surrendering everywhere to the will of the wind.

What you hate about holidays is not the absurd traditions, nor the fact that people celebrate them in the same way year after year, nor their faith in this creed or that. You hate the crushing boredom and the need to imagine life as a series of new beginnings. Every New Year's Eve, people list the wonderful new changes to come because they need a reason to stay, a reason for happiness, whether real or imagined. Because the endless slew of days and nights is unbearable. What's even harder about a holiday is staying in a good mood. Chances are, something will happen just moments before all the guests arrive and will ruin everything. Your cheeks will get streaked with kohl, and you'll lose all the excitement that's been building for weeks as you meticulously planned for this day. The holiday spirit you've been nurturing for months like a fern will just wither and die. All you can do at that point is drink and drink.

You end up going out, jumping from one lap to the next, from one cold embrace to another. You can't even taste alcohol anymore, like a cracked jug that can never be filled. You want to get rid of something inside of you, fling it far away, but the only thing that gets tossed in the street after midnight is you. This isn't going to be a regular party to bid the year farewell. You'll have to say goodbye to many things that are falling away on their own. What kind of stupid girl arrives dressed to the nines to face a big loss, to be a laughing stock? You should have stayed home...

Do you remember that one particularly bad night when you were staring at the sky after you had tripped and fallen on your back? The noise of cars, the bustle of passersby, the music coming from the amusement park – it all blended into one indistinguishable sound. You were listening to that Johnny Cash song – "God's Gonna Cut You Down." Remember how badly you wanted to change and escape the prison of this country in search of freedom? Lying there on the road you asked, *Is this death? Is this how it is? It's not that bad.* It's total emptiness. The end of everything. The end of all senses. Of everything that was lit up. Drunkenness in death can't be worse than alcohol. You vomited and cried as if trying to get everything out. Everything, not caring which passerby on the street the projectile of your entrails hit. You stayed in a hotel room on the highest floor that night. You entertained the thought of jumping off the balcony because you liked the sight of your scarf floating this way and that, and it occurred to you that you wanted to follow it all the way down.

Every time you find something, you go looking for what's next. You're never satisfied. You're like a rocket tearing through the sky, losing pieces of itself as it transcends each stratum. Believe the gypsy fortune teller who told you that neither the stars nor planets rule you. Instead, you are driven by a mysterious force inside. Don't wait for the planets or destiny to have mercy on you; they do not control you. She said something to you, then with a smile on her face, she left. *Listen to the call of your soul, girl!* She was trying to get your attention, but you told yourself it was just prattle and you kept going with your friends to the club downtown.

You will eventually get tired of leaving the house in fancy clothes because you're going to get harassed. And if you try to speak up, it will just get worse, and you're going to lose the battle simply because you have less testosterone in your body. You can't win against nature. Anyway, no one will take your side because it's your fault to begin with. You're not going to get into eating and drinking during the fast anymore, because you'll only blame yourself. Do you remember that summer when Ramadan fell and you were on a long bus trip? Back then you were full of passion and a desire to rebel till your last breath, no matter the cost. You opened a can of food; you remember the smell of bread with cheese and chicken thigh bone. You started eating on the bus, in spite of everyone. You remember their looks and their sharp, threatening tones and the warning that they would call the police. You thought you were a rebel, but in the end, you were just offering yourself up to violence. It was a suicide mission that wouldn't change anything. You realized how hard it would be to swim against the current.

It was pointless to weep over your despicable society when life was elsewhere. You couldn't sit around waiting for a savior to pull you from the quicksand. You had to move. Life was elsewhere, and you had to live it and enjoy it. Here in the Holy Land, logic is dead. Any attempts to be logical brands you as a deviant, an outcast, and every other category of evil. Life here is dangerous, especially for a woman. Every road leads towards madness or suicide; it's better to escape with what's left of your sanity.

Do you remember that sunny morning when you said to yourself, *All I need is a walk to the sea, like this, and watch the waves glimmering*? You were surprised by the feeling of freedom for the first time. It was magical. It was like unraveling silk from a cocoon, but it was only a superficial layer. What's worse was having to fight battles that others had won centuries ago. You fought for things that weren't worth all that time and effort. You believed that freedom came after all these inner struggles with society. But they were only a distraction from the true meaning of life and from being free. Getting rid of them is just the first step. Life as a whole is about overcoming. Every time you understand something, you reach for what's next. Surviving is what's beautiful.

If things hadn't been so challenging in the past, and you hadn't gone through what you did, you wouldn't be sitting here enjoying the sunset. You wouldn't be sitting here on a bench unafraid of being mugged or getting into confrontations with men that might end in profanities and physical violence. Deprivation is the only way to appreciate what you have and where you are. Life's boring and easy routines smother your feelings. They make you glance in the mirror with that look on your face, unable to list two beautiful things about yourself. Not even one thing you're proud of. A coldness emanates from you like ice. You can't control your thoughts or clear your head. There on the bench, all you dream about are peaceful moments like this.

Once again, you cried like a child when you took out your nose ring and couldn't get it back in. Hours passed. You tried and tried to no avail. You said, *I won't let the opening close. I won't give up like I always do.* No one knows how you had the nerve to keep trying until the early morning hours. Every time you got the ring in, it got stuck and wouldn't go all the way through. Your life flashed before your eyes, and you flew into a fit of rage and tears. A thin filmy layer formed over the hole after it became inflamed. You took a needle-shaped ring and pushed it into the hole violently. You were in such pain. When the sun rose, you laid on your back.

You broke the promise you made to yourself of not getting blindly attached to anyone. Or reach a point where you couldn't live without them. But life goes on, even when we hit rock bottom. We get up after falling. We step back from cliffs. Hundreds of trains pass without us throwing ourselves onto the tracks. We throw away shards of glass without breaking our skin.

Each time you have a drink, you remember that night, and a terrible feeling comes over you. Only later will you realize it's loneliness. A deadly loneliness. It's a feeling you never knew. You never understood why those who feel lonely leave with anyone just to escape it. They join any silly gatherings to tell and hear jokes, to burst into laughter for no reason. They buy things just for show. They only read to boast their knowledge about overpopulation in China or the health benefits of an unknown plant. They do anything just to please the person they're attached to.

Take a good look in the mirror, into your shrivelled eyes. For days, you've been a prisoner in your room. You swallowed your bitter saliva and asked yourself why it was bitter. You exchanged looks of hatred with yourself. You could simply go for a walk in the neighborhood. You could go to a party. You could have a drink at home or outside. You could look for a lover and go all the way with them, with no shame. But here you are, a prisoner of your room, a prisoner of yourself. Haven't all the barriers to your freedom been torn down? What is keeping you in bed? What about your inner freedom? Do you still believe that freedom is out there far away, and all we have to do to reach it is jump over a fence? Does that work for everyone? Why is your soul tired, slowly dying?

Being displaced is cause for enough trouble and confusion. You aren't necessarily who you think you are. You are the type of person who needs to find a connection, so don't ignore the signals that come from your deepest crevices. Listen carefully to them and when that seems impossible, look for ways to get them back and make them stronger. Go to a safe place and reconnect with your body and soul. Move. Run every morning. Strengthen your awareness of your body. Be beautiful inside and out. What was the last thing you did that boosted your self-confidence? Something that made you say, *I'm not useless. That proved you aren't as hopeless as you think?* Do it and the rest will come.

Just because creative chaos is a complex notion doesn't mean you should lay back and wait for miracles. You've done it many times, and here you are, dissatisfied with yourself. You're used to taking untrodden paths. Don't be stubborn with this now. Prepare your fingertips to write. Look at the universe. It's true that it's drowning in chaos, but if it were perfect, we wouldn't be here. And guess what else? If it were lazy and incompetent, then we wouldn't be here either! Ask everyone; they'll tell you: nothing comes easily. Talent is not enough. You have to do something with it. Don't let it die while you die a thousand deaths every day! Next time you consider everything you failed at, remember, the things you excel at compensate for it. But you, with all your potential, are lying there, staring at the mirror, hating yourself more and more.

Do yourself a favor: tell the woman in the mirror, *I know I feel bad, but I also know that I am exaggerating my anxiety. I am ill. But I won't let this illness destroy me.* Do you need someone to tell you that life is about chances and obstacles? You have to accept your weaknesses. Once you do, you will understand your place in life. When you wish to be someone else, your stubbornness and desire to swim against the current will exhaust you. At every moment you walk parallel with the things you are good at, the things you were born to do. You have no business with things that upset you. Don't chase them. You'll just end up hating yourself. You will overcome all this only when you remember this isn't the first time it's happened. You've gotten through it before. Not all the dead in their graves were entirely bad.

Go and reclaim what you lost in a moment of vanity. Then stop and come back to yourself. Admire the stars as if they were God's ins piration. His words are spread out across the sky, waiting for someone to arrange them in vases like flowers. Make peace with the curse of life. It's better to be cursed with living than dying. Embrace your solitude. Everything else has come at you like a stray bullet. You took it and bled. You slept on a white bed until you were healed. It's now your bullet, your story, and the scars will stay forever. So go back and retrace them on paper...

With all the love that can't be reflected in the mirror,
You

Translated by Amahl Khouri

CONTRIBUTORS

Roseanne Saad Khalaf is Associate Professor of Creative Writing at the American University of Beirut (AUB) and the founding coordinator of the Creative Writing Program in the Department of English. Her experience spans creative, academic, and editorial work in Lebanon as well as in the US and UK. Khalaf is the author and editor of numerous articles, two children's stories, and eight books including *Once Upon a Time in Lebanon* (1982), *Lebanon: Four Journeys to the Past* (1998), *Transit Beirut: New Writing and Images* (2004), *Hikayat: Short Stories by Lebanese Women* (2006), *Arab Society and Culture* (2009), and *Arab Youth: Social Mobilization in Times of Risk* (2011). She is currently working on a memoir.

Dima (Deema) Nasser is a PhD candidate in the Department of Comparative Literature at Brown University. Her interests lie in contemporary literary and visual works from the Arab world and comparative translation studies. Her editorial skill draws on two years of experience at Turning Point Books during which she edited Desmond Astley-Cooper's debut novel *In the Time of the Mulberry* (2016) among other works. Nasser has also published an academic article in *Kohl: A Journal for Body and Gender Research*, and has a forthcoming article co-written with James Hodapp in *African Literature Today*.

Michelle Hartman is Professor of Arabic Literature at the Institute of Islamic Studies, McGill University and a literary translator from Arabic and French into English. She has translated novels by Iman Humaydan, Alexandra Chreiteh, Jana Elhassan, a memoir by Radwa Ashour, and the short story collection, *Beirut Noir*.

Rula Baalbaki teaches writing and translation in the Department of English at the AUB. She also translates Arabic poetry and prose as a freelancer, having published translations of three literary works and a number of Arabic poems for literary magazines and stage productions. She is currently working on a translation project that seeks to establish the place of a trans-lingual component in writing courses as well as a proposal for starting a Translation Studies major in the Department of English.

Yasmine Haj is a writer, editor, and translator from Arabic and French into English, based in Montreal. She has completed her MA in comparative literature and is a co-founder of *Dalaala Translations*, a women's collective for translating Arabic and English texts, with a focus on literature, poetry, and film.

Amahl Khouri is a Jordanian documentary playwright and theater director based in Munich. She has written several plays including *She He Me* (Münchner Kammerspiele 2016), received a Rosenthal Emerging Voices fellowship from PEN USA and was a member of the Lincoln Center Directors Lab in 2013. Her work has been published in several U.S. journals including, *Queer Dramaturgies: International Perspectives on Where Performance Leads Queer*.

Hanan Al-Shaykh is an award-winning Lebanese journalist, novelist, and playwright whose work has been translated into 28 languages. She is the author of the short story collection *I Sweep the Sun off Rooftops*; the novels *The Story of Zahra, Women of Sand and Myrrh, Beirut Blues*, and *Only in London*; and a memoir about her mother, *The Locust and the Bird*. She has most recently published *One Thousand and One Nights*, an adaption and re-imagining of some stories from the legendary *Arabian Nights*. She was raised in

Beirut, educated in Cairo, and lives in London.

Zena El-Khalil is an internationally exhibiting visual artist, writer, and Nāda yoga instructor based in Beirut. Her work includes paintings, sculptures, installations, and performance pieces that focus on creating a culture of peace through love, compassion, forgiveness and empathy. She founded xanadu*, a non-profit art collective, as a direct response to the 9-11 attacks, to help Arab artists during a time of extreme xenophobia in NYC. During the 2006 invasion of Lebanon, El-Khalil was one of the first largely followed Middle Eastern bloggers; her writings published in the international press, including the BBC, CNN, and Der Spiegel. In 2008, she was invited by the Nobel Peace Center to participate in a conference on freedom of expression over the internet, and has been a TED Fellow since 2012.

Hind Shoufani is a Palestinian filmmaker and writer currently living between Beirut, Dubai and the UK. She was a Fulbright scholar to NYU where she obtained an MFA in film directing, and has also been awarded a residency at the IWP in Iowa University in 2011. She's edited two anthologies: *Nowhere Near a Damn Rainbow*, a collection of over 30 poets from her spoken word performance platform "Poeticians," and *Uncommon Dubai*, a literary and fine art photography guidebook to Dubai. She's also written two poetry books titled *Inkstains on the Edge of Light* and *More Life Than Death Could Bear*, published by xanadu* in Lebanon. She's directed an award-winning poetic multimedia video-art feature documentary titled *Trip Along Exodus*, and is currently working on two other feature films, and a third poetry book.

Rima Rantisi is a faculty member in the Department of English at the AUB. She is the editor and co-founder of *Rusted Radishes:*

Beirut Literary and Art Journal, which publishes artists and writers from Lebanon and the region and is currently in its fifth circulation. A student again, she is an MFA in Creative Writing candidate at the Vermont College of Fine Arts.

Zeinab Al-Tahan holds an MA and PhD in Arabic language and literature from the Lebanese University. She has worked in print and electronic journalism for 18 years, having published dozens of critical articles that examine cultural and literary concerns, as well as the human condition at large. She is also a short story writer and currently works with *Risalat*, an art collective in Lebanon, and is a professor of literature at the Lebanese University.

Mishka Mojabber Mourani is a Lebanese writer. Her short story, "The Fragrant Garden," appeared in two anthologies: *Lebanon Through Writers' Eyes* and *Hikayat: Short Stories by Lebanese Women*. She published *Balconies: A Mediterranean Memoir* and co-authored *Alone, Together* with Aida Y. Haddad, who translated Mourani's poetry from English to Arabic and vice versa. "Once Upon a War Night" was published in the *Exquisite Corpse* anthology by Medusa's Laugh Press. Her work has appeared in several print and online literary journals, including *The Studio Voice, Mused Literary Review, Sukoon*, and others. Mourani is a contributor to *Arabic Literature in English* and the *Your Middle East* culture and literature page. Her writing deals with issues of memory, identity, war, exile and gender in the Arab world.

Raya Hajj has been a financial manager in a leading IT group in Lebanon for over seven years, which has made her an expert at technical writing. But she pursued her love of writing and decided to participate in a short story writing workshop to develop creative storylines. "On the Seventh Floor" is Raya's first short story.

Zaina Erhaim is an award-winning Syrian journalist, named among the 100 Most Powerful Arab Women in 2016 by Arabian Business and Unsung Heroes of 2016 by *Thomson Reuters*. She has received many awards, including Index on Censorship and Freedom of Expression in 2016, the Press Freedom Prize by Reporters Without Borders, and the Peter Mackler Award for Ethical and Courageous Journalism in 2015 along with the Mustafa Al-Husaine Award for best article written by a young journalist. She has been working as the Syria project coordinator for IWPR for the last four years, trained over 100 media activists on journalism basics in Syria, and made a series of short films called *Syria's Rebellious Women* and *Syrian Diaries* told by its women.

Shahd Al-Shammari is Assistant Professor of English Literature at Gulf University for Science and Technology in Kuwait. Her research interests include Disability Studies, Women's Studies, and critical race theory. She has published creative fiction in journals such as *Pomona Valley Review*, *Sukoon*, and others. Her first collection of short stories entitled *Notes on the Flesh* (2017) deals with illness and identity in the Middle East.

Gabi Toufiq is an Iraqi student who came to Lebanon in 2013 to pursue her degrees in Psychology and Creative Writing at the AUB. Toufiq hopes to continue her graduate studies and eventually work in the legal sphere with both sexual assault victims and perpetrators to help shape sexual assault protection laws in the Arab region. She has worked on-site with refugees and internally displaced people residing in the United Nations' camps in Iraq. Her piece, "Silent Letters," is a short memoir she began working on in one of her writing classes and is published under a pseudonym.

Youmna Bou Hadir is a musician, poet, and writer. She is also a creative writing trainer for youth at FADE IN: Creative Writing Hub. She holds a BA in English Literature from the Lebanese American University and was awarded for Best Senior Project for the Academic Year 2014-2015 for an extended work of creative adaptation incorporating music, set, and poetry. She is continually developing her online blog with song pieces and short stories. She also works in journalism, copywriting/editing, translation, as well as administration and management. Her dream is to work with special needs children and adults to teach them how to better express themselves through the art of story.

Nadia Tabbara is a writer who grew up in the U.S. and moved back to Lebanon in 2011 to share her love of writing. In 2013, she founded FADE IN and grew it into a competitive writing hub with an education program for aspiring writers and a content creation department for screenplays. With a BA in Film & Writing from Emerson College in Boston, Tabbara continued her training in a specialized writing studio in New York City. Through her work, she hopes to lend her voice to those who are misplaced, stuck in the hyphen between being Lebanese and living other cultures. Currently, she is based in Beirut as a professional screenwriter for film/television, a script consultant, and a creative writing lecturer and trainer.

Cyrene Bader is a Beirut-born Palestinian writer who spent her childhood and early adult years between Limassol and Lagos. She moved back to Beirut in 2008 and has been working as a beautician since. She is also a single mom currently living with her son.

Fatima Mahmoud is a Libyan poet and journalist. She founded *Modern Scheherazade* magazine in Cyprus, which focuses on Arab women's issues. Her first collection of poems was published in 1984.

She sought political asylum in Germany in 1995 and continues to live there.

Zeina Abi Assy is a Lebanese writer and media artist based in Brooklyn. She has an MFA in Creative Writing Nonfiction from The New School, and a BFA in Graphic Design from the AUB. She explores the complex intersection between personal and global manifestations of culture, art, and politics in her work. She manages the Interactive Programs at the Tribeca Film Institute and is the digital media editor and one of the founders of The Seventh Wave, a literary and arts organization.

Yasmina Hatem is a Lebanese writer and storyteller. After receiving her MA degree from Columbia University in 2007, she started a career in journalism between Lebanon and New York, all the while writing about women and relationships on her blog "Beirut Rhapsodies." Her first novel, *I Believe in Angels* (2006), was sponsored by the Lebanese Canadian Bank, the proceeds of which were donated to the Children's Canter Center. She currently lives in Dubai and is working on a creative nonfiction novel.

Hafsa Bouheddou is a Moroccan writer who is currently teaching and working on a novel in a remote village in Morocco where her story will be based. Her interest in informal and alternative education practices is taking her on a trip around Asia to volunteer her teaching skills at English-speaking schools.

Inaam Kachachi is an Iraqi born writer living in Paris and working as a journalist. She has published four fiction books, two nonfiction works, and three documentary films. *The American Granddaughter* was shortlisted for the Arabic Booker Prize in 2009 and translated into English, French, Italian, and Chinese. *Tashari* was also shortlisted for IPAF in 2014, and was translated and published in French by Gallimard.

Huda Al-Attas is a Yemeni writer based in Beirut. She has published four award-winning short story collections, titled *Hajes Rouh, Hajes Jasad, Li'annaha..., Barq Yatadarrab Al-Idaa*, and *Thalath Khutouwat*. Al-Attas is a social and human rights activist, director of the Yemeni Foundation for Social Studies, and has worked in Yemeni and Arab journalism. Her stories have been translated into several languages. She currently teaches sociology at the University of Aden while pursuing research on the intellectual woman in the Arabic novel for her PhD at the Lebanese University.

Adania Shibli is a Palestinian novelist and playwright. She is also author of many short stories and essays, which have been published in various anthologies, art books, literary and cultural magazines in several languages. She was also recipient of the Young Writer's Award by the A.M. Qattan Foundation in 2002 and 2004. Her latest novel, *Tafsil Thānawi* (2017), was published by Dar Al-Adab in Beirut. Apart from writing, she is engaged in academic teaching and research and lives between Jerusalem and Berlin.

Irada Al-Jubouri is an Iraqi writer, scholar, and social activist with a PhD in journalism and media studies. She has published seven short story collections, a novel, a children's book, in addition to many journalistic pieces in local, regional, and international print and online newspapers and magazines. Al-Jubouri is also a documentary and feature film screenwriter and has directed several art and journalistic projects including, "Open Shutters Iraq" with British photographer Eugenie Dolberg and Iraqi-British filmmaker Maysoun Pachachi. Al-Jubouri is currently teaching in the College of Mass Communication at Baghdad University.

Aisha Isam grew up in Bahrain and currently resides in California. She studied English Language and Literature at the University of Bahrain and started writing fiction in 2009, focusing on social and ethnic conflicts in the Middle East. In 2015, her first published story, "Catastrophe," was featured in a collection titled *A Room of One's Own*, which was produced in collaboration with the University of Iowa's writing program and consisted of stories by local women writers. In 2017, it was selected again to appear in the anthology *No Matter How Long the Separation*, published by the Palestinian Youth Movement in the United States. Since graduating, she has been working as a translator and teacher of both Arabic and English.

Sima Qunsol is a Jordanian writer, and prospective academic and musician. Her main area of interest, inspired by living between Beirut and Amman, is exploring the relationship between individuals and their surrounding urban landscapes.

Fatima Bdeir was born in Michigan and came to Lebanon in 2007 after ten years of living in the U.S. She has lived between Beirut and South Lebanon and is currently pursuing her BA degree in computer science at the AUB, while minoring in creative writing.

Amany Al-Sayyed first came to Lebanon in 2009. She moved from Canada to become an independent researcher and instructor at the AUB. As a Palestinian-Lebanese woman trained in World Literature, she continues to write from local experience, especially on the topic of family heritage, displacement and hope.

Nisreen Sanjab is a Syrian scholar based in Beirut. She teaches in the civilization sequence program at the AUB and Rafic Hariri University. She is also an English literature and drama teacher at

Rafic Hariri High School. Sanjab is interested in the connections between language, identity, gender, and movement, and is currently working on a theater piece that investigates storytelling in a gender-free plot in Arabic.

Reem Rashash-Shaaban earned an MA degree in Applied Linguistics from the AUB where she taught English for 32 years. She is a Saudi, married to a Lebanese, and lives in Beirut. In addition to being a photographer and mixed media artist, she is a poet and fiction writer. Her works have been published in regional and international journals.